Wait a Minute, You *Can* Have It All

Other books by Shirley Sloan Fader

Successfully Ever After

Jobmanship

From Kitchen to Career

Wait a Minute, You Can Have It All

How Working Wives Can Stop Feeling Overwhelmed and Start Enjoying Life

Shirley Sloan Fader

A Jeremy P. Tarcher/Putnam Book
published by
G. P. Putnam's Sons
New York

A Jeremy P. Tarcher/Putnam Book
Published by G. P. Putnam's Sons
Publishers Since 1838
200 Madison Avenue
New York, NY 10016

The author acknowledges permission to reprint from the following
sources:

Permission to reprint from her column granted by Ann Landers and
Creators Syndicate.

"Occupation: Housewife," copyright © 1946 by Phyllis McGinley,
from *Stones from a Glass House* by Phyllis McGinley. Used by
permission of Viking Penguin, a division of Penguin Books USA Inc.

Library of Congress Cataloging-in-Publication Data

Fader, Shirley Sloan.
Wait a minute, you can have it all : how working wives can stop
feeling overwhelmed and start enjoying life / by Shirley Sloan Fader.
p. cm.
"A Jeremy P. Tarcher/Putnam book"—T.p. verso.
Includes bibliographical references
ISBN 0-87477-696-1 (alk. paper)
1. Working mothers—United States. 2. Wives—Employment—
United States. 3. Work and family—United States. I. Title.
HQ759.48.F33 1993 92-17910 CIP
306.872—dc20

Printed in the United States of America
1 2 3 4 5 6 7 8 9 10

This book is printed on acid-free paper.

For my husband, Seymour J. Fader
& my children, Susan Deborah Fader & Steven Micah Kimchi Fader
who've made all the years of trying to Have It All
worth trying for
& for Lawrence, Julie, Edward, Miriam, Laura, Jacob
who've expanded "All" in wonderful new ways.

Contents

· · · · · · · · · · · · · ·

Author's Acknowledgments   9

Part One: The Problem You're Struggling With

1. Overview: What You'll Find in This Book   13

2. Overload Impact: How It Crushes Wives, Husbands,
   & Marriages   15

3. Found: The Mysterious, Missing Male-Convincer You Need   23

4. The Three Real Reasons Most Husbands Scorn Housework   31

Part Two: You're Entitled

5. 10 Big Ways Your Job Makes Your Husband's Life Easier,
   Better, Happier   41

6. Your Man Is a Success! Even If Your Family
   Needs Your Paycheck Too   51

7. Why Wanting a Career Is So UNselfish—Even If Your Family
   Can Live Well on His Income   61

8. Working Wife Bill of Rights: What Are You Entitled To?   68

Part Three: Your Man & Family Responsibilities:
The Encouraging Big 1990s News

9. 1990s' Disappearing Macho Man: 16 Big Reasons Why He's
   Ready to Share the Housework   73

**Part Four: Your Hidden House-Power Fears:
How to Recognize Them & Free Yourself**

10. *How & Why Working Wives Prevent Husbands from Doing More at Home*   87

11. *Sharing vs. Helping: What's in It for You & Your Family?*   96

12. *How to Get Him to Do It "Right"*   107

13. *Your New Invincible Husband-Convincing Powers*   118

14. *What to Say & Do When You've Already Tried Everything*   123

15. *How to Say It So He Hears It—& Likes What He Hears*   133

16. *How Sharing House-Power Makes Your Marriage Happier*   148

17. *Why Your Children Will Love Mother More*   157

18. *Emotions vs. Logic: Figuring It Out*   168

19. *Hiring Help When You Can't Afford It, They Won't Do a Good Job, & There's No Help Available in Your Area*   172

20. *Conclusion: Should You or Shouldn't You Use This System?*   180

Backgrounder:

How Media, Business, Government, Society Generate Working Wife Guilt & Prevent You from Solving Your Overload   182

Research Notes   192

Survey Questionnaires   230

Bibliography   237

Author's Acknowledgments

· · · · · · · · · · ·

I am grateful to many people who helped create this book—people whose names I know and whose names I don't know.

I am deeply grateful to the more than five hundred working wives I have interviewed during the past 20 years as I wrote articles, columns, and other books about women's new combined family and employment lives. The women shared their working wife problems and personal experiences with candor. Their names have been changed throughout the book to protect their privacy.

I also did a written anonymous-response survey among working wives. Jean Shepherd, Bergen County Editor of North Jersey Newspapers Company, did much to produce a diversified range of respondents. Ms. Shepherd ran a news article in the company's newspapers inviting women's organizations of all kinds to contact me and distribute my questionnaire among members who were working wives/mothers.

Janet M. Hill, then vice president of the New Jersey Family Day Care Providers' Association, Bergen County Chapter, was among those who responded. Singlehandedly, Janet M. Hill arranged for and produced more completed questionnaires than anyone else. Ms. Hill distributed batches of the questionnaires to her chapter's owner-members for use by their working wife/working mother clients; she then followed the process through until the questionnaires were returned to me. The network of family day-care groups Ms. Hill reached through BCFDCPA serves a wide variety of middle-class families in many suburban towns in northern New Jersey—towns that differ significantly in demographic characteristics. As a result the survey yielded a wide sample of middle-class families of different education levels and with aggregate family income ranging from $35,000+ to $100,000+.

The association owner-members who helped obtain completed surveys are: Janelle Chin, Dorothea Fulmore, Debbie Kwapniewski, Lori Dent,

Debbie Newman, Beth Clarke, Mary Ann Trulby, and Carmen Vala. Leaders of other organizations or individuals who helped distribute and/ or collect the completed anonymous questionnaires are: Eleanor Antolino, Helen Gazda, Barbara Harrison, Joan McCaffrey, Eleanor Roes, Patricia Sinnott, Suzanne K. Sykes, and Marie Vojitovitz.

And, of course, I am grateful to the working wives/mothers who completed the survey questionnaires anonymously and thereby provided so much valuable information. It is useful to note how revealing a well-balanced sampling such as my 62 can be. Two valuable and acclaimed books are good examples: Gail Sheehy's *Passages* is based on 115 interviews; Dr. Arlie Hochschild's landmark book documenting the dimensions and characteristics of working wife Overload, *The Second Shift,* is based on interviews with 50 couples. Copies of the questionnaires used in my survey can be found at the end of the research notes.

My family helped me from beginning to end with practical efforts, insights, and/or important encouragement. They are: Seymour J. Fader, Susan Fader, Steven Fader, Lawrence Krule, Julie S. Fader, Joyce S. Anderson, and B. Robert Anderson. I received help in formatting the questionnaire and targeting a meaningful sample from Joyce S. Anderson, a sociologist, and from Susan D. Fader, a principal in a New York City-based strategic marketing and analysis corporation. My sister, Joyce S. Anderson, made many very valuable editorial contributions to the final form of the manuscript.

Susan Ginsburg, my literary agent, worked with great professional skill—together with warm personal interest. The sum of her efforts eased the tasks of creating the book. The book's editor, Sandi Gelles-Cole, painstakingly worked through the text and helped me clarify many of the important ideas.

Jeremy P. Tarcher, the publisher, has supported, guided, and helped shape the book with the kind of personal attention, knowledgeable and perceptive insights, and practical actions that writers always hope to find for their books but too seldom do.

As always, my husband, Professor Seymour J. Fader, constantly encouraged and helped me in every possible way by attitude, word, and deed.

PART ONE

. . . .

The Problem You're Struggling With

. . . .

1

Overview: What You'll Find in This Book

WHETHER you work solely because you have to earn money, or because you want to combine family and career, this book will give you the answers you need to balance marriage, children, job/career and enjoy them all.

Since 1971 I have worked as a careers columnist and/or careers contributing editor for *Glamour*, *Working Woman*, *Ladies' Home Journal*, *Working Mother*, *Woman*, *New Idea*, and for *Family Weekly*, the weekend magazine featured by 350+ major American newspapers. I have also written career articles for many other women's magazines in the United States, Australia, and Great Britain such as *Cosmopolitan*, *Harper's Bazaar*, *Company*, *Portfolio*, and *Family Circle*. And I've written two women's career books, *From Kitchen to Career* and *Successfully Ever After*.

During 20+ years, as I researched sociology, economics, and psychology for my women's books, columns, and articles, I also interviewed hundreds of working wives. More than five hundred is a very conservative estimate. In these interviews I heard women describe how exhausted they were from their attempts to combine paid employment and the responsibilities of wife, mother, and homemaker. As we talked, I learned about working wives' hopes, anxieties, and deep feelings about their overloaded lives.

My several decades of formal sociological, economic, psychological research, the 500+ interviews with working wives supplemented by a written survey I conducted for this book, and my relevant bachelor's and master's studies at the University of Pennsylvania led me to this book's new insights and solutions for working wives' Overload.

With that knowledge base, this book approaches working wife Overload in new ways that can bring your husband into a *willing* home-and-family partnership with you. Whether you use all the book's system, a little of the system, or none, the information will be useful to you and helpful to your marriage.

Once you understand how one-paycheck marriage rules—that are irrelevant to your two-paycheck marriage—are manipulating you into working wife guilt, you will be free from that guilt. By itself, even if you make no other changes in your life, your new knowledge will reduce your Overload stress and give your husband and children a happier wife and mother. Your new information will also eliminate most of your Overload anger and exasperation. You will understand *why* your husband doesn't do more at home and with the children and *how* you can make changes, if you want to!

That's the wild card in *Wait a Minute, You Can Have It All*. If you want a more equal sharing at home with him, the book offers the how-to specifics you need to make it happen. But if you want to keep it "my kitchen" and "my home" with only slight shifting of your home responsibilities to him, the book's system will also help you.

When you choose the balance between your own family efforts and his that feels comfortable to you, you'll find the new family mood and routine expands your children's love for you and adds more zest, companionship, and love to your marriage.

You'll find that the full life men have of marriage, children, job or career, all at the same time, can be just as realistic—and enjoyable—for women.

Throughout the book, whenever you feel you need to know more about the research I mention, you will find full details arranged chapter by chapter in the Research Notes at the back of the book.

2

. . . .

Overload Impact: How It Crushes Wives, Husbands, & Marriages

. . . .

*K*AREN Wilmot of Ridgewood, New Jersey, has a daily routine other working wives will recognize. Karen wakes up at 5:30 A.M., changes, feeds, and dresses the baby, throws in a load of wash, grabs a five-minute breakfast, dresses for work, takes her baby, Jimmy, to day care, puts in a full schedule as a teacher at a suburban high school, picks up Jimmy, comes home, makes dinner, feeds Jimmy, bathes him, and puts him to bed, shares a twenty-minute dinner with her husband, cleans the kitchen, finishes the laundry, gets ready for the next morning. "By nine o'clock I'm ready to drop. I just fall into bed exhausted."

Karen's friend Lori has a job, a husband, and school-age children, and Lori's life may be even more pressured. Besides seeing to her children's food, clothing, and physical needs, Lori races mornings, evenings, and weekends to give her children quality-time companionship, to help with their school needs, to see to their play dates and to all their religious, sports, and other extracurricular activities.

Most working wives with children live as Karen and Lori do. Consequently, most working wives will tell you they're chronically exhausted from carrying paid employment and nearly all the family work. Many admit they're also discouraged. "Is this really a way to live?" Some are resentful. "It's just not fair. Somehow we've had this big sexual revolution and change in women's lives. But at home it's still the same old thing." Though modern husbands often do pitch in, it's usually not nearly enough to make a real dent in their wives' Overload.

During the last few years men have caught a lot of criticism about their limited home efforts. Television talk shows, magazine articles, newspaper features, public opinion surveys all say, "The husbands of working wives refuse to do their fair share at home."

But that accusation is an unintentional distortion. The truth is far more complex. The truth is that neither men nor women are to blame for working wives' predicament.

The Problem You're Struggling With

We take for granted that every ordinary man we meet is entitled to marriage, children, paid employment all at the same time. When he goes for it, we say he's pursuing a full life. He isn't considered unrealistic. Nobody suggests that he wants too much.

Why then should we give up and decide it's unrealistic when women try for the same full life? Yet today an alarming new doubt is spreading among working wives. Whether a married woman with children works solely because her family needs her income or because she wants to combine family and career, she is usually struggling with the same problem. She's probably trying to carry her job and most or all of the family's home responsibility. This Overload—the combination of her job and most of the family work—makes many 1990s working wives wonder if "having it all" is an impossible dream for women.

It's a nationwide feminine problem:
Time magazine cover story: "WOMEN FACE THE 90s . . . In the 80s American women learned that 'having it all' meant doing it all."

Working Mother magazine: "HAVING IT ALL USUALLY MEANS DOING IT ALL . . . Though most of the women in our survey work as many hours outside home as their husbands do, women still bear most of the responsibility for household chores."

Professor Cynthia Fuchs Epstein, author of *50-50 Parenting:* "No matter what kind of job a woman has, executive, professional, clerical, blue-collar, she has the same Overload problems."

Sociologist Dr. Arlie Hochschild in her landmark book, *The Second Shift:*

Most women who work at jobs during the day also work a "second shift" at night doing most of the shopping, cooking, housework, and if there are children, parenting . . . putting in an extra month's work a year, in the form of chores at home. This double burden strains them to their limit.

Then there's this vivid letter to Ann Landers and Ann's bull's-eye reply:

> . . . not only do I take care of the oil changes in my husband's car, I also change flat tires, tighten oil pans, and buy the gas.
>
> I cut the grass, clean the gutters and take care of the furnace and humidifier filters. I have refinished the woodwork and replaced the faucets all over the house. I do all of the cooking, dishes, laundry, cleaning, and grocery shopping. I buy all the gifts for special occasions, including those for his grown kids from a previous marriage.
>
> If I waited for my husband to do his share, the kids would be walking around naked and the house would be condemned. There is no 50–50 in this marriage and I'll bet it's the same all over.
>
> Signed: 100 Percent Fed Up in Overland, Mo.

Ann Landers's response:

> Dear Fed: I have received five tubs of mail on this subject, and about 70 percent of the women claim they are doing 90 percent of the work around the house plus the shopping, driving the kids around et al. *even though they also work outside the home.* [Emphasis added.]

A 1990s Roper Organization survey gives us women's pungent view of their Overload burdens: "TODAY'S WOMAN IS FED UP . . . men's minimal contributions to housework and childcare are fueling yet another gender gap built on stress and resentment." And quoting Roper's executive director: "There's a lot of frustration and dissatisfaction at home and at the workplace. It's the dilemma of the decade . . ."

The specifics of what working wives fit into their daily 24 hours can boggle the imagination. Research by the respected, conservative Conference Board reveals that many working wives are carrying all the usual home and childcare tasks and in addition:

26% of working wives arrange and manage family auto repairs
34% frequently prepare family tax returns
47% regularly take out the garbage
23% paint or put up wallpaper

But what of the New Man that we constantly hear about, the minority of husbands who purportedly make significant contributions at home? A *Wall Street Journal* headline describes the facts: "MEN VOLUNTEER FOR THE FUN JOBS." They explain that the percentage of men who do chores declines swiftly the dirtier or more unpleasant the job becomes. For example, they say he's likely to make company dinner while she prepares the daily family meals. He's doing children's baths and story time or he's away with the youngsters for an outing while she's home with the mop and pail.

Husbands of working wives also gravitate to chores that can be scheduled to their convenience, like changing the car oil once in several months and painting a room once in several years. Meanwhile women see to the constant life maintenance tasks like meals, kitchen cleanup, childcare, laundry, food shopping, that are day in, day out demands.

And men frequently lose interest when faced with more than one household task at a time. "I'm trying to vacuum. If you want me to do it, get the baby out of here."

Yet, as everyone knows, working wives frequently hold family life together by juggling many tasks: making dinner, watching the toddlers, running back and forth to keep their laundry machines busy. That's a routine many women can manage until the fourth typical simultaneous challenge is added. Her husband also has just returned from work and he wants to discuss something. Too often because she's learned to cope fairly smoothly, he's oblivious to the fact that she's already doing three other things. Her distracted responses produce not an offer of help but hostility as he gives his impression of what's going on. He flares, "You never really listen . . . You're just not interested." And off he stalks.

As a result of working wives' crushing physical and emotional Overload, Dr. Hochschild noticed that the women tend to talk more intently than their husbands about being overtired, sick, and "emotionally drained." They speak about sleep, she says, "the way a hungry person talks about food."

Even if you're one of the fortunate working wives who has cleaning help and good childcare, women like you consistently report they also feel overwhelmed. The whole huge children-home-job complex of children's medical, religious, sports, extracurricular, clothing, and play life, and all the aspects of the adult home and social life, keep going only because you have "everything on your head." You do, investigate, hire, instruct, watch over, foresee, and follow up. When your husband finally puts forth efforts, you've usually done the research, purchasing, and scheduling of the hidden 80–90% of the task.

That's what Overload is costing you. Now

How Your Husband & Marriage Suffer from Your Overload

His Risk of Losing You

The 1990s man has a large portion of his identity and self-esteem invested in his success as a husband. Gone are the days when a divorce or separation automatically meant he had left her. Today's wives tolerate just so much. Then, unlike the unhappy wife of yore, she frequently says to herself, "I don't have to take this. I can earn a living." As a major *New York Times* feature reports, nowadays more wives than husbands end a marriage.

Vernal Brown, who makes auto bumpers in a Ford auto plant, reflects a 90s wifely attitude. Though her paycheck was essential for family bills, when her husband told her to quit her job if she couldn't also take care of the home needs and have his food ready, she made a 1990s feminine decision. She quit the marriage.

A *Husband's Costs* If she walks out, the man's emotional distress is heavy and long lasting. Though a woman may take longer to remarry, psychological research reveals that when a man is rejected in love, he suffers deeper emotional wounds over a longer period of time than when she is rebuffed. Therefore, the husband who allows his wife's resentment and anger to build as she staggers under her job-home responsibilities has much to lose if she eventually terminates their marriage.

Yet many men fail to see how their attitude can make it relatively easy for some working wives to slam the door behind them. As one separated wife puts it, "My husband had nothing to do with the house and home. He worked and felt that the rest of his time was free, that he could do whatever he wanted . . . It's easy for me to be separated, since nothing has changed. I still do everything by myself."

When Overload anger does destroy a marriage, counselors find that many men go into shock. Blind to the interpersonal nuances that are so important and clear to a wife, many of the newly separated men believed their marriage was in good condition—though his wife saw the marriage as failing and probably had been telling him so.

His Risk of Losing Touch with His Children

As fathering becomes a national male passion, men seek the emotional closeness with their children that traditionally has been reserved for mothers.

A Husband's Costs If Overload drives a mother to separation or divorce, a father usually loses daily closeness with his children during their childhood—and then permanently for life!

Most mothers who want it still receive custody. And an in-depth study of the later-life effects of divorce on father and child found "divorce has a pronounced negative effect" on how often men see their adult offspring. Divorce also sharply reduces the probability that the fathers consider their adult children as a source of support in times of need.

His Risk of Living within an Unhappy Marriage

Even if she doesn't leave him, her anger over his inadequate home efforts and the battles it produces can make domestic life miserable for him (and, of course, for her and the children). Marriage research finds that only money generates more fights between husbands and wives. "Domestic chores" ranks second as a husband-wife battlefield.

A Husband's Costs Women's impatience with husbands' inadequate family efforts is escalating. An Associated Press account of a relevant poll was headlined, "Women Find Men Mean, Oversexed, Lazy." The accompanying article explained that today's women have far less tolerance for and are quicker to fight about such behavior than were their 1970s sisters.

Doonesbury  BY GARRY TRUDEAU

Less Sex & Less Ardent Sex

A Husband's Costs Now here's a masculine loss caused by her Overload that any man can regret. Yet no-time-for-sex has become a nationwide phenomenon. Dr. Merle S. Kroop, associate director of the Human Sexuality Teaching Program at the New York Hospital-Cornell Medical Center, is one among many sexual performance experts who've observed that lack of desire is common in working mothers.

Fatigue is an obvious culprit. But Dr. Sharon Nathan, who is with the same program, comments that fatigue can be triggered from emotional sources—such as resentment about Overload—even more than physical causes.

Less Money

As children are born and working wives take on more responsibilities at home, many women find they are forced to refuse promotions. Some even quit high-paying executive and managerial work for less interesting and poorer paid part-time assignments. In her book-length research study *The Gender Factory*, sociologist Sarah Fenstermaker Berk reports the major cause of working wives' restricted income and reduced employment hours is their responsibility for most or all of the family's domestic labor and especially for the childcare.

So stressed are working wives that "Putting a Career on Hold" has become a commonplace national female decision, inspiring a *New York Times Magazine* report with that title. On the West Coast a *Los Angeles Times* survey finds that while only 2% of fathers report parenthood demands have hurt their careers, 41% of mothers believe their family concerns have "forced them to scale back their careers."

A *Husband's Costs* Heavy. To make up his wife's lost family income, he either pushes himself harder to carry two jobs or, as the family standard of living drops, his personal standard of living also falls.

In addition, the arrangement asks too much of human nature. It is unrealistic to expect that a career-oriented woman can watch with equanimity as he has undistracted daily freedom to build *his* career—while she must sacrifice opportunities to accumulate career experience, credentials, and income. When she contemplates that his freedom is built on her carrying his & her family responsibilities, the realistic sense of injustice she feels cannot fail to sear their relationship and him.

What It All Means to You

Everyone hammered by working wife Overload—you, your husband, children—is coping with significantly diminished emotional and psychological lives.

An Overload problem that threatens the marriages and physical, emotional, psychological well-being of close to 60 million adult Americans— the two-thirds of American couples who are dual wage earners—is as huge a social problem as can be found.

So far, all the books on the subject have either documented and proved the dimensions of the problem, offered women time management plans for doing it more "efficiently," or suggested the problem is intractable except by some form of putting her career on hold.

It's time to solve the problem! He is not a villain and you are doing your intelligent best against strong countervailing social forces. Wives and husbands need realistic new solutions that free families caught between one-paycheck reasoning and two-paycheck life.

3

Found: The Mysterious, Missing Male-Convincer You Need

WHAT will solve your Overload? What does it take to convince him to do more at home?

An extra measure of sex appeal?

More dollars in your paycheck?

Nagging?

Sometimes the search for the missing male-convincer seems the biggest treasure hunt ever.

Since the 1960s when two-paycheck families multiplied, business, government, universities, and family organizations have sponsored hundreds of research projects costing millions of dollars. *The family researchers are looking for the personality traits or living conditions that would influence your husband—and other husbands in two-paycheck marriages—to carry a real share of family work.* I call the unknown persuasive conditions they're searching for the "male-convincer."

The family experts—sociologists, psychologists, psychiatrists, family counsellors—know a set of conditions exist that do influence a husband to cooperate. They know because in nearly every family study of two-paycheck marriages, a relatively few wives surface and report, "No problems. We both do our part. We're a team in everything."

Discover and use the male-convincer that produces those team-couples and your own Overload problem—and all working wives' housework and childcare Overload—could be solved.

The Search So Far

Thirty years of male-convincer research has helped us all. They have now tested everything you and I in common sense would have thought important. And based on the research, the family experts now know you *cannot* depend on any of the conditions listed below to move your husband—or any husband—to do enough family work to rescue you from feeling overwhelmed.

Nagging

Just the opposite. The researchers notice that the cooperative couples have marriages high in "stability and happiness." Whereas if you try nagging, it often has little effect or actually boomerangs.

As some women in my working wives' survey put it, "When I scream . . . he does it, but only when I'm at the end of my rope." "He says, 'Yes, sure . . .' and then forgets to do it." "He says he works too hard all day . . . but I work as long and hard at my job." And the hoary ploy? "He does it and makes sure it turns out so badly I won't ask again."

Your Husband's Attitude Toward Sexual Equality

This one is a real brain teaser. Reams of studies indicate that your husband's belief in equality of the sexes, including his sincere conviction that both parents should share homecare and childcare equally, does *not* of itself cause him to share the work.

Your Husband's Age

The number of birthdays he's celebrated is useless as an influence or predictor. You find some two-paycheck husbands in their 20s and 70s and everywhere in between who carry their fair share at home. And you find many more of all ages whose behavior ranges from grudging or occasional cooperation to outright refusal.

Your Husband's Education

More education sometimes seems to help men see the fairness of taking over some of their working wives' home responsibilities. But even in these "good" situations his efforts are usually nowhere near equality and education definitely does not always produce a more cooperative husband. Some husbands with modest educations happily do their share and more. And the research indicates that millions of well-educated men are skillful at reluctant home cooperation or complete refusal.

Your Education & Career

Your career and education do not move him to team effort. Wives in pink collar, blue collar, and clerical jobs are usually doing most or all of it at home. Then again, the family studies show that so are married female executives and working wives in the professions: the female engineers, CPAs, teachers, nurses, scientists, physicians, journalists, and even those women trained to defend themselves, the lawyers.

Your Non-traditional Career

Even if you succeed in a traditionally male job, it usually has no effect on persuading your husband to assume a real share of home responsibilities.

Your Income

The amount you earn is not the male-convincer! There's only a small increase in a husband's home efforts as his wife's financial contributions rise, approach, or surpass his. Though you may become your family's major breadwinner, you as a working wife will usually go on doing the lion's share of homecare and childcare.

Type of Community You Live In

Whether you live in a city, town, suburban or rural area, the studies find that you as a working wife are usually doing most or all of it at home.

Socialization

This is the catchall. But it doesn't work. The researchers say it "yields no valid data." Translation: Whether you were raised by old-fashioned sexist standards or by liberated parents, now as a working wife you are probably overburdened and doing most of the family work.

The Things about You That Really Matter

How can it be that a man's belief in sexual equality, his age, education, his and your occupation, and all the other personal factors each fail as a male-convincer?

What has been dubbed "the first X-rated dissertation" gives us some clues. For her Pennsylvania State University doctoral dissertation, Dr. Beverly Romberger investigated women's beliefs about men. In thorough one-on-one interviews lasting between three and nine hours she surveyed women who differed widely in age, education, income, religion, lifestyle.

She admits she was "amazed" to discover that women absorb in childhood and live by a core of common beliefs about female behavior. And she found these beliefs are unaffected by women's other personal experiences.

For example, a girl who quit high school at 16 to work behind a fast-food counter, then got pregnant at 17 and was hustled into a shotgun marriage by her parents, had two more children, and at age 30 left her husband who drank and beat her, probably has the same basic male-female beliefs as the woman who shone through undergraduate and professional university studies, delayed motherhood until her thirties, and has a gentle, sober husband.

Prominent among these beliefs is the conviction that keeping the house clean and caring for the children are a wife's job. Dr. Romberger found that on an intellectual level many women believe in equality in the relationship. But in everyday life, especially after the children are born, women tend to fall back into the old male-female roles and arrange their lives on the assumption that home and childcare are a wife's duty, not joint wife-husband responsibilities.

Once you're aware of this attitude that even though she is employed, home and children are her duty as a wife, you start noticing confirmation in friends' and family's conversations. You hear the working wife's account of being overburdened. Yet if someone suggests that she get her husband and teenagers to do more, hire help, or in some way eliminate or shift work, her response is a variation of "No. It's my job. I'll do it."

This typical attitude was expressed by many women in my survey including a young mother, a college graduate, with a family income of $80,000–$100,000. Though she writes that she "detests" cleaning the bathrooms, she doesn't hire anyone. It's "my job." And "racing with time" to get home and prepare dinner for her husband and children "is a daily grind." But she believes it's necessary. Otherwise ". . . my husband will have to start dinner before I get home . . . I feel it is my responsibility." Her comments are interesting because they are so typical, because you hear the same ideas so often from women at all income levels.

Essentially, the women are saying they don't believe it's right; they don't feel Entitled to lighten their load by shifting any of their traditional home and child duties to other people.

It all comes together in a study reported by an American Management Association publication that found working wives openly confessed that they felt "lazy" and "guilty" if they took shortcuts in their home chores *or got husband or children to do some of the work.*

A man who owns a personal service business talks about the guilt feelings he notices among working women. He explains that men who hire his company to balance checkbooks, write checks, track investments don't see it as an indulgence or extravagance. To the men it's not an emotional issue.

Yet when he deals with a woman who holds a job that is just as demanding, her comments tell him that she feels she's being "lazy" in hiring him. He reports that her attitude is, "If I were really organized, I could do this myself."

The same dreary truth emerges in a *Wall Street Journal* roundup of executive women's comments about their job-home Overload. "I think I feel guilty about having my husband doing household chores."

The full extent of working wives/mothers' feeling that they're Not Entitled to household efforts from others is dramatically revealed in the prestigious research publication, *Journal of Marriage and the Family.* The researchers find you can send the average tired working mother home after a day at her job to a household of healthy teenagers and often she won't disturb their phone chatter or TV watching. She requests and receives *less* efforts from those teenagers than full-time homemakers receive from their adolescents. "Kids Learn by Helping Out—Stop Doing Everything Yourself!" shouts a *Working Mother* magazine coverline at their overburdened readers.

So here in working wives' belief absorbed in childhood that women are Not Entitled to shift home responsibilities to someone else, we have the beginnings of the real causes of Overload and with it, the path to solutions.

This Is the Two-Part Male-Convincer

During my 20 years of interviewing 500+ working wives and writing books, articles, columns on aspects of working women's lives I've become aware of this pervasive, socially induced working wife sense of Non-Entitlement about shifting home responsibilities.

And I've observed, interviewed, and analyzed the attitudes and communication styles of enough exceptional team-couples to have discovered that the male-convincer—that makes some relatively few two-paycheck husbands carry a realistic share of family life—is a *double-barreled working wife mindset.*

The team-couple working wives who escape Overload and enjoy those marriages high in "stability and happiness" have somehow individually worked past the cultural message of Non-Entitlement. Those wives have arrived at a team effort with their husband through two behavior traits the women have in common. These two working wife behavior traits together are the male-convincer:

TRAIT NUMBER ONE:

These working wives believe that because they are bringing in family money, they are Entitled to have their husband assume a real portion of family responsibilities. *The dollar amount the women earn compared to their husband's earnings does not matter.* Since there are only 24 hours in everybody's day, what counts is whether the wife is devoting a significant number of her weekly hours to earning family money.

Notice that when a working wife feels Entitled, the men in these marriages "assume responsibilities." They do not help her. "Helping" is another way of saying, paid employment

or not, home and children remain *her* duty. Or why would he be "helping her with *her* work?"

By "assuming responsibilities" the men in these families not only take on the physical effort for the chores they've accepted, they plan for, obtain the supplies, and remember on their own to attend to the work. The family obligations he's accepted are on his mind, not on her mind.

TRAIT NUMBER TWO:
Once the woman believes she is Entitled she speaks up and explains to her husband why she is Entitled and why he should become a real family-life partner.

Elsewhere quantities of family and general communication research (which we will discuss in later chapters) have found that a wife who speaks up about something often succeeds: The evidence is that men respond to wives' openly expressed attitudes. That's encouraging.

WHY DON'T MORE OVERLOADED WIVES ACT?
Because most women do not feel Entitled to speak up. The women feel a husband puts up with a lot because a wife is away from home at a job.

The women feel it is a man's job to support the family and a woman's job to care for it and that current economic needs shouldn't interfere with that time-honored arrangement.

They feel he won't do it "right" and so it's often easier to do it herself than explain it all to him.

They feel that carrying home and children responsibilities is a big part of their femininity and that they are a failure as a woman if they shift any real portion of the work.

Besides, even if a woman felt Entitled, how on earth does she go about talking up and "changing the division of family labor" with her husband?

Parts Two, Three, and Four of this book explore and solve these and other sensible worries.

But first one other important twist of the problem must be understood before you can solve it.

Do You Recognize Your Own Attitudes Here?

Perhaps you're carrying a job and far too much of the family responsibilities while your husband does his job and a relatively light portion of family life work. Yet you've been slogging along feeling, "Well, it's fair. It's my duty and besides that's the way marriage is and so why rock the boat?"

This contradiction of wives suffering heavy overwork stress while declaring their husband's behavior is "fair" is a surprisingly common situation.

Dr. Myra Marx Feree of the University of Connecticut reports a striking example. She interviewed 103 employed married mothers in a telephone survey to determine what conditions they would describe as fair or unfair in their own families.

She learned that women would complain throughout the interview about how lazy her husband is and how angry she is that he does so little around the house or for the children. Then—incredible—the woman would sum up by claiming that she was "satisfied" with her husband's behavior.

Dr. Feree concludes that apparently women who say and believe they are "satisfied" with conditions that make them "angry" are those who see the situation as beyond their ability to change.

In my research I've found an additional enormously important factor. "Satisfied" and "fair" as working wives use the words—and perhaps as you use them—mean that your husband's behavior matches your own views about your proper feminine home duties.

As a result, a woman will ruin her looks, her health, her disposition, her relationship with her husband and her children as she grinds through her impossible regimen of paid employment plus a second shift at home and call it "fair" if she believes she is Not Entitled to shift home responsibilities to others. If she believes that though she is bringing in family income, it still remains "her duty" to carry most or all of family tasks.

The key question which must be answered before many women can start feeling Entitled is WHY, HOW, & WHO loaded women with this sense that though they're earning family income, it's not right to accept much household effort from others?

4

The Three Real Reasons
Most Husbands Scorn Housework

. . . .

AS we've seen, family researchers sometimes come upon working wives who say, "He does his share; we're a team."

Somehow these lucky women have worked through feelings of Non-Entitlement for others' efforts. They've somehow withstood media, business, government, society that keep pounding us with one-paycheck family rules; *rules that were true for full-time homemaker-husband/breadwinner; but which simply do not fit the facts of your two-paycheck life.*

> These *one-paycheck family rules* that every major institution
> of society is still hammering into two-paycheck couples:
>
> 1. Make it impossible for most two-paycheck couples to solve
>   her Overload.
>
> 2. Create working wives' sense of Non-Entitlement for oth-
>   ers' efforts.
>
> 3. Teach husbands they have no responsibility for home and
>   childcare.

Are You Running Your Life This Way?

The one-paycheck family rules tell us:

1. **A Husband Whose Wife Goes Out to Work Is Putting Up With a Lot**

   Working wives should remember that though they are enjoying a new expanded women's lifestyle, it's really costing the man.
   The men are losing in the status and power within the family that went along with being the only breadwinner; plus they're losing all kinds of wifely services to the men's comfort and to the housekeeping and the children. Wives should try to make it up to the men.

2. **The Husband Who Cannot Support His Family Is a Failure as a Man**

   Therefore, the husband must be the family's *real* breadwinner.

3. **Seeing to It That Children & Home Are Properly Cared for Is a Wife's Job**

   Her femininity and success as a woman depend on her doing the work and doing it properly. If she is fortunate, her husband will help. But with or without his efforts, she is the one responsible. And she will be criticized as a bad wife and bad mother if home and children appear to be receiving below par attention.

It is not the task of this book to investigate or prove the motives of leaders of media, business, government, social institutions that continually generate working wife guilt by discussing your new working wife Overload in terms of these old one-paycheck standards.

But for clarity here are two quick examples of how this ongoing din teaches all of us that working wives must go on living by full-time homemaker rules. Then the "Backgrounder" chapter immediately before the Research Notes gives you in-depth proof and illustrations of How, Where, When we're brainwashed.

Example: Though you're both out earning money to support the family, the institutions continue to discuss childcare as a "working wife" problem and as a strain and burden of "working wives/working mothers" instead of what it really is: a "working *parents*" issue/strain/burden.

As they continue to label childcare a *"working wife"* problem, the institutions are delivering a powerful message to both you and your husband. They're reminding you that though you're both supporting those children, caring for them is *not* his concern. It remains a "working wife's problem"; it remains *your* job.

Another typical example of how the institutions keep telling us that two-paycheck wives have to live by one-paycheck full-time homemaker rules: Business, media, government, social institutions continually offer us programs, plans, hints, ideas that they say are meant to "help working wives" "put more time in your day" in order "to get it all done." As they do, they are really pointing out to both you & your husband that your Overload is strictly your feminine problem.

They do this by offering help in a form that says: Notice, Ms. Career Lady, you as wife and mother are the only person who must do these family tasks. Despite your paid job, you're Not Entitled to shift any of these responsibilities to either family or paid help.

We remind both you and your husband that you alone are responsible for home & family by offering "help" that always takes the form of the "newest," "quickest," "best ideas"—for *you* to do the work!

How the Three Rules Victimize You, Your Husband, & Your Marriage

These three one-paycheck rules when forced upon the realities of two income marriages are the real reasons most husbands of working wives do so relatively little home/childcare.

The rules produce your Overload which then assaults and damages marriages with all the husband costs discussed in chapter two. This is precisely how the tragedies evolve:

Since media, government, society constantly remind us that HOME & CHILDREN ARE A WIFE'S JOB (with the sub-message that, paid job or not, your success as a woman depends on doing it yourself), we women learn the work continues to be "our duty" and it's not only wrong to try to shift it to husbands, it's wrong to shift it to anyone. (It's OK to complain but not OK to mount a thought-out, effective effort that will really transfer a fair portion of the work.)

This social pressure produces startling results. During all the 20 years of my interviews with working wives I've heard it and in my recent written survey of working wives I obtained evidence in black and white. In the survey women were asked the family's income. About half the women indicated family incomes of $60,000, $80,000, or even $100,000+ together with a small family of healthy children. Most of these prosperous women also noted they were coming home from a day's employment to launder and iron his shirts, scrub kitchens and bathrooms, and do all the rest of the housework.

Working wives with strong family incomes like these, and certainly those $100,000+, can surely afford to send his shirts out and hire cleaning help. *But if everything in the culture keeps telling you that job or no job a decent woman is still expected to do the housework herself, then you do it!*

And that is why the family research shows that even among affluent female executives and professionals so many of them come home, lay down their briefcases, and pick up the piles of dirty laundry and the vacuum cleaners.

If feeling guilty about hiring help stops so many affluent working wives from buying significant chore relief, how much more so does this wretched IT'S A WIFE'S JOB rule forbid working wives with lower incomes from using their ingenuity to find a few household dollars for some chore aid?

There's no need to guestimate. The United States Department of Labor has considered the question nationwide at all income levels and has the dismal news waiting for us.

It's Not Just You: That's the Way It Is Everywhere

My survey results reflect the national pattern for all income levels. The Labor Department's *Monthly Labor Report* tells us that when a woman adds a job to her life, the new demands on her time have no effect on her and her family deciding to hire help for laundry, cleaning, and other household necessities.

As the Labor Department puts it, the family research shows "a positive relationship between [wives'] employment and some relevant services such as child care, but not between employment and domestic services [of any kind]." In other words, adding a job to a woman's life doesn't change her attitude or behavior. If she didn't already use paid home chore help, when she takes a job and starts putting in all that time outside the home and earning thousands of dollars of family income, she still does all the housework herself. She still doesn't hire help.

Apparently working couples are forced to buy childcare for the hours they're employed because a mother's body can't be in two places at once. But her sense of Non-Entitlement sees to it that other "women's work" can wait till she returns from her job. And it does . . . being employed has no effect on women purchasing home service efforts!

Women used to have busy, demanding lives as full-time homemakers attending to all their home and family needs. Now with commuting women are devoting 20, 30, 40, 50 or more hours weekly to their jobs. Yet since they are not buying help, that means they're still doing everything at home. As we know, except for the relatively few team-couples, most husbands and adolescents are doing very little housework. No wonder working wives feel so overwhelmed, so starved for sleep, so stressed.

And here's the husband wallop. As business, media, society constantly remind him that housework and childcare are still a wife's job, he simultaneously learns that the work therefore still is not appropriate for a Real Man like him.

His renowned bungling and disinterest when he does her a favor and "helps" are the logical result. If he put himself enthusiastically into what society still labels as his wife's job, he would undermine his self-image as a manly male.

All the rest of women's exasperations also logically follow. No matter how mediocre his performance, wives, their friends, and family feel obliged to note how really good of him it is to undertake the work. As one working wife vividly sums it up, "You can't just ask men to do housework and then expect them to do it. You have to be over them with a whip and chain. And then they want praise."

And why not? According to the one-paycheck rule HOME AND CHILDREN ARE A WIFE'S JOB, he's entitled to appreciation for undertaking *her* duties.

The Breadwinner Ostrich-Act & You

Meanwhile rule #2, THE MAN WHO CANNOT SUPPORT HIS FAMILY IS A FAILURE AS A MAN, enormously complicates your

Overload by continuing to use breadwinning to measure your husband's masculinity. If you're like most two-paycheck couples, because of this rule neither you nor your husband admit aloud how much of the family support you're doing. Though a working wife weighed down with pay discrimination and needing all those hours for family efforts usually does not earn as much as her husband, the average working wife brings in almost a third of the family income. And wives who work full-time earn an average of 40%—close to half—of family income. There are also those 21% of working wives who earn more than half the family's money.

Yet prestigious psychological and sociological family research indicates that most men go on seeing themselves as the breadwinner. And their wives make little or no effort to get the men to see it more realistically.

It's not surprising that women are as reluctant as husbands to call attention to how essential the wives' paychecks are. After all, we've been taught that A MAN WHO CANNOT SUPPORT HIS FAMILY IS A FAILURE AS A MAN. And what wife wants to think her husband is a failure as a man?

So nationwide, couples create family fictions with each other about how he is the breadwinner and her income is for extras when it is in plain fact buying family necessities. For instance, in "The Provider Role: Its Meaning and Measurement," family researcher Dr. Jane C. Hood gives an illustration of how these family fictions operate when she quotes a husband who says:

> . . . we just use her paycheck to pay the house payments. So that's about all we do with hers . . . just pay the house payments. So that's a whole lot of money that I don't have to worry about.

In the same way couples label her paycheck's purchases of things like children's school clothes, adults' winter coats, basic appliances, college tuition, auto payments, home and auto repairs as "special extras," and then blandly tell each other and everyone else, "He's the one who is supporting us."

As we turn away from the credit, we lose our best chance to solve Overload. We give up our best bargaining issue which could say: "Since I am now carrying a significant part of your traditional masculine job of supporting our family, it is fair for you to assume a significant part of my traditional responsibility for our home and children."

But since Rule 2 says pointing that out would insult his masculinity, most women cringe and reject even the thought of expressing such an idea.

The It's Costing Him Farce & You

Wives are then completely sealed into marriage battles and anger about husbands' non-cooperation by the continual, multi-institution nonsense about THE MAN WHOSE WIFE GOES OUT TO WORK IS PUT-TING UP WITH A LOT.

As media, business, society constantly remind everyone that husbands "lose a lot" due to a wife's job, it's natural for women to shrink even further from trying to shift a fair portion of family work to him. According to the It's Costing Him rule, husbands are already giving heavily at home as he loses his patriarchal family power and many of his wife's full-time homemaker services.

It would then seem dangerous for the marriage and wrong to dare talk up and try to shift a real chunk of Overload to him.

Simultaneously, the It's Costing Him message lets him feel it's fair to make excuses and refuse while she struggles with her Overload. By convincing him he's already doing a lot for her just by "putting up with her job," the rule gives him a clear conscience and generates his irritation as he wonders why she keeps wanting him to do "more."

With this incredibly unrealistic one-paycheck view of two-paycheck marriage constantly beamed at them, it's not surprising so many women feel they're Not Entitled.

PART TWO

. . . .

You're Entitled

. . . .

5

. . . .

10 Big Ways Your Job Makes Your Husband's Life Easier, Better, Happier

. . . .

EVERYBODY'S DOING IT

Working wives are often apologetic about trying to combine family life and paid employment. A woman may apologize to her husband if she falls behind in some family tasks. Then she apologizes to him again if she's so pressured she has to ask him to do some family work. "I'm sorry to bother you, honey, but would you mind please . . ."

This chapter discusses the enormous hidden benefits your husband enjoys because of your outside employment. It makes clear why it's time to stop feeling defensive about how your job is "costing" him.

Rather it's time to feel confident and Entitled to work out with your husband a more equal sharing of family home/childcare responsibilities.

If your husband is like most two-paycheck family men, he now collects so many advantages and pleasures from the family money you bring in, that he derives more from your two-paycheck family life than you do.

Yet because of media/business/society brainwashing, both husbands and wives are programmed to see only the domestic inconveniences men suffer because of a wife's time away at her job.

Here then are important joys, privileges, & material goodies *your* working life is putting into *his* life:

He Owes His Lifestyle & Standard of Living to Your Job

Without your paycheck, back he would go to all the stresses and anxieties of being your family's sole breadwinner. To match your financial contributions and keep himself and your family in your current standard of living would be a near impossible task for him. As we've seen, wives now produce an average of 30–40% of their family's income. And 21% of wives—approximately one wife in five—produce *more* than 50% of the family's money.

Even if you earn only a few thousand dollars a year, you're paying for children's clothing, car repairs, college tuition or other family life items that he would have to cover.

As for housing, that most expensive middle-class necessity, a spokesperson for the American Association of Home Builders says, "For the majority of home sales today a wife's income is critical. Without it the couple could not afford the house they've chosen."

If your husband singlehandedly had to bring the family finances to its current level, it would mean heavy moonlighting for him at one or two extra jobs. The penalty if he failed to moonlight and push himself would be a severe drop in his own and the family's living standard.

Therefore, it is foolishness to go on believing your husband is "putting up with" you going to work; or he is "letting" you go out to work. He cannot live the middle-class family life he wants without your employed efforts.

Your Family Income Means He Can Choose His Work Conditions

When a wife makes real contributions to family support, her husband feels less pressure to devote himself intensively to work. Ronald C. Pilenzo, long-time president of the largest personnel society in the world, Society for Human Resource Management, has a strong overview of what is happening. He says, "When a family had only one wage earner, that man often had to accept many kinds of unattractive work obligations. Now men are saying no to overtime, to heavy travel, to unpleasant work conditions; even to putting in longer salaried and self-employed hours. They're saying, 'I'm not willing to do that anymore because I don't have to. I'd rather have a better quality of life.' "

Pilenzo drives the point home with, "But the freedom to put lifestyle first comes only with the fact that the man now has a second income, namely his wife's."

Research by a Fordham University professor matches Pilenzo's observations: Compared to a man whose wife is a full-time homemaker, the man whose wife has a full-time job:

1. **Tends to work fewer average annual hours.**
2. **Takes longer or more frequent vacations.**
3. **Chooses the job with the shorter commute time.**
4. **Changes jobs more readily when it pleases him to do so.**

Your Family Purchasing Power Protects His & Other Men's Jobs

Your job not only improves your own husband's work life, it keeps other women's husbands employed. And other women's jobs are helping keep your husband employed. The distinguished economist Eliot Janeway has pointed out that if it weren't for the added family purchasing power that wives' second income provides, untold numbers of men would be unemployed as sales of their products and services lagged. Janeway says the family purchases your paycheck buys "can make the critical difference for thousands of businesses and . . . [prevent them] from going broke and laying off males with seniority."

Your Income Builds Your Husband's Health, Lengthens His Life

Whether it's a few thousand a year, or the 30–40% of family funds wives typically earn, your income makes a big difference in your husband's good health.

More money, less stress. When they have a family income of over $50,000, people report life becomes easier, less wearing. Dr. Sheldon Cohen, professor of psychology at Carnegie Mellon University discovered this income-stress correlation in a government sponsored survey of 2,100 people. More than 70% of the time, it's the wife's earnings that raise the family into the stress-reduced comforts of $50,000 and beyond. It's also the wife's earnings in lower-income marriages that raise the family to the lesser stress of at least $25,000 and beyond.

Besides softening immediate pressures of paying the bills, the elasticity your money adds to your family budget allows your husband to join a health club, buy workout and sports equipment. Then, because his "second income" frees him, as we've seen, from long and inconvenient work schedules, he is able to use his health club and his equipment regularly.

Harder to prove, but worth considering. The happy, steep decline in heart attacks among men in their forties and fifties since the 1950s–60s is, of course, due in part to our new diets, new emphasis on exercise, new medicine, and bypass operations.

Still uninvestigated is the role of less career tension in men's lives. Surely as your paycheck lifts all the employment tensions your husband used to bear as the sole support of the family, you're lessening his stress and so increasing his health.

Your Job Gives Him a More Exciting, Interesting Life

In the past attending business parties and trips as a guest was strictly a wifely perk. Today millions of husbands (who have jobs of their own) enjoy this new extra *male* perk. The men accompany their wives to luscious expense-account dinners, conferences, conventions, business trips, and company parties that are part of their wives' occupations.

While their wives work, the husbands not only relax, the men often make their own excellent business networking contacts with other guests.

Take away the perks your job gives him—from everyday family budget-stretching extras like discounts on merchandise purchased where you work to glamour perks—and your husband would find his own life noticeably diminished.

Your Job Gives Him a Wife Who Understands Him Better

A famous James Thurber cartoon shows a tired husband dragging himself home after a day's work and a huge ravening wife gripping the roof of the house, watching for him, ready to pounce.

"Talk to me. You don't talk to me." Those were the traditional complaints of the wives who had been housebound all day. Her husband was her lifeline, her only regular avenue to the outside world. But after a day's work, he yearned not for chit-chat but to be left alone at least for a while in peace and quiet.

Under women's old housebound conditions, both wife and husband were right. He had a legitimate weary adult need for relief from pressure to perform in his own home. Yet, she had an understandable hunger for adult conversation.

Today as a working wife with your own many hours of adult activities in the work world you have no need to pressure him for conversation.

Yet ironically, when you're together, it's easier now for him to make conversation. Now he can discuss what he does all day with you as someone who is also out there and who is well equipped to understand workplace pressures, anxieties, triumphs. Your matching conversation about your job is something he can identify with and be interested in. Simultaneously, the more he shares the home and childcare, the more he understands and can take an active conversational interest in the small dramas of domestic life.

Your Income Eliminates His Unemployment Desperation

Amid company downsizing, buyouts, restructuring, and insolvency, pink slips are handed to every type of employee, including the conscientious and the competent. If that happens, all the problems of unemployment are eased for your husband if you have a job.

It's not just that you'd be bringing home dollars to purchase family necessities if he were unemployed. Equally important, you'd be subsidizing his self-esteem and ego. Though men continue to be emotionally devastated by job loss and reluctant to lean on a wife's income, nevertheless a wife's earnings allow him invaluable job search time. But for her paycheck he'd have to swallow his pride and snatch at any job—including uncongenial jobs and ones beneath his previous career level.

That's true for both the professional white collar and the blue collar worker. For instance, a truck driver can reject the immediate warehouse, night shift, and janitor job offers; the sales executive can reject the immediate sales rep possibilities. Their wives' income buys both of these

men time to search for a position akin to or better than their previous
employment. Sometimes her paycheck even allows an unemployed husband time to retrain for a new occupation.

Other gritty insights into how your job could help your husband
through unemployment come from John Crystal, whose ideas are the
acknowledged basis of the classic career book *What Color Is Your Para-
chute?* He says, "When a man was the only family breadwinner, men
often went out to interviews in horrible condition. They had to get a
job fast and their anxiety put them in a sweat that showed itself in all
kinds of behavior that counts against you in an interview. With a working
wife, a man's interview anxiety is not so intense, not anything like the
way it used to be."

Your Paycheck Frees Him to Follow His Career-Changing Dreams

In 1971 I wrote a research article on midlife career change. My assignment
was to try to find proof that such a life choice actually existed in American
society. Today everyone knows someone who has changed careers. Department of Labor statistics indicate that annually at least 10 million
Americans do it.

Though some of these career changes are the result of job loss, most
are what columnist Barbara T. Roessner calls the outcome of "an underlying shift of [personal] aspirations, expectations, and frustrations—
a subliminal command from the deep."

In 1971 when I first wrote about the subject, a man suffered almost
universal criticism if he dared change career in midlife: "Irresponsibility
about your family . . . Must be something wrong with you psychologically and morally" were among the politer barbs he could expect. And
with good reason. Families then usually depended solely on his income.

Today a man with children to feed and educate can follow his deep
psychological needs. When he jettisons a successful career to experiment
with entrepreneurial skills or to embrace a lower-paying but more creative
or human services occupation, people compliment the man. "Go for it,"
they say. "Why not do what you want?"

In a survey for his book *The Career Changer's Source Book*, author
Gene R. Hawes found that when a man discards a salaried job for life
as an entrepreneur, in almost 100% of the families it is his wife's income

that makes it possible during the early tight cash flow years. Her job is also essential for family group health benefits as opposed to the astronomical costs an individual entrepreneur must pay.

Other experts like James E. Challenger, president of Challenger, Gray & Christmas, Inc., a major international outplacement consultant firm, reports that until recently entrepreneurship was considered a young person's activity. Now, "because of the wife's second family income," Challenger finds that an increasing number of people in their forties, at the height of family expenses, are choosing self-employment.

Your Job Increases the Children's Love for Him

The omnipresence of nurturing TV dads dramatizes how thoroughly Americans now accept the idea of committed, competent fathering.

As a New York Times TV critic points out, TV doesn't introduce new social concepts. Instead television dramatizes social attitudes which the audience already believes in. So the popularity of active TV fathering mirrors a viewpoint about fathering that the audience has already embraced.

"Family Time Is More Important Than Rapid Career Advancement. Survey Shows Both Men and Women Support 'Parent Tracking'," says a recent press release from the international employment recruitment firm Robert Half International.

These are just fragments of the mountains of evidence of America's interest in fathering. During the last 10 years there's been an outpouring of personal essays, and books from men dwelling on men's newly discovered joys of fatherhood—in scores of diverse publications including Life, Texas Monthly, Newsweek, Esquire and People. And there are the full-length celebrations. How else except by realizing that fathering is in, can we explain the best-selling stature of an opus entitled Good Morning, Merry Sunshine: A Father's Journal of His Child's First Year, which was for seventeen weeks on The New York Times best-seller list, and was a multi-book-club selection.

In many of these current paeans to fatherhood, the author recalls how different it was when he was a boy. His father drove himself to provide for his children but had little free time to know and enjoy those children. Simultaneously, lightly sketched are the portraits of the authors' mothers whose only outlet was their children and home.

Hungry for opportunities to use their competence, these mothers often seized control of most decisions, activities, and emotions involving the children. Father then became a family outsider not only because he truly was very busy supporting them—but because his wife arranged it that way!

Nowadays a Gallup poll probing current male attitudes finds that the ". . . force underlying men's increased involvement with their children is their desire to achieve the kind of emotional bonding with their children that traditionally has been reserved for mothers."

Yet male longing for a deep emotional relationship with their children is doomed if women's world contracts.

If she's defeated by the burdens of Overload and gives up her career, leaving her only children and home to focus on, can anyone doubt she will again see to it that she is the only important one at home and with the children? Deprived of wide outlets for her abilities, wives will again dominate their children's practical and emotional life just as before—by forcing father back to the role of family outsider.

Your Income Buys Him Freedom from Traditional Male Chores

Now we're at the ultimate benefit that your paycheck buys for your husband.

As you struggle with your endless to-do list of job/home/childcare, your paycheck is freeing him from many of his traditional male to-do family chores.

Let there be no misunderstanding. Most working wives agree there's no money to employ household services for themselves. But it's ironic. While you continue to struggle with paid job and all your traditional female home responsibilities, you as a working wife almost certainly pay the bills for services that relieve your husband of many "male" family chores.

It's not that your working wife income is funneled directly out of your pocketbook into the hands of his service people. No, research indicates working wives usually combine their income with his into family finances or the women directly pay various household food, clothing, mainte-nance, supplies, utilities, insurance, vacation, car, children's college tuition bills that once were his obligation as the family's sole breadwinner.

Now because your paycheck covers some of these various family outlays, there's enough slack left in family money so he can "afford" to hire others to relieve himself of many of his traditionally male home tasks.

For example, Ron Hall, editor of *Lawn Care Industry Magazine* recalls that in the 1950s–60s lawn service for the middle class was next to nonexistent. "The industry took off in the late 70s when dual income families became popular and gave couples the extra money they need for the service. It now takes in $4 billion + annually."

This four billion + is not surprising since prices can be heartstoppingly expensive for middle-class budgets. Routinely, it can cost $150 to rake autumn leaves from tiny ¼ acre tract house plots, another $20–$40 weekly to cut and trim a lawn. Spring cleanup of winter debris, another $100–$150. Spring fertilizing, weed killing, ground thatching, still another $150. All this for very modest tract houses. Naturally, on larger plots, prices shoot upwards accordingly.

But how do so many modest-income husbands manage these lumping big charges? No problem. The service money is right there in his wallet. His working wife paid enough of the other family bills to make it possible.

As a result, today in millions of two-paycheck middle-class families, husbands are garden-free. Both days of his weekend are his for sports, TV, shopping, perhaps fun time with his children, and maybe a few hours spent "helping" his wife with "her work."

The same arrangement where she pays various family bills changes the family car wash scene. True, some men still wash the family car in the driveway. Many more can "afford" to have the car professionally washed and waxed regularly at a commercial establishment. When winter's snow arrives, no more backbreaking toil for him with a snow shovel. Just wheel out the expensive new snowblower. Or if it's really deep, phone the lawn service people who spend the winter snow-plowing. Dad can afford it.

Yet when it comes to your household chores, you may feel you cannot afford to send his shirts out. You may also believe you personally must shampoo the living-dining room carpet because commercial service prices are too high. And you probably wouldn't dream of an indulgence like weekly or bi-weekly cleaning service or sending your children's jeans and dresses out to a seamstress to have hems raised and lowered.

If you're skeptical that it's your paycheck that's freeing your husband from many traditional male chores, consider the alternative. On his income alone, could your husband—and most middle-class men—pay *all* the family bills and still "afford" to buy and hire these "ordinary" male chore-savers? Or on one income, would he still be doing the jobs himself?

There's more. Today all over America men are far quicker than in their one-income days to call the plumber to install a new bathroom faucet rather than spend a good part of their weekend struggling with it. Nor do many men spend months of evenings and weekends refinishing worn kitchen cabinets. Instead, the two of you decide to lay out your paychecks for a commercial kitchen overhaul. The men thereby win a twofer: they fulfill your desire for updating the kitchen (with your money) and at the same time the men avoid months of personal backbreaking refinishing labor doing it themselves.

Painting the home inside and out is still sometimes done by a husband. Yet far more often than in the 1950s–60s days of one family income, the two-paycheck husband hires a painter. Why should he knock himself out? Both he and you agree on the decision. After all, he can "afford" to pay someone to relieve him of this traditional male drudgery.

But where oh where, did *his* "extra" male-chore-relief family money come from?

☙☙☙

This long list of big benefits your husband derives from your paycheck should free you from the mistaken belief that you alone are benefiting from women's new liberated lifestyle. You now see the emotional, psychological, material benefits your harried job-plus-home life is bestowing on your husband.

The new knowledge of what your job is doing for him should set you free from guilt and apologetic need to "make it up to him." Instead, based on all your job is doing for him, it's time for you to feel Entitled to have him "make it up to you" by working out a fairer division of your family Overload.

6

. . . .

**Three women's lives: How the 1990s
are working out for them.
The Eventhorpes, the Kosnicks, and the Jensenns.**

*Your Man Is a Success!
Even If Your Family
Needs Your Paycheck Too*

Many working wives say, ...

> "Though the money I earn is very useful for my family, we don't
> see it as my sharing the burden of supporting us."
>
> "Knowing I must work or we can't pay our bills sometimes makes
> me angry because it's a man's job to earn the money."
>
> "If I came right out and said to my husband, 'Since I'm doing a real
> part of your man's job of supporting our family, it's fair for you to
> take on a real part of my home and childcare work,' it would make
> us both very uncomfortable. It would mean we had accepted that
> he's a failure who just can't support us."

**As long as you believe or act in accordance with any of these statements,
you will not be able to solve your Overload.**

In this chapter's stories of how the 1990s are working out for Jill &
Lenny Eventhorpe, Marie & Gregg Kosnick, and Sally & Douglas Jensenn, you'll find the facts you need to free both you and your husband
from these outmoded ideas, and make you both happier.

The Eventhorpes: Jill Blames Lenny

Jill Eventhorpe remembers how ashamed she was that night. She and her husband, Lenny, were at a party and Lenny was going on about how tough it was for him to take their baby to childcare every morning. Lenny explained that the nursery was on his way to work and nowhere near Jill's route. "But I have to park the car and it takes time every day to settle the baby. So I have to get out of bed and out of the house a half hour earlier than I used to."

At that point Jill tried smoothing things over with a gentle comment, "Well, I guess if I didn't work . . ." That was as far as she got.

Lenny turned on her, his face in a scowl, and loud and clear he demanded, "What do you mean, 'If you didn't work.' You must work! We can't manage without it."

As Jill recalls, "I thought I'd die. Lenny'd had a bit to drink and it made him say things that he'd normally never admit, like needing my income. It's bad enough Lenny doesn't earn enough to support us. But making his inadequacy so public . . . I really am losing respect for him.

"Lenny has much more education than my father. Yet my father earned enough so my mother was able to stay home and raise four children comfortably in a nice suburban house. Lenny and I can barely afford two children. We've been married twelve years. He's changed jobs. But we still can't live comfortably on his income.

"With just a high school education and his work at the factory, my father supported us well. Why can't Lenny, who has a college degree and an executive job, manage it?"

Why It's Not Lenny's Fault:

Like millions of other American husbands, Lenny can't manage to support his family on his income alone because this is the 1990s. Lenny works hard. His bosses and coworkers like him and Lenny's paid the full going rate for his efforts. Lenny's problem—the same problem millions of other American husbands have—is caused by the new 1990s world economy where low wages among competitors abroad force USA employers to limit all their costs including wages.

Jobs that pay enough to support a family are disappearing. Most jobs that are being created are at the bottom or at the high top. In "The Declining

Middle," a ten-page research analysis of the problem in *The Atlantic Monthly*, the author explains that though America has always had low wage service jobs, in the past we had a large middle range of relatively well paid manufacturing production jobs.

That's why for three decades after WWII, men like Jill's father could graduate from high school and choose among a number of relatively well paid production positions in their own community.

Now many of these jobs have vanished. For instance, in the 1980s, FORTUNE 500 industrial companies alone eliminated some three million manufacturing positions—that's equal to the entire working population of Massachusetts. The newly created service and technological jobs pay far lower wages, often as little as a tiny one-third of the paycheck an individual could earn in a manufacturing job.

If you've had this wage-ceiling problem and been thinking it's just you and your husband who are struggling, stop feeling it's your fault. U.S. Labor Department data shows the tight wages problem is hitting competent people throughout the country—because more than half of the new jobs created since 1980 pay "poverty wages" of less than $15,000 annually while a mere 12% pay more than $46,444.

No matter how Lenny and other husbands may push themselves and search, landing those relatively few positions that can support a family is very difficult.

And though both husband and wife work, one or both may be in the new low-wage positions the economy now offers. When you add up their two very modest his & her incomes, you can see why the Eventhorpes and so many other American families find that Mom's job is *not* temporary and why it's so necessary. As Lenny Eventhorpe put it at the party in that rare burst of frankness, "You must work! We can't manage without it!"

The Vanishing Career Ladders

Jill also doesn't understand Lenny's job changes and she's troubled by them. Presumably each time Lenny moves to a new job it's a better job. Yet Lenny doesn't seem to move up in job status. Again, it's probably not Lenny's fault. As companies battle foreign or domestic competitors, they trim their costs by cutting back on personnel. You can't pick up your local newspaper without reading about a firm that's cutting staff.

Nor do you need the newspaper. Too often it's people you know who are being laid off or maneuvered into early retirement.

The business term "lean" translates to fewer layers of executives and managers and therefore fewer promotion possibilities for Lenny, for Jill, and for everyone. American companies are becoming "flat as pancakes," says *The Wall Street Journal.* People reach a modest job plateau and salary range and are stuck there.

Economists and labor experts estimate that between the mid-1980s and 1992, two million middle-management positions have been permanently eliminated. "Like the blue-collar steel and auto workers of the early 1980s, most of these white-collars will never get back the earnings position they once had," says D. Quinn Mills, professor of organizational behavior and management at the Harvard Business School.

How Lenny, Jill, and You Should Look at It

None of this is in any way Lenny's—or other husbands'—fault. The fact that families like the Eventhorpes need both his & her incomes reflects 1990s employment conditions. As the conservative *New York Times* put it in a lead editorial, "Women who work, even in the most fulfilling professional jobs, do so because they have to."

Therefore, Lenny and Jill must stop pretending to each other, to themselves, and to the world at large that Jill's money is for extras. They must acknowledge they're a team working to support the family. By recognizing that this is the new, normal 1990s lifestyle, they can realize that Lenny—and other husbands like him—are each a success as a family provider within the 1990s economy.

The Kosnicks: Marie Wants to Stay Home

Despite their problems, Jill Eventhorpe enjoys her work and like so many other American working wives (75–85%) would not willingly become a full-time homemaker. Marie Kosnick is part of the remaining 15–25% of working wives who say, "I'd much rather be home full-time raising my children."

Family research indicates that women like Marie often are angry with their husbands because the men aren't singlehandedly supporting the family. This hostility often boomerangs against the women and then, like Marie, they have an especially hard time with job-home Overload.

Marie rises before six on workdays to put in two hours of family care before she leaves. She keeps moving every minute after work to attend to all her family's needs. In her mind the grim one-paycheck refrain keeps playing, "It's his job to support us. It's my job to take care of our home and children. *He's* not doing his job. But I'll do my job!"

With this attitude, Marie rarely asks for home effort from her husband unless she's absolutely desperate. She feels she *should* do it all. And she does.

Lately Marie has been angrier and more disappointed than ever with Gregg. As she views it, he's certainly not a success. First, the company he was with lost a big U.S. government defense contract and Gregg was among 2500 employees laid off. Then Gregg persuaded Marie it would be best to tighten the family belt, and live on Marie's pay while he retrained. After six months at an advanced electronics program, Gregg found work testing missile oscillators at a military contractor in the area. Marie was distressed to discover the salary was $2,200 less than he'd earned previously, and this employer's benefits program had no dental or eyeglass provisions and fewer holidays. Now there are rumors this employer may lose the defense contracts and Gregg may be unemployed again.

When Gregg asked Marie if she could go along with his taking time for more training that would give him more job chances in non-military work, Marie exploded. "It's my job to be home here. It's your job to support us without running back to school like a kid. What kind of man are you anyway?"

It's Not Just Gregg:

If Marie will cooperate, Gregg could be one of the winners on the new 1990s job scene. ". . . Workers Will Need Lots of Training to Get Started, and Still More to Stay Employed" warns a headline in *Fortune* magazine. *The New York Times* summarizes 1990s career trends with "Tomorrow's careers will entail a lifelong commitment to retraining, and the prospect of frequent short bouts of employment . . . Not many are likely to find the comforting positions in big, stable companies like their fathers filled."

Gregg understands this instinctively and constantly pushes himself to increase his skills. As soon as Marie drops her blinders, she can start seeing Gregg as a husband to be proud of, a man who understands and is willing to do what is necessary to succeed in the employment world of the 1990s.

Gregg's pay cuts and benefit losses are also a new, nearly-universal part of the times—and nothing for Gregg or anyone to be ashamed of. It's the increased international competition. As soon as a company's costs rise, lower-priced competitors attract the customers. The company either closes down or moves where labor costs are less. Nationwide, under these cost control pressures, employers' contributions to pensions, health plans, and benefits of all kinds have eroded.

Once Marie recognizes that Gregg is a successful 1990s breadwinner, she should start to bring her own my-job-his-job attitudes up to date.

Since the economy requires Marie to carry a real part of supporting the family, she has to stop blaming Gregg because she has to work; and she must stop holding tight to all the traditional family "women's jobs." As Marie herself would be the first to admit, the constant struggle to keep up is turning her into a stressed-out, caustic woman. She says, "In my calmer moments I know my exhaustion and short fuse are damaging my relationship with my children and undermining my marriage."

As soon as Marie updates her attitudes, she can start saving her marriage by talking sense to Gregg about her Overload. Masses of family-behavior research conclude that husbands change and take on home and childcare tasks *only when the wives make it clear to them that the wives really do want the men to change and accept the responsibilities.* Marie will rescue herself when she realizes that just as she supported Gregg economically in his job changes and retraining and as she continues to carry an important part of their family's financial support, so it will be fair and right for her to expect, actively campaign for, and then *accept* his regular efforts toward a sizable share of family and homecare.

The Jensenns: Even When He's Doing Very Well

Sally Jensenn is one of the lucky women whose husband has a high income. Douglas Jensenn's annual gross is $66,000. With Sally's part-time $15,500 added to the family exchequer, they ought to be living a pleasant life with few financial worries. Instead, they seem to lurch from paycheck to paycheck. Last month they weren't able to send the full amount for their credit cards. Sally can just feel those finance interest charges accumulating. Yet, they both wanted the new CD player, and just two dinners last month at a gourmet restaurant didn't seem extravagant for people with their income. Why then is it so hard each month to cover their ordinary essentials and their few luxuries?

It makes Sally wonder about Douglas. Where is the money going? Why are they always so short? Is it possible Doug is spending money on gambling? Another woman?

Sally has read several articles that report money triggers the most marital battles. It's certainly true in the Jensenn house. Sally and Doug argue about money constantly. Where *is* the money going?

His Raise + Debt + Her Job = No Improvement

Business Week magazine researches part of Sally & Doug's problem and reports "Breadwinners Are Still Running to Stay in Place." They explain that though many families are battling costs by winning raises, borrowing, and making wives' jobs a permanent part of the family budget, millions of families like the Jensenns are nevertheless falling behind.

"U.S. Living Standards Are Slipping and Were Even Before Recession," says *The Wall Street Journal.* Median weekly family earnings adjusted for inflation—meaning what you could buy with the money then and what you can buy with the same amount of money now—has fallen from $516 worth of things in 1979 to only $501 worth of things in 1990. Only the top 20% of families gained from the roaring eighties. Sixty percent of American husbands face the 1990s with a *loss* in real hourly pay, adjusted for inflation—meaning a loss in what the money they earn per hour will buy. And like the Jensenns many American families are feeling the pressure.

Lately economists have noticed another income problem you face, something they call "unequal pay." Labor Department data reveals that people in the same field, age, sex, and with the same education and experience are receiving widely diverse wages. A salary survey in New York City offers an illustration. They found young staff lawyers with the same qualifications in the same specialty were receiving anywhere from $110,000 down to $42,000. Economists warn the trend exists *in all occupations* and is "widespread in the U.S." It means you're often at an employer's mercy as to what they are willing to pay in a job market where people are struggling to find work. "U.S. Wages, Not Getting Ahead? Better Get Used To It" and "Except at the Top, Wages and Salaries Are Dropping" are two typical 1990s headlines that sum up the problem.

What Sally & Douglas Expect from Life

The biggest financial problem faced by the Jensenns, and so many other families, lies in Americans' new definition of what they expect from a middle-class life. For example, if you lived in American suburbia during the 1950s–1960s, you remember that when your family went to a fast-food place like McDonald's, it was a big deal. When McDonald's-style fast food arrived on the American scene in the mid-1950s, offering Mom a night off from cooking at a price Dad could afford on the family's single income, eating there was a family treat, a highlight of the week.

Even allowing for inflation there's been an enormous increase in meals Americans now consume away from home. Today the humblest newspapers routinely feature restaurant ratings because ordinary middle-class life now means eating out regularly at a "real restaurant." In 1954 we spent approximately 12 billion dollars on restaurant meals. By 1970 it had risen only to $26 billion. Considering the ongoing inflation in restaurant prices, the $26 billion indicates most people still regarded eating out as an exceptional treat. But with the 1980s the amount shot to $112 billion in 1985 and zoomed up to $171 billion by 1991. In the process the status of fast food sank. In middle-class minds fast food has been transformed into a necessary middle-class convenience *in addition* to "real" restaurant meals.

What people expect from middle-class family vacations has also been enormously upgraded. In the 50s and 60s family holidays usually fit four modest patterns: A few day trips with most of Dad's time off spent painting the house or attending to other chores. Or a week or so with grandparents. Or a week or two in a rented waterside lodging 50–150 miles from home. Or lastly, a camping trip in the family tent or RV. At the campground camping fees were no more than $1–$5 daily and Mom cooked the family meals. Nobody but the rich dreamed of flying a family hundreds or thousands of miles away for a holiday. A hundred miles from home, three hundred tops, was the standard and the family car took you there.

Today giant hotel chains target the mass middle-class market in print and TV with invitations for weekend mini-holidays. "Two jobs, two kids, too much . . . bounce back with our weekend mini" trills the ad jingle. With two incomes, middle-class families like the Jensenns now routinely slip those weekends into their lives *in addition* to summer travel holidays and maybe winter skiing or Caribbean island jaunts. The hotel chains & travel agents who market these weekend packages know outings like these are well on the way to becoming a taken-for-granted middle-class family activity.

So altered is the Jensenns' and most people's view of what constitutes "ordinary" middle-class possessions that you often read earnest newspaper or magazine analyses of family budget problems that list items like soda pop, frozen food combinations, disposable diapers as basic family requirements. Nowhere in these articles is there a hint that as recently as the 60s and early 70s most Americans regarded scores of current "everyday items" like these as luxuries for special occasions only.

When the Jensenns charged the new CD player last month, like many middle-class Americans, they were thinking of it as a commonplace expense. Yet an article on the electronics industry reminds us:

> Much of what many Americans have come to regard as standard equipment for the home was virtually unavailable 10 years ago: the portable cassette player, the videocassette recorder, the telephone answering machine, the home computer, cordless phones, CD players.

No wonder Sally Jensenn can't figure out why "routine" purchases and a few extras should make their monthly charge payments so difficult to cover.

In good part middle-class economic stress results from our enormously expanded definition of what we need. If the average 1990s middle-class family were forced to return to the lifestyle that *one-income* families were content with in the U.S. in the 1950s, many would feel they were suffocating in narrow "subsistence" living. Economists agree that it now takes two earners to attain the family lifestyle Americans have come to take for granted.

So whether it's the Eventhorpe and Kosnick style or the Jensenns' higher income standard, Lenny Eventhorpe, Gregg Kosnick, and Douglas Jensenn are each a success. The sooner the men themselves and their wives too start seeing the men as succeeding as 1990s style husbands, the sooner they all can acknowledge they also depend on the family dollars Jill Eventhorpe, Marie Kosnick, and Sally Jensenn earn.

By understanding that 1990s families usually need two incomes, they stop being ashamed that her money is essential and start being proud of both wife's and husband's economic contributions. They start moving toward saying out loud that if she is carrying a real portion of family support, it's fair for him to accept a real portion of caring for their home and children.

7

Why Wanting a Career Is So UN*Selfish—Even If Your Family Can Live Well on His Income*

*Y*OUR working life is good for you, your children, your husband, and your marriage. Here's why:

PROBLEM: "The accusation of selfishness triggers the most guilt in women. We are constantly fearful that we have not done enough for others." Grace Baruch, author and associate director at the Center for Research on Women at Wellesley College.

DEFINITION OF NEW TRADITIONALIST WOMAN: advertising term for 1990s woman who is supposedly eager to return to concentrated domesticity.

FACT: A *Newsweek* poll finds 75% of working mothers say they'd work even if they didn't need the money. A *Working Mother* poll of its readers finds 85% would work even if they didn't need the money.

Suddenly, 10–15 years after we thought the question was happily settled in favor of a full life for women, it rises again: "If your family can live well on his income, is it selfish to deny them your full-time home-maker efforts because you want a paid job?"

This time the campaign to reconvince us that women's place is in the home is fueled by the hoopla for the New Traditionalist Woman. With drumbeating from groups that have an economic or ideological self-interest in her, the New Traditionalist Woman is being resurrected from the 1950s and promoted to us as a 90s heroine.

There she is in those New Traditionalist ads happy in her quasi-Victorian home, surrounded by her glowing children. The message the ads deliver subliminally and often nakedly in the text is: This woman is happy because she's rejected the idea of trying to do everything. She's doing what a woman should do, she's concentrating only on her family.

Fortunately, considering the SELFISHNESS question in the 1990s is different from doing so in the 80s or before.

We have accumulated exciting new knowledge. We have the 20 years of unprecedented numbers of working wives and working mothers. During the last two decades with the mass movement of married women into jobs there came a concentration of psychological and sociological studies probing the effects. So whereas family life counselors, researchers, psychologists, and experts of all kinds in the 80s & 70s could only speculate on the results of your combining family and job, now we have documented scientific answers.

If you arrange good childcare and balance your life by having husband, children, and perhaps hired services do their shares, you do yourself and your family a favor by combining career and family.

Your Health & Happiness

Looked at from any scientific angle you like—medical, psychological, sociological—scores of research studies reveal you'll probably be happier, healthier, and pleasanter to live with if you "have it all": marriage, children, paid employment.

A Yale University book, *Spouse, Parent, Worker: On Gender and Multiple Roles,* a round-up of relevant research, declares flatly that women who combine wife, mother, and worker have the highest happiness, self-esteem, and life satisfaction. They tell us the evidence "clearly show employment predicts well-being and health." They warn that lack of employment seems to have "serious negative implications for all other aspects of life." Not a surprising result, they comment, in a society such as ours where employment means status and identity.

The proof in favor of family plus career and against family alone keeps coming. Anthropologist Patricia A. McBroom, in her book *The Third Sex*, reports her research also concludes that if it's happiness you're after, take the children plus career path.

Though a happy marriage is life's jackpot prize, it turns out it isn't enough. The family research reveals that when a woman wants a paid job and her family's attitudes or her Overload keep her from it, even happily married women often succumb to depression and a general sense of misery.

Dr. Rosalind Barnett of the Wellesley Center for Research on Women finds that full-time housewives are more likely than working wives to suffer anxiety and to feel unhappy. Women apparently instinctively know this. Witness the 75–85% of working wives/mothers in *Newsweek* and *Working Mother* polls who say they'd work even if they didn't need the money.

Dr. Barnett explains, "There are two ways to look at women and work. One way supposes that you have a limited amount of energy. Each role drains part of that energy, so that the more you do, the worse off you are. But the other way, which our work supports, is that having more roles offers women more opportunities to be challenged, to feel competent and to have their work acknowledged." She points out that employment plus family allows women to divide their emotional supports. "If something is going poorly in one area of her life, things are likely to be going better in another."

Additional research by experts at the National Center for Health Statistics and the University of Michigan finds that "at all ages," working women are physically healthier than full-time housewives. The working women have fewer days of limited activity because of illness, spend less time sick in bed, have fewer chronic problems, and generally feel healthier.

So living with you as a working wife and mother has to be better for your children and husband. We fantasize that full-time homemaker means the children come home from school to smiles and homemade apple pie. If we turn the research facts into a mental picture, we realize that since a full-time housewife is sick in bed more often than working women, has more chronic health problems, and a lower general sense of health, her children must frequently come home and find Mom feeling depressed, sick, dragged out. Not quality parenting for any child. Nor is the same welcome for Dad good for their marriage and his general happiness.

Your children begin benefiting from your job immediately—while you're still pregnant. The foremost British medical research publication, *The Lancet,* reports that women who work have fewer premature births, stillbirths, or babies dying within the first week than do housewives.

As the children grow and you struggle to teach practical and moral life codes, working mothers whose jobs have some status have an edge. Advice from her on drugs, drink, sex, and the like has more impact on her children. Though the researchers don't discuss why this happens, probably the children shrewdly decide that a mother who is succeeding in the work world knows how the world operates. Hence they see her behavior advice as grounded in reality and accept it, whereas they may reject the housewife-mother's strictures because they may see behavior rules of a mother who is isolated at home as a housewife as unrealistic and unreliable.

Children's school performance too seems to benefit from having a working mother. A study led by John Guidabaldi of Kent State University and including work by Dr. Helen K. Cleminshaw, director of the Center for Family Studies at the University of Akron, compared grade school children from thirty-eight states and found that children of working mothers tended to do better in school and be more self-reliant.

Both your sons and daughters profit immensely by watching you manage your diverse life as mother, wife, worker. The sons have the background to choose and live comfortably with a woman who can be their companionable equal, an achieving, interesting wife. Daughters receive invaluable reassurance that guides them toward a focused, successful life. Dr. McBroom's *The Third Sex* reports that women who do move confidently into having both careers and children often were brought up by strong mothers, grandmothers, or other close female relatives.

These older women may not have had careers by our modern definitions but they made key family decisions or shared family power with their husbands. From them, says Dr. McBroom, today's "have it all" women learned it's safe to relax and nurture children and also it's safe to be forceful in other portions of their lives, as in a job.

By contrast, so many of the unfocused, adrift young women who can't get their lives together are suffering from their childhood experiences with *unfocused,* full-time homemaker mothers. Dr. McBroom finds that the woman who lacks a memory of a strong mother or other female relative often fears she will be unable to combine marriage and career. Consciously or unconsciously she is afraid that effective business behavior might make her feel "masculine" and nurturing behavior toward her children might rob her of ability to function in the "masculine" world outside her home.

Lacking a role model of a mother who combined both, she may vacillate for years between the roles or attempt both roles without confidence and with many anxieties, an attitude that often leads her into self-fulfilling problems. Working mothers give their daughters the role model that saves adult daughters from such unnecessary career vs. motherhood conflicts.

As children mature and leave home, University of Michigan research finds that a working mother's mental health will probably remain strong. With career identity to fill the new spaces in their lives, the empty nest "doesn't seem to be a major issue" for working mothers.

Sexually, because of your job, your husband is a lucky guy. A *Working Mother* magazine survey discovered working mothers have sexual relations almost twice as often as the average American wife. And they enjoy it. The women declare nothing would make them happier than sharing a weekend of great sex and romance with their husbands.

🕉🕉🕉

It is sad to realize that some of the most distinguished relevant academic and government institutions and researchers need to spend millions of dollars and years of energy and expertise on all this research in order to prove that HAVING MORE makes women happier and healthier.

Nobody finds it necessary or sensible to fund or spend years scientifically investigating whether men would be happier and healthier if they confined their energies and emotions only to marriage, fatherhood, and domesticity. It is deemed self-evident that male human beings will be happier if they have access to *all* life's central riches: spouse, children, and paid accomplishment.

If we weren't so blinded by our ingrained sexist notions about woman's natural place being in the home, it would be equally self-evident that a woman WHO HAS IT ALL will be happier.

Your Far Longer Youth

Writing about the 1940s–60s when full-time homemaking was the only socially approved wifely role, Pulitzer prize–winning poet Phyllis McGinley poignantly captured the desperation that the 75–85% majority of American wives who work because they want to would feel if they were forced back to homemaking alone:

Occupation: Housewife
Her health is good. She owns to forty-one.
   Keeps her hair bright by vegetable rinses.
Has two well-nourished children—daughter and son—
   Just now away at school. Her house, with chintzes
Expensively curtained, animates the caller.
   And she is fond of Early American glass
Stacked in an English breakfront somewhat taller
   Than her best friend's. Last year, she took a class

In modern drama at the County Center.
   Twice, on Good Friday, she's heard *Parsifal* sung.

She often says she might have been a painter,
   Or maybe writer; but she married young.
She diets. And with Contract she delays
The encroaching desolation of her days.

Phyllis McGinley's sonnet also tangenitally reminds us that family plus career adds 30–40 or more prestige years to women's lives. The woman in *Occupation: Housewife* is beached, finished in her early forties!

It is a marketing and sociological commonplace to note that before World War II a woman was no longer considered young as soon as she hit 30. At about 45, she was often seen as totally over the hill. Women today are considered sexy, attractive, and assets to their worlds in their 50s, 60s and beyond—for example, both the Elizabeth Taylor and Sandra Day O'Connor types. Cosmetics and hair coloring are aids. They are not the explanation.

When home was woman's only sphere, her only value lay in her looks and her ability to bear and raise children. With the passing of her first beauty and the end of her reproductive ability, she lost her value in others' eyes. And in her own eyes. Return her full-time to the home and she'll again have to rely for status entirely on physical appearance and pregnancy.

It is because you're now permitted to accomplish in the outside world and can earn a real wage (not an old-fashioned woman's job pittance) that you can command respect long after 30 and 45. It is because you can still produce after menopause—not babies but job results—that people continue to find you current, interesting, and attractive.

Formerly when women tried cosmetics and diet to maintain their post-40 appearance, they were often *ridiculed* as deluding themselves. "Dressing mutton like lamb" was the popular acid phrase. The comment meant, a woman really is of no value after age 40, so why pretend. Send her back to full-time homemaking and you shorten her youth and middle age and turn her again in others' eyes and in her own eyes into an old, useless woman at 40—or younger!

The new research proves what common sense should already tell us—that, for your family, for yourself, wanting to combine marriage, children, career is the most UNselfish choice you can make. Your children's personal and emotional lives are enriched. Your husband and children have a happier healthier wife and mother; you have decades of additional status; and your husband and you have a marriage based on fairness where you *both* have it All.

8

· ·

Working Wife Bill of Rights: What Are You Entitled To?

· · · · · · · · · · · ·

Basics

You're Entitled to remember that men have never had to choose. They expect to have all three—spouse, children, paid employment.

You're therefore Entitled to realize that whether or not your family can live on his income, it is sexual discrimination to feel he has an inherent male right to have all three and you have an inherent female obligation to settle for one or two out of three. Sexual equality means since he's entitled to have all three—spouse, children, career—and enjoy them, so are you.

What You're Entitled to Do About It

1

You're Entitled to notice all the ways
media, business, society keep trying
to make you feel guilty about not living
according to one-paycheck rules.
Then you are Entitled to pay no attention
because one-paycheck rules don't fit your two-paycheck family.

2
You're Entitled to realize your husband
is gaining, not losing,
by your going out to work.
You're Entitled to feel proud
that your job and your paycheck are making
your husband's life easier, pleasanter, healthier,
more interesting, and far, far less pressured.

3
You're Entitled to recognize
that the multi-faceted role model
you give your children
and the high mental and physical health you enjoy
from having both family & career
means your children also are profiting
from your working life.
So You're Entitled to realize that your wanting it ALL—
marriage, children, career—makes you UNselfish,
and makes you a better wife and a better mother.
And that this is true whether you work because
you have to, want to, or for both reasons.
You're therefore Entitled to stop feeling guilty and apologetic
about combining career and family life.

4
Last of all You're Entitled to realize that
in today's economy most families need
both a husband's and a wife's paycheck
to live a middle-class life.
Therefore, because you are now doing a real part
of his traditional male job of supporting your family,
You're Entitled to expect him to take on a real portion
of your traditional female job of caring for your home and family.

PART THREE

. . . .

Your Man & Family Responsibilities: The Encouraging Big 1990s News

. . . .

9

1990s' Disappearing Macho Man: 16 Big Reasons Why He's Ready to Share the Housework

*D*AVID Warren often feels like an undercover agent who is living a double life. As a new-style father who wants to be an active parent to his children, he usually leaves work promptly, taking the extra tasks with him for late-night attention. He's said "No" to assignments that involved too much travel. And he ignored a good promotion opportunity because it meant inconvenient relocation for his family. David never publicly ties his behavior to his family goals lest management write him off. Instead, each time he sidesteps an unwanted job change, he produces another plausible explanation.

David Warren, 31, is among the 60% of fathers 35 years and younger who report they shape their career plans around their family concerns. Many 35-and-older fathers, as yet uncounted by researchers, do the same. Like David, these fathers who want to be active in their children's lives now regularly make disguised pro-family career decisions. They're choosing an "Invisible Daddy Track" and becoming part of a "national phenomenon," says Douglas T. Hall, Professor of Organizational Behavior at the Human Resources Policy Institute at Boston University's School of Management.

There's nothing camouflaged about Mark Greeley's career as a home-based CPA. The garage attached to the family house has been converted into Mark's office with its own entrance from the street. As Mark's client list has expanded, Mark has hired a full-time receptionist/clerk. He says, "If business continues to grow, I'll add another desk and hire an accountant to help me." Though Mark is *not* unusual, few people seem to notice how many men earn their living as Mark does by working from home. Mention "working out of your home" and you raise what *The New York Times* calls the "myth" that these people are mostly young women trying to combine motherhood and career. Yet nearly half of homebased workers are men, and 88% of the men are like Mark, professionals, executives, and managers, often self-employed.

David Warren's and Mark Greeley's recent career experiences with Invisible Daddy Track and working from home are *not* transitory career blips. Knowledge-banks like *Fortune* and *The Wall Street Journal* foresee these and other significant anti-macho trends in business conditions, masculine life goals, and national attitudes gaining strength throughout the decade. As these conditions continue, they will change men's attitudes and make most men—probably including your husband—much more willing to accept housework as an ordinary part of their male lives.

As a result, if you understand these big '90s changes and make a new effort to move your husband to a real home life partnership with you, you will probably succeed.

Here's what you need to know:

1. How His Working at Home Can Make Him More Cooperative

Like Mark Greeley, most homebased workers are part of a dual-income family. If during the 90s your man is homebased—there are already close to 20 million men who are homebased and the number has been increasing by 13% annually since 1985—his domestic work scene will help you bring him into a fuller family partnership.

It's easy for a husband to slough off home responsibilities when he walks out the door Monday through Friday and remains out of sight and sound for 8–12 hours. But there's a world of difference when he's a daily, permanent part of the home scene. Use our Part Four ideas and a husband who's permanently in the territory is bound to be drawn into family errands, childcare, and housework too.

"More and more you're talking about . . . the distinction between somebody's personal life and his employment life . . . thinning down," says Harris L. Sussman, strategic consultant for personnel and manager of special education projects for the Digital Equipment Corporation.

2. How His Salary Ceiling Improves His "Attitude"

Amy Mieden is a self-employed, freelance PR consultant who built her expertise during eight years of full-time employment with a large PR firm. Nowadays when Amy must leave her home office to meet prospective clients or attend functions she's set up for current clients, she's not always able to arrange for good childcare. Often her husband, Roger, is forced to solve the problem by changing his schedule and spending several hours that day working from home.

In the 1980s the toughest marital bargaining issue was said to be: "In two-paycheck families, who makes the adjustments when there's a work conflict?" Usually couples decided in the age-old way: His job comes first; she makes adjustments.

Roger used to assume it was Amy's wifely duty to adapt and carry most of the domestic workload. He was skillful at persuading Amy that his work was the "primary" family career. But now as American companies nationwide keep a lid on salaries to compete with low wage workers overseas, Roger, like so many other Americans, finds his income is stagnating.

Roger has responded by taking on more family chores. He food shops, cooks, vacuums, cleans the bathrooms. "I'm really doing it for selfish reasons," Roger admits. "I do the housework to free up some time for Amy so she can get on with her current project. We need the money."

As international trade pressures keep the cap on most Americans' incomes, husbands all over America will want their wives to earn more family money. Many will react as Roger did. To give their wives the time to earn the money, the men will significantly increase their share of family work.

3. Flattened Career Pyramids: How They Affect Your Family

As Jill Eventhorpe discovered in our report on three families, companies are eliminating layers of managers, and employees therefore are losing many of their hopes for promotions. "People may continue to move from project to project or employer to employer . . . I put it as hopping versus climbing," says Dr. Rosabeth Moss Kanter, former editor of *The Harvard Business Review* and a prominent management consultant to big business.

As men lose satisfactions that they used to receive from job promotion possibilities, they'll look more than ever to the personal part of their life for emotional rewards. Because of this new *additional* need to draw his emotional support from wife and children, your husband will have increased psychological incentives to make his relationship with you successful.

He'll therefore be more willing than ever before to listen and alter his behavior if you make it clear that for you a happy relationship includes a fairer distribution of family responsibilities.

Also, as promotion potential erodes, so too does the need for your husband to work a 70–80 hour week in order to look promotable. He'll therefore have more free time to respond to your efforts and build that more equal home life.

4. Tomorrow's Bosses: A New Generation

Another business influence tilting your husband toward assuming more family tasks: As more baby boomers reach power positions in the century's last decade, your man will have many supervisors with the same home goals and complicated two-paycheck daily routines your husband has. As supervisors they will be less rigid and more flexible with subordinates if men like your husband need time for family responsibilities. Professor Hall explains that though many people are working harder than ever in the new leaner organizations, employees "have so much more autonomy (along with increased responsibility) that they have more freedom to achieve work results in their own ways, more flexibility to schedule work around family needs."

5. Male Baby Boomers Ready for Housework

Because baby boomers are by far the largest single population group in the United States, public opinion has mirrored their interests since they arrived between 1946–64. Now their interests have shifted to the home.

During their youngest years in the 1950s & early 60s, the United States was a child-centered culture. As the boomers, male and female, reached their teens in the mid-1960s–early 70s, the nation was convulsed as we shared their adolescent rebellion against authority. As young adults struggling to make their place in the world, in the late 1970s & 1980s boomers stampeded the nation along with themselves into a love affair with money, child-free life, the single life, & sex without commitment. Now the baby-boom generation is in a new life stage.

As they reach their 30s and beyond, the boomers are embracing the marriage and parenthood they delayed. "The Homing of America," as *Marketing Insights* magazine calls the boomers' new interests, makes it natural and popular for men to take an active part in raising their children and running their homes. More family tasks for men is the logical result you can expect from this 90s home-centered female *and* male boomer mood.

6. Close-to-the-Hearth College Students

Like everyone else, the relatively small baby-bust generation rising behind the boomers is being influenced by boomers' desires. A large national survey among college students finds 74% of them rating "values such as family and friendships" as "top priorities" compared to only 61% in 1980.

These college men will be twentysomething husbands and fathers during the 90s and will be living out their high interest in family. If one of them is your husband, he will be just as good a family-responsibility candidate as his thirtysomething and fortysomething elders.

7. Active "Fathering" Now a Strong Male Life Goal

David Warren and his pro-family career decisions are typical of this massive 90s male interest in fathering. Research investigations such as *Fatherhood Today: Men's Changing Role in the Family*, which brings together reports by 27 distinguished family researchers, confirm men's new passion for active parenting. So do major surveys like "The Family Life Survey," conducted through the National Opinion Research Center at the University of Chicago that found that American men (and women) have begun to ". . . yearn for deep affection between parents and children, as well as closeness in marriage."

The happy implication for you and all working wives is that men who start out trying to build emotional links with their children inevitably end up doing housework too. How can they possibly do one without the other? The children they're fathering get hungry and demand meals, they come dragging dirty play and school clothes and ask his help for tomorrow's game or school occasion. Next thing you know, he's cooking, laundering, and keeping house.

8. His New Desire for Emotional Closeness

Separate from all the foregoing business and fathering pressures for family closeness, notice your man's new interest in emotional intimacy per se. Men's right to openly express emotion was a new idea born in the turbulent 60s & 70s and moving into the mainstream by the 80s. Today men's need for emotional expression is accepted as a healthy, desirable new male way of life.

In searching for opportunities to receive, offer, and enjoy emotional closeness, your man will turn more and more to family and will discover what we women already know. He'll learn that emotional closeness at home cannot be created or sustained in a vacuum. You have to do something to produce it. In families, "doing something" usually turns out to be some kind of shared duties for home and family.

9. Changed Male Definition of "Success"

There's another group of pro-family men who are different from Roger Mieden, who sacrifices some of his career drive only because the family must have Amy's earning power, and different from David Warren, whose goal for reining in his career is time with his children. These other men are the 63% of men with and without children in a *Men's Life* magazine survey reported in *USA TODAY* who have revised their overall life ambitions to put their marriage "before sex, career, fame or fortune." Barry Golson, at that time editor of *Men's Life*, commented, "This obviously signifies a pretty sweeping shift in [masculine] values."

Since a big 63% majority of 90s men are putting their marriage first, chances are your man is one of them. These men don't aim for the apex of the career pyramid. They want a solid slice of everything, a balanced life. Their new male hunger for a balanced life will make the men more responsive to your plea for more balance in your marriage through increased homefront efforts from him.

10. Avoiding Housework No Longer Part of "Masculinity"

As young husbands, Dad & Grandpa wouldn't be caught washing dishes, vacuuming, doing laundry lest others roast them as "henpecked."

Even if he did housework, the husband and wife used to cooperate to hide it from others. If the doorbell rang, she helped him ditch the apron and she took his place at the sink washing the dishes. When in-laws or friends visited, she zipped her mouth, never asked for help and did 100% of child and homecare in order to carefully preserve his patriarchal power image in front of others.

Nowadays men who carry their share at home feel no need to hide their behavior. Instead, public opinion polls, such as the one conducted with 2,962 adults and children at Epcot Center, indicate that America's view of a father's role has shifted dramatically. Men who do their share at home are now viewed as good guys who fit America's emerging definition of modern, healthy masculinity.

With this growing public harmony between housework and "masculine" behavior, you can expect more and more 90s men to start seeing housework as a non-sexist, OK activity.

11. Seeing Each Other Eye-to-Eye

Married people are growing toward genuine equality within marriage, says the important family research forum, *Journal of Marriage & the Family*. *American Demographics* magazine, a publication dedicated to the scientific analysis of how population patterns affect people's behavior, spotlights "Gender Trends" in its January 1990 overview for the decade. They state flatly, "In the 1990s . . . women's and men's responsibilities, occupations, and opportunities (will) become more alike. Bottom line: Women's and men's concerns will coincide." Elsewhere other large nationwide surveys like "The Changing Life Course of American Women" discover that men's and women's *overall life goals* are also becoming similar. Therefore, throughout the decade as you see this increasing equality in marriage and growing similarity in female and male life goals, you'll simultaneously see men—including your husband—become still more comfortable doing what used to be considered "women's work."

12. Real Men Are Allowed to Say They Enjoy It!

As more men try housework—voluntarily or under feminine pressure—many discover they like some of it. Nowadays you frequently see newspaper and magazine features that profile men's newly discovered pride in their culinary skills, home decorating abilities, and their fathering talents. As media stories like these of men openly admitting they're *happy* doing housework continue, you'll find they further influence your man to believe that doing a bigger share at home is right for a "masculine" guy like himself.

13. Househusband: From Scorn to Cheers

Pitching in at home is now good for a two-paycheck husband's masculine image. But role reversal with him in charge as househusband has always been another matter. "I get stares all the time—they don't know what the hell I am," says Robert Coulombe, who cut back his hugely successful insurance sales career with a 40–50% income drop because he tired of his sixty- to eighty-hour work week. While Robert cares for their two young children, his wife, Carol Evans, commutes to New York City for her work as publisher of *Stagebill,* a program guide distributed at many New York City dance, musical, and theatrical productions.

Househusband Robert Coulombe is not alone. During the last ten years accounts of other househusbands have surfaced in the media. Each time the angle is, "Gee whiz, look at this unusual family." The men's experiences match Robert Coulombe's as they recount how friends, family, business colleagues politely doubt the wisdom of such an arrangement or openly disapprove.

Yet now in the 1990s a large national survey conducted by one of the leaders in social attitude research, Yankelovich Clancy Shulman, found that about 50% of women and 40% of men admit to having reversed their thinking. They now "respect" a man who stays home to care for his children while his wife works. This is an enormous about-face since 1970 when a majority condemned him outright by saying they'd lose respect for him.

The new public respect provides a social climate that encourages other couples to choose househusband-working wife lifestyle if that best fits their personal temperament, career, and economic needs. It's happening already. From being an oddball rare family decision, the US Labor Department tells us that 257,000 men ages 25–54 are now raising children while their wives work.

As full-time male homemakers become an ordinary, accepted part of the American family scene, housework for men in general will rise in status. When it does, other husbands will feel increasing public opinion pressure to carry a fairer portion of their own two-paycheck home life.

14. At Last, Family Job Leave Is Expected

On family issues our government follows public opinion. It doesn't lead. Indeed, for years the United States and South Africa have been the only industrialized nations in the world without supportive national parental job leave laws. This long lag is further proof that if the federal or state governments are finally taking an interest, it is solely because nationwide so many two-paycheck voters are insisting on it. Various states have already adopted progressive family leave laws and some congressional members indicate Congress may move toward a national parental job leave law. When more state or federal legislation passes and men use the family leave to stay home from work because there's a new baby or family illness, the men will be agreeing to do a lot of housework. After all, that will be the reason they took the time off!

15. Women's 1990s Sex Ratio Advantage

Great days are coming for young single women in the 1990s. There will be more young men interested in marriage than single women in their age bracket, according to widely reported US government census data. Housework-for-Him will be the result.

Through personal experience and media coverage young men will discover that young women have many marriage possibilities. A young man will therefore be under psychological and practical pressures to commit to marriage to win himself a permanent relationship with a desirable woman. Then he'll be under the same psychological tension to hold onto his wife by accommodating at least her mainstream views of what she needs for a happy marriage. If he doesn't, she's less likely than previous generations to tolerate an unhappy marriage. With more marriageable men than women, she'll know she has an excellent chance of making another, better marriage.

All this means she won't have to put up with Overload as women of the 80s did. Way up front among her mainstream marital desires is women's well-documented eagerness to rid themselves of working wives' exhausting career/home/children Overload. And the 90s woman, with the sex-ratio on her side, needn't be shy about telling him about it.

So the coming years, where more young men will be chasing fewer young women, will give her that extra marital power she needs to get *him* into the kitchen, nursery, laundry room and throughout the home to do his share.

16. Men's Attitudes & Behavior Change Constantly

It's easy to believe the average two-paycheck husband will soon do a significant amount of family work when you remember that during the past century men have made a habit of attitude and behavior somersaults.

The 1890s Victorian woman, for example, had to faint and flutter to please men. Around 1900 women stopped fainting and men accepted her new rules for how women "should" behave. If he could find a woman who swooned, today's man would no longer be charmed. He'd label her a kook and flee.

From 1900 to the 1960s, a woman had to act helpless and indecisive to be thought of as feminine. The clinging vine was a very popular type among marriage-minded men. As women changed and insisted they were competent, men accepted the new version of femininity. Today few men want anything to do with a female clinging vine who needs to be propped up as she goes through life.

In the same way men's reactions to working women and working wives have undergone vast & quick alterations. Millions of men who in the 1970s declared that they'd never take orders from a woman boss, now do so. Most are no longer self-conscious about it. As for a working wife, as recently as the late 1970s most men were still ashamed(!) to have their wife in the job world. Popular opinion viewed her employment as a sign that he had failed as a family provider. Now just 15 years or so later, sociologists find the majority of men are proud of a wife's ability to bring home a healthy paycheck. Her successful career has developed into a "sexy" plus for her.

So do expect a giant 1990s improvement in your man's family work attitude. Then if working wives actively attempt to draw husbands into more family responsibilities, these powerful anti-macho trends will help the women succeed. And husbands as full home partners will become a popular and typical male lifestyle.

PART FOUR

. . . .

Your Hidden House-Power Fears: How to Recognize Them & Free Yourself

. . . .

10

How & Why Working Wives Prevent Husbands from Doing More at Home

. . . .

Wives Have Good Reasons for Their Fears & Actions

Of course, working wives want to ease their heavy family-plus-job schedule. They want their husbands—please, finally, at last!—to do MORE around the house and for the children. What . . . prevent him from doing more! Never. Certainly not.

Yet accidentally, unintentionally, it happens every day in many two-paycheck homes.

During 20 + years as I've interviewed hundreds of working wives for my career books, columns, articles, I've become aware of a very important subtext in what is said. Those years of researching made me realize the conventional wisdom about working wives' job-home Overload is wrong.

Check it out for yourself. You'll find the conventional wisdom—the experts' analyses, surveys, and the average person's opinion—agree. They tell us husbands are to blame; two-paycheck marriages are strained and working wives live with constant fatigue and tension because husbands *refuse* to do their fair share of home and childcare. But my decades of research have taught me this explanation is inaccurate.

He is not to blame.

And though she is *unintentionally* preventing him from doing more, she is not to blame.

Beyond the one-paycheck family rules hammered into two-paycheck families that make women feel they're not Entitled to have him assume a real share of home tasks, there is a second real reason husbands "refuse" to do their share. And that is women's hidden—very legitimate—house-power fears.

To use the two-part male-convincer a woman has to feel Entitled; then she has to talk effectively with her husband. We've taken care of entitlement. *Now to talk effectively it's necessary to unmask and eliminate women's realistic and sensible house-power anxieties.*

The average husband may never accept a full 50 percent of family life responsibilities (and many women don't want him doing anywhere near that much), but the average husband would do far more if his wife overcame her fears and no longer limited him.

How Wives Limit Husbands' Efforts at Home

During interviews women routinely talk about how overburdened they are. Then they say they "can't let" him do more because he doesn't do it "right."

It's a very rare wife who won't smile and identify with that worry: "He doesn't do it right."

Typically a working wife will remark, "He uses too many pots when he cooks." "He doesn't stack the dishwasher the way I want it." "He doesn't fold the towels right." "I don't like the way he vacuums." "I'm not satisfied with how he rinses the cleanser out of the bathtub." "He brings home supermarket items that aren't on the list I give him."

"So I can't let him do it."

or

"So it's easier to do it myself."

or

"It takes too long to explain it. It's easier to do it myself."

What we have here is a constantly recurring drama where the men have not refused the chores. She's decided she "can't let him do it."

In the written survey of working wives for this book, four of the questions included were:

Lots of women say they really can't let their husbands do much at home or with the children because it turns out to be more trouble than it's worth. Why do you think they feel it's more trouble than it's worth?

When you've given over some home or childcare tasks to your husband, and it didn't work out, what was the problem?

And the follow-up questions:

If you said, "He didn't do it right," what exactly did he do wrong?

How do you think the common husband problem of it being more trouble than it's worth could be cured?

One woman set forth the "can't let him do it" attitude in very few words when she dismissed the whole set of queries with, "Women think they can do it better."

Another, age 29, said, "I just want him to go away and take care of our children so I can go and do the housework the way I want it done."

A third with one five-year-old child confessed, "I'm set in my ways." (Yet she checks her age as only 25–30.) "I like things done my way—not his."

Another delivered a succinct summary of women's typical reasons for limiting his efforts: "He didn't do it the way I'd like."

Others echoed the same refrain with comments like, "I think a lot of women who feel this way worry too much that their husbands won't do it exactly the way they do and aren't willing to let it go and accept how their husbands do things."

Women's conflicting Overload pressures were obvious in answers to other survey questions:

Everyone has some housework & family jobs they really don't care for:

What jobs would you be happy about if you didn't have to do anymore?

What parts of the day are hardest for you?

What makes them the hardest?

Why don't you make changes that make it easier for you?

A woman who first had come out strongly against putting up with his housework "because he doesn't do it right," revealed a pathetic picture of what it was costing her. For tasks she'd like to be rid of, she wrote her homemaker life off completely with "laundry & house cleaning."

What parts of the day are hardest? "Early morning & late night." What makes them hardest? "Tired." Why don't you make changes? "I am a slow riser & work hard all day so I'm tired at night."

She checks her age as 41–50, two young adult children, household income $60,000–$80,000. Yet she apparently does not feel Entitled to find at least a few dollars to hire some house chore aid that a $60,000–$80,000 income like hers can provide.

Revelations like these of what it was costing women to insist he do it "her way" ran throughout the answers to the questionnaire. About 85–90% of the survey answers described a daily routine where the women were pushing themselves to and beyond exhaustion. One woman's answer to her most difficult time of day poignantly spotlighted the emotional cost of doing it herself and doing everything her way. Her hardest time and what makes it hardest? "Getting myself ready for work & my daughter out to day care. I'm too tired to play with my child as she'd like me to."

Why doesn't she make changes? "I can't easily afford domestic help." Another lists one two-and-a-half-year-old child, family income of $80,000–$100,000 per year. Is it that she "can't afford" help as she says or that she doesn't feel Entitled to spend money that way? She herself seems to be aware of her sense of Non-Entitlement. In her next answer she explains, "Women are socialized to feel like it is their responsibility; that they have to be 'super women' or they are failures."

A word picture that seemed to sum up the "I can't let him do it" attitude and its cost to women emerges from another woman's answers:

Why doesn't she make changes to help herself through the hardest parts of her day? "I try to, but I feel compelled by all the things I know that need to be done . . . women have been conditioned to believe that home and children are the woman's responsibility . . . so feel guilty if their husbands end up doing much housework or childcare."

A woman who checked her age as 31–35 with a two-and-a-half-year-old baby combined the problem and a suggested solution in her answer when she wrote, "Women, by traditionally doing certain tasks, develop set ways in which things should be done. Men may use alternate methods and are then put down by the wife for not doing it right. Women have to be more flexible and give up this 'attitude.' "

This is a fine idea and could be a complete solution. Unfortunately, many women find it impossible or extremely difficult to follow that advice because life is so complex.

Why Women Are So Afraid to Accept His Methods

Fear of Looking Like a Bad Wife & Bad Mother

To start with, the universal feminine desperation that he do it right is well founded. The one-paycheck family rule that holds wives responsible for house/childcare says no matter who does the physical work, you as wife & mother will be judged by the results.

Don't underestimate the pressure this family and community attitude places on you and on all women.

A vivid dramatization of how women are pressured by this rule is found in one of Arthur Conan Doyle's Sherlock Holmes stories. In "The Adventure of the Blue Carbuncle," the great detective is deducing a man's character from the battered hat he left behind. Holmes concludes with the comment that the man's wife no longer loves him.

Pushed beyond even his good nature, Dr. Watson wants to know how a man's hat can testify to a wife's emotions. Whereupon Holmes delivers his analysis: "This hat has not been brushed for weeks. When I see you, my dear Watson, with a week's accumulation of dust upon your hat, and when your wife allows you to go out in such a state, I shall fear that you also have been unfortunate enough to lose your wife's affection."

The logic of Holmes's reply satisfies Watson, as it has satisfied readers around the world in scores of cultures these hundred years or more. Everyone recognizes that Holmes's insight is true.

If a man has buttons missing from his coat, a dingy shirt collar, holes in his socks, an unbrushed hat, his wife will be criticized. People will say, "How can she let him go around like that? Doesn't she have any pride?"

He is not faulted if he looks like a slob; she is. He is pitied. She is condemned.

As a result, Monday through Friday, working wives everywhere see to it that they themselves have something clean and appropriate to wear to work, that the children have suitable clothing, and "Does he have a clean shirt? Did I remember to see if his suit needs cleaning? I pushed myself to do laundry last night. So at least he has clean underwear."

This scenario would be ridiculous if it weren't so familiar. Little children need adult attention to leave home suitably outfitted. But if he goes to work and she goes to work, why doesn't an adult male get dressed, brushed, mended, dry cleaned, and laundered all by himself? Does he go about remembering to attend to the hem that's loose on her best suit, to the elastic that's going on her black bra, and that her silk blouse needs to be cleaned for the meeting next week? The hypothetical picture of his constantly rummaging around on her side of the closet to keep her wardrobe in order makes us smile.

Why doesn't the real omnipresent reverse also make us smile? Because family rule #3 says care of home and children is a wife's job and therefore she should be criticized if either appear neglected.

In the same way, working wives know that dust balls rolling around the visitor, fingermarks on door and light plates, dirty bathrooms and kitchens won't make people think, "*They* are terrible housekeepers." Though she's employed full-time, others are likely to react with, "How does *he* put up with it? What a slob she is."

Women know this and much of working wives' passion for having housework done "right" springs from anxiety lest others see an inadequate job and decide she's an incompetent, uncaring wife and mother.

Your Personal Need to Protect Your House-Power

Besides the pressures of public opinion, all of us have sensible personal reasons for instinctively trying to protect our power at home by getting him to do housework and childcare our way.

Sometimes, and this is easiest to cure, men really may be botching the job from disinterest, ignorance, or a combination of both. No one who knows better can stand by and tranquilly watch black and navy garments tossed into a laundry load of whites. Nor can any good housekeeper watch grease spattering over stove and counters during cooking and then silently accept a clean-up that doesn't touch the grease. "Teach the basics and arrive at some mutual standards" was a wise solution proposed by several women in my survey.

Beyond the legitimate need for him to learn and agree to basic standards, women are actively engaged in protecting their right to have things done "*my* way," for another much bigger reason. For the thousands of years of western civilization until just recently in the 1970s, house-power—the right to make decisions for cooking, cleaning, childcare—was the only power women had.

Dependent on male wage earners for every penny, prohibited by social laws of appropriate womanly behavior from many activities, paid employment, or even controversial opinions expressed outside the home, women controlled nothing except the details of housekeeping and childcare. Even there, since husbands controlled all the family money, wives had to adjust home behavior and plans to his wishes. "Your father wants his dinner at 6:30 sharp, not before, not a minute later."

As late as the 1970s, house-power was women's only source of prestige. You judged yourself and others judged you by your housekeeping and the way you attended to your children's and husband's needs. There literally was no other status area open to you. A career added nothing to your social status. In fact, it diminished it. A Gallup survey of the 1930s found that 80% of men and 75% of women disapproved of a married woman who went out to work if her husband could support her.

These attitudes were the norm until only yesterday and if you're 25 or older you were born into them. Yet many people have lost sight of how dependent women have always been on house-power. To remind yourself all you have to do is watch the reruns of 1960s TV family sitcoms. You'll see that June Cleaver, the wives in *Make Room for Daddy*, *Father Knows Best* (that title alone speaks sexist volumes), wife Laura in *The Dick Van Dyke Show*, even Lucy, stand back and say almost nothing in public situations when a husband is present. Whether an individual episode deals with problems with salespeople, angry neighbors, the children's teacher, no matter what, when both husband and wife are there, the man does all the public discussion and decision making. She behaves like a proper pre-1970s woman. She listens, nods, puts in a phrase or two to agree with what he said, but she never publicly solves the difficulty.

He is the man of the family and in public it is her place as a wife to keep quiet and not put herself forward as having ideas of her own.

It's behind the scenes in these episodes that you often see her trying to influence what he will say and do for this week's problem. Frequently the whole plot turns on her frantic, disguised schemes to put her ideas, insights, plans, into his mouth. She has to work in these devious ways. Until the 1970s at home as in public "father knows best" and she must speak cautiously.

Look through an etiquette book from a few years ago and you'll see that up till and sometimes well into the 1970s—long decades after WWII—women were still being instructed that it was wrong to speak directly to the waiter in a restaurant. The women were reminded that it was their place as females to tell male escorts what they wished to order for dinner; the man would then deal with the waiter. This was an extension of the fundamental view that a woman's total rightful sphere was the home; and outside it she should speak only to those people she knew socially.

It's only yesterday, in the 1960s and early 1970s.

So today your hidden need to have home and childcare done *your* way is based on good reason. House-power and the right to make those decisions is the only world women ever had.

Furthermore, because most women born before the 1970s were raised in the era of house-power as women's only sphere, many of us have a good portion of our self-image invested in "feminine" household skills. Ability and talent as cook, home decorator, hostess, as a good house-keeper matter. And certainly our abilities as a good mother are central to our self-esteem and sense of success.

One woman I interviewed remembers bursting into tears at her desk when her husband phoned to say he'd taken their daughter for her six-month medical checkup. "She needed the next inoculation and I couldn't take time off just then. But still I was broken-hearted. I'm her mother. Her doctor visits should belong to me."

Other women who conscientiously try to share parenting with their husbands nevertheless are infuriated if they say the child needs to wear a sweater and their husband contradicts. "That's something I should decide. His giving me a hard time about it threatens my whole feeling as a mother."

Given the conditions that existed only yesterday, it's reasonable that women feel ambivalent and sometimes angry when men try to annex some house-power by doing things their own way.

It's reasonable. But as women are expanding their lives to include home, children, marriage, and career, insisting that house-power continue to be woman's alone now costs us too much in physical and emotional Overload stress.

No human being can do it all. But women can "have it all" if they'll stop trying to do it all and find comfortable ways to share house-power.

Just as men reluctantly allowed women into the outside world of careers and real income, and then men found it gives them fuller, easier lives, sexier, happier wives, so women will find that if they give over some house-power to husbands, their marriages, their relationship with their children, and their total lives will greatly improve as Overload fades.

It's necessary then to discover practical ways of Sharing house-power with men and to locate the specific home-childcare areas where you personally will feel comfortable about Sharing your house-power.

11

Sharing vs. Helping: What's in It for You & Your Family?

A young Pennsylvania mother recalls that her first baby was only two months old when she and her husband treated themselves to a weekend at a local luxury hotel together with their new son. "We'd agreed before I got pregnant that he would help me as much as he could after the baby was born. That weekend the baby must have been going through some kind of growth spurt. All he wanted to do was nurse. I barely got out of the hotel room.

"But when I asked my husband to change a diaper, he said, 'Honey, I'm on vacation.' "

This dramatic example typifies how useless "helping" can be for really diminishing your Overload.

With "helping," childcare and homecare are all your job. He does a chore only when and if it's convenient for him; when and if you can convince him; when and if you ask nicely and then thank him very, very sincerely.

Worst of all—and this is what really exhausts women—when he "helps," too often it is with limited attention and marginal effort. For example, he agrees to oversee the younger children while he's also watching his TV football game. Yet Mom, who is running the washing machine, vacuuming, and has a roast in the oven is the one who notices as she passes through the room that the four-year-old is on the floor rocking back and forth against the lamp which is about to crash. Or it's she who notices that the newly toilet-trained two-year-old has a concentrated look in his eyes and needs to be hustled to the potty. Or that the ten-year-old is in the yard on a chill November afternoon wearing only jeans and a T-shirt. The way he treats his "helping" assignments makes it clear he *expects* you to go on noticing, planning, and giving him his orders. His helping then is based on your mutual understanding that he'll contribute some physical effort but all the preparation, equipment, scheduling, and responsibility for the task is *yours*.

In an awe-inspiring project, professors Linda Thompson of the University of Wisconsin-Madison and Alexis J. Walker of Oregon State University reviewed more than two hundred research books, articles, and reports on how gender affects marriage, parenthood, and wage & family work. Because of their efforts featured in their report in *Journal of Marriage and the Family*, we can be sure of several sensational and key facts. They tell us family researchers have devoted a great deal of attention to the "drop in marital satisfaction, especially among wives, when partners become parents."

Dr. Thompson and Dr. Walker say that not one research project but the sum of the two hundred research accounts indicate that:

> Mothers end up doing most of the child care and housework regardless of what pattern was established or expected before children arrived . . . while conflict increases after children arrive, and disagreement over who does what domestic work is at the top of the list.

They comment that for many mothers the drop in their marital happiness is tied to the fact that the new fathers turn their concentration to their jobs. The men pull away from home just when they are needed most and in spite of promises to do their share.

Thompson and Walker explain that the investigations reveal that parents typically *create a family fiction* about how intimately the fathers are involved with their children, when in fact the mother is doing almost all the daily childcare. In other words, the parents seize on the statistically proven approximately twenty minutes of fun time a day that the average father spends with his children and turn that into a family belief that he's doing a full portion of the childcare.

Next Thompson and Walker give us the single most important insight we need to see how a working wife is misled about the amount of "help" her husband is contributing compared to the family load she is carrying.

They report husbands and wives "tend to view men's minimal help with raising children as substantial . . . and women's substantial help with provision [income] as minimal."

Play out their quote as a family scene and you'll surely recognize it. Your husband takes the children out for several hours to the playground/mall/food shopping/it doesn't matter where so you can get on with the housecleaning or whatever else you have piled up on your To Do list. When they all return, gracious glory are you ever grateful. You got this, that, and the other thing done as you hurtled around in your few childfree hours. You thank him; he beams modestly. The kids are already hanging on to you, demanding, telling, talking. You can hardly get your gratitude out coherently. But you manage. And he wanders off, a good husband and father in both your eyes.

Has either of you said a word about the seventeen family services/chores/work you raced through in those hours? It's not that you're looking for thanks. The point is that neither of you have really noticed your contributions to the family during those hours. Both your and your husband's attention are focused on his big fathering and good-husband contribution. Your work is invisible to both of you, just "of course it's your job."

Imagine a family scene for the other half of seeing "men's minimal help with raising children as substantial . . . and women's substantial help with provision as minimal" and you'll also recognize it. He did some of your "women's work" by keeping the children occupied for a few hours and drew rave family reviews. Now you put in *not* a few fun hours of his traditional man's job of supporting the family, but, with commuting, fifteen, twenty, thirty, forty or more hours a week of real toil at your job. You bring home your paycheck. Does the gratitude flow?

Not only is there no reenactment of your gratitude when he did part of your "woman's work," the fact that you're now doing part of his "man's work" goes completely unacknowledged. Both you and he pretend that he's the family's only real breadwinner. Your money slips quietly into the pot and out the door to pay family bills. His minimal efforts with the children were treated as substantial; your substantial efforts to earn family income draw minimal attention.

Elsewhere, since 1980, Dr. Jay Belsky, Professor of Human Development and Family Studies at Pennsylvania State University, has been studying how babies and men's inadequate "help" changes and undermines your marriage. From his research he gives us the similar conclusion that modern working wives often hope for and may even expect fifty-fifty parenting but in reality are getting "about ten to fifteen percent."

Does This Sound Like Your Husband?

When you depend on his help for home responsibilities as well as child-care, there are other major problems. Two of my survey questions dealt with the communication difficulties you face in obtaining that help.

> When I do try to get my husband to do more in our home or with the children, I usually say something like (write down exactly the words you usually use.)

> He usually reacts by saying & doing what? (Really describe the scene; use other side of this paper for more space.)

Because both the wives & husbands see home and childcare as *her* responsibility, the women admit they have to "ask," "beg," "scream," and "plead" to move him to action. Some women succeed moderately well with their requests and pleas. Many others describe different types of resistance. And except for those scarce successful team-couples, none of the women manage to transfer to him the responsibility for remembering to do the job again when needed.

One woman described the self-defeating traps you entangle yourself in when you keep asking for help. She wrote, "I have a habit of constantly asking for 'favors'—'Can you do me a favor and take out the garbage?' I have found that he considers this nagging and is not receptive. He prefers to have assigned chores that he can complete on his own time schedule. I often become frustrated at having to be the one to remind him and ask him to help me."

The unreliability of the "help" method, even when offered by cooperative husbands, comes across in another woman's answers. She writes that she usually says, "I would appreciate some help with (whatever) because I simply cannot get to everything around here."

He replies, "Tell me what you need help with and I'll do it." This sounds great till you read her next sentence: "And then *maybe*"—her emphasis—"he'll get around to it."

Another woman suggests you obtain help from men if you "Plead your case and maybe they'll assist you." Her husband has fixed undemanding jobs such as "empty the waste cans in each room . . . load and empty the dishwasher." Another copes with her Overload by explaining she gets "some satisfaction from complaining. Truly." And that her husband's reaction to her requests is usually, "I'm busy." Whereupon she "drops what I'm doing and slam and bang around and dress the kids, take out the trash, etc."

Still another says she tries to cope with all that needs to be done, "usually asking (screaming)—for his participation about getting dinner prepared." His normal reaction: "OK, OK, OK and leaves the room."

Throughout wives indicate that as they ask, request, beg, plead, they also must display ample gratitude. The men expect it under the umbrella one-paycheck premise that it's her work.

The Hidden 80–90% of His Helping Jobs

Your child brings home an invitation to a birthday party. In order to arrange a carpool so you need drive only one way, you phone the birthday child's mother to learn who else is invited. Then you phone around among the invitee list. This may require multiple calls to each woman because mothers may be out dealing with their own busy overburdened lives and the fathers who answer the phone "don't know." (Of course they don't. They're not carrying any of this around in their heads.)

At last you locate a few other mothers whose schedules make it practical to carpool with you. Those who don't drive either way will owe you for another time . . . and that's another thing for you to keep track of. With each carpool mother you review the route to her home and when you'll pick up her child. You quiz your child on what kinds of presents are being favorably received these days. Translation: what are you *not* allowed to buy because it is suddenly déclassé and will "disgrace" your child. You buy and wrap the gift including a suitable birthday card. You wake up the morning of the party remembering the event and planning time in your day to prepare your child. You then watch the clock to have your child presentably clean and appropriately dressed on time.

Beforehand you may have enlisted your husband's help. He's agreed to do the carpool route. You hand over your child, the wrapped gift, names and addresses and directions to each child to be picked up, as well as directions to the birthday home. Off he goes. Thirty minutes later he returns glowing with virtue. He has done a big "helping" job. He has collected and deposited all four of the children.

He sits down to watch TV with a pure conscience. In his mind he's done a fair share of the work for your child's birthday outing. He did all the driving. Whereas, as he sees it, you "just" bought a present and . . . oh yes, arranged the carpool. In his mind the carpool is a very hazy task, something that coalesces on its own and besides women like talking on the phone. Usually he's unaware you made the calls—and the calls back—with your last flicker of energy after working and talking all day and as something you absolutely didn't want to do.

Because he doesn't realize that you have spent portions of *days* preparing your child for this party, he is unaware of the hidden 80–90% of this chore. And he's equally unaware of the hidden 80–90% of all chores he helps you with. As a result, he probably has little concept of the complexity and seriousness of your Overload.

Many women themselves do not think about the hidden 80–90% of any job he helps with. Therefore the women are often puzzled as to why they go on feeling so overburdened and overwhelmed even when a husband contributes a sizable amount of physical help.

⚵⚵⚵

Your Overload solution lies in clearly facing the fact that *as long as you continue to use all that emotion and energy just to get him to "help" and you then carry the hidden 80–90% of the tasks he does plus 100% of what you do, you're really doing almost everything.* And it's therefore hopeless. With "helping" you will never make a real dent in your Overload. You will go on feeling overwhelmed because you are overburdened.

You can solve your Overload only when you move to Sharing the work and Sharing the house-power. With Sharing, you give up asking and he takes permanent responsibility for various family tasks including the hidden 80–90% of remembering, planning, obtaining supplies for the tasks he accepts as well as physically doing them.

But will you be comfortable with Sharing responsibility and house-power? What will your friends think of your new homefront behavior? What will your neighbors and family say about you right out loud?

Why It'll Surely Work for You

You can feel safe about how others will react to his assuming full responsibility for various of your homelife needs—because all around you people are shifting their own family patterns in a variety of new ways. For example, women who were trained by their mothers to make the bed first thing in the morning and also put a spread on, now don't make the bed at all. At night before they climb in, they may smooth the sheets. Then again, they may not.

Most used to feel guilty. Some still do. Many don't think about it anymore. A *Woman's Day* magazine survey on "How Working Wives Cope" reports 89% of the women confess they're doing less housework than before they combined home and outside job. Among chores they never do and that just don't get done: picking up the children's rooms 98%; spring cleaning 69%; ironing 34%; making beds daily 34%.

Laura Lein, director of the Center for Research on Women at Wellesley College, finds big changes in family lives: "Americans have reordered their priorities. They're juggling work and house and family, and when forced into a choice, the first thing to go is the house." Selling Areas Marketing, a division of Time Inc. that measures purchases of supermarket items, agrees. They report that products used for heavy home cleaning jobs have become "less and less popular." The result is a wonderful easing of pressures on you. As fewer women keep white-glove spotless homes, the more tolerant they and their families become of yours and other people's less than perfect housekeeping.

With the new, more relaxed attitudes toward housework, you also can stop worrying so much about your husband "doing it right." Women can start feeling comfortable about possibly telling Sherlock Holmes and the world, "His unbrushed hat, buttonless coat, and dingy shirt collar have nothing to do with my love for him. They're his clothes and he's old enough to keep himself looking presentable."

Also very encouraging is the University of Michigan's study and report of "Changing Attitudes Toward Family Issues in the United States." The researcher, Dr. Arland Thornton, examined three decades of "changing norms and values concerning family life in the United States . . . 1950s through the middle 1980s." He finds a "greatly expanded range of acceptable behavior" in family life, many fewer "shoulds" and "oughts."

For housekeeping, the increased range of "acceptable behavior" means a wide diversity of standards among your friends, neighbors, family.

So why struggle? You'll never satisfy everyone.

Keep a white-glove home and women who are holding down a job and also concentrating time and energy on children's and husband's emotional needs will sniff and say, "If you have that much time to clean, you must be ignoring your family's real needs." Or behind your back they'll whop you with the timeless putdown of the so-so housewife for the spotless housefrau, "Can't she think of anything better to do than spend her life polishing and cleaning?"

In turn, the white-glove lady will look down her nose at the lived-in home with the disdain of the woman who knows each of her cabinets, closets, and dresser drawers will do her proud.

There are other possibilities. Suppose you exhaust yourself and somehow pull off the Superwoman act: children, husband, home, career all by yourself. Many people will still label you a loser. "Poor thing. Her husband doesn't love her or he wouldn't let her do it all."

Get him and the children to do their fair share and you'll find the stereotypical traditionalists who gossip that you're taking advantage of your family.

Give it up. In the variegated family world of the 90s, you are never going to please everyone. So please yourself. Choose from among our Sharing-responsibility-and-house-power ideas. Have it all and enjoy it too.

Why Bother Changing?

Are the rewards of changing from helping with *your* work to Sharing the work, responsibility, and house-power worth the effort? This question is at the heart of your decision.

With a few minutes' effort, the unmade bed can look picture pretty and fresh. With a cleaning crew or, at most, cleaning and painting crews, the neglected home looks fine. But what happens to the children of overloaded mothers and underinvolved fathers? After neglect, there's no blitzkrieg way to quickly fill the children's unmet needs.

Yet frantically busy working mothers can be misled into believing that if the children are kept warm, fed, bathed, clothed, and physically healthy, they're well cared for. Parents who have time to ponder know that well-cared-for children from cradle through college need quantities of undistracted parental time and attention as much as they need food and clothing.

The children need mothers who are less overburdened and fathers who are more involved. At all ages through to adulthood, children need parents with the time, energy, and inclination to listen with a "third" ear, to see with a "third" eye; to be aware of the subtleties that indicate the young person is troubled or confused. They need parents who will quickly realize when the child is losing the way in some school subject; when peer pressure is turning the child or teenager toward self-destructive choices; when the youngster is bewildered or frightened by something that occurred among family, friends, relatives, or at school or in the street.

At all ages children also need two parents with time and attention *to actively create positive situations* where the young person can be successful and develop self-esteem. Two parents who listen for, hear, and respond not only to nuances of anxieties but to the nuances of the child's or adolescent's efforts to draw forth the parent's favorable attention and praise.

This is the kind of third eye and ear that is beyond the logistical capability of many overburdened working mothers. There are just twenty-four hours in a day; only so much one human being can do. And with a husband's help that is often grudging and often amounts to 10–20% of the task, you have a setup that discourages his really focusing on the children's subtle psychological needs and emotions.

Parents who go for weeks or months without recognizing that their child or teenager is emotionally troubled or is acting out distress with temper outbursts, petty thefts, truancy, drugs, sex, liquor, vandalism, or learning difficulties have been relying only on their two eyes and two ears. Mom has been too busy and Dad has been too uninvolved to see the invisibles of the child's moods, the need for a parent to suspect and investigate the existence of situations that must be cleared up to *prevent* the child from drifting into self-destructive behavior.

It's not only your children's psychological and emotional welfare that's at stake in this helping vs. Sharing decision. Too many overloaded working wives lack the time and energy required to think through and respond effectively to a marriage they feel is disintegrating. If she had more time and energy, she might be able to make more effort to enlist her husband's cooperation and together they might work through their problems and revive their marriage.

What Will Take Care of These Family Emotional Needs?

It's not time for a visit to the zoo or a hectic social life that you need with your children and husband. It's time and energy for *unscheduled* activity, to be relaxed "doing nothing" at home together. Then your third eye and ear will have ideal conditions to see, sense, hear, feel.

Where, after all, did we women acquire the notion that our husband and children will love us more if we're constantly busy cleaning, laundering, in the kitchen? Marital happiness research reveals the opposite. One of men's top complaints about working wives revolves around his immense dissatisfaction because she's too busy to spend leisure time with him. Dr. Morton H. Shaevitz, practicing clinical psychologist, has written a woman's magazine article, "How Men Really Feel" about working wives. In a sub-head italicized to emphasize its importance, he points out "Men Are More Vulnerable and Dependent on Their Marriages Than Women Are."

He explains that, unlike women, men usually lack many close personal relationships and sources of emotional support. Consequently, they are super-dependent on their marriages, need a great deal of emotional support from their wives, and are devastated when she's too busy to provide it. "Men are unhappy when they can't have enough time with their wives. Often they become angry or they sulk; but they rarely verbalize their feelings of loss, abandonment, loneliness, and perceived lack of importance . . . 'Where the hell were you all afternoon?' [can mean] 'I missed you.' "

So when you continue to depend on his "helping" together with all the battles it creates and end up doing the hidden 80–90% of tasks he helps with plus 100% of your own tasks, his helping becomes a dangerous Catch-22 and a threat to your marriage. You're doing it all—or almost all—and husbands' complaint about working wives is that they're too busy doing it!

Choose Sharing and, with your how-to-talk-to-him-about-it skills discussed in chapters thirteen–fifteen, bring him into a *willing* home partnership with you. Then as he shares the work *and the house-power* for the tasks you turn over to him, you gain the time and energy you need to give your husband the attention and time together that he craves . . . and that will so strengthen your relationship.

And with his new increased home and childcare responsibilities, there's also more energy/time for third eye/ear attention for the children—from you both. This has to markedly raise the quality of parenting they receive and greatly improve your chances for drawing a winning answer to the big question:

"How will your children turn out?"

12

How to Get Him to Do It "Right"

Doing It My Way

Horizontally along the suburban streets stretch the lines of tract houses. Dozens of houses with the same floor plans, the same builder-supplied appliances. Vertically from earth toward the clouds rise the condominium complexes, dozens of apartments with similar floor plans and appliances.

In each of these near-identical houses and condo units, someone is keeping house in her own individual way.

Though floor plans, appliances, closet dimensions match, you'd be hard put to find two women who use the facilities to prepare meals, arrange their kitchen cabinets, clean, vacuum, launder, and keep house in exactly the same way. Each woman has her own likes, dislikes, pace, schedules, methods, and priorities. Is one of these women "right"? Are all the rest of the women wrong?

When women manage their homes in different ways—and they all do—it's just individual styles. Different does not equal wrong.

The same is true for your husband. Turn your husband loose on a task and he'll almost surely use methods different from yours. That doesn't automatically mean his system is "wrong." Just as the woman next door performs the task her way and it's OK, so too his way can be both different from yours and "right."

Feeling comfortable with your husband's methods requires that he learn the basics of the task and that the two of you agree on some family standards. Then it requires that you *let go*.

As management consultant Nancy Lee points out in her book *Targeting the Top,* each household chore has two parts: doing it and the responsibility of remembering and planning for it. She says, "If a woman gives over a task and then keeps checking on it, it's a sure way to get the responsibility back again."

In her report "Negotiating Household Roles and Responsibilities: Resistance, Conflict, and Change," Dr. Myra Marx Feree, professor of sociology, University of Connecticut, mentions that men increase their home efforts when women are willing to give up control over the task. It makes sense.

As long as you treat him like an underling, bossing, correcting, insisting that everything be done your way, he's just a temporary, reluctant body with an attitude of "Let me get it done, then forget it, till she grabs me again." When you give over the authority—the house-power—he makes decisions, uses his methods, and the work becomes something he will feel some pride in doing well.

It also becomes something that he, not you, is judged by. "It's Mike's day to do the kitchen and he hasn't got to it yet," says the working wife to her visiting girlfriend. With today's new approved wider range of family behavior there's an excellent chance the visitor will follow the lead and see that the messy kitchen reflects on Mike. She may even criticize Mike aloud. "Hey Mike, you're getting to be a slob. *Your* kitchen looks awful."

Still, it certainly isn't easy to give over your right to make home/childcare decisions, or to sit by calmly when his performance doesn't measure up to your standards. Most women automatically react like working wife Sally Forth in the cartoon strip of that name. She sets her husband to vacuuming with a long speech, "It's best to start vacuuming in that corner and work your way out, going over each area in several directions, also, you should . . ."

Her husband interrupts, "I know how to vacuum."

Or Sally Forth comes home from work to find her husband has started a beef stroganoff dinner. She's pleased but begins offering advice: "You know when *I* fix stroganoff, I put the . . ." As he gestures her out of the kitchen, Sally admits, "You're right. You're right . . . Letting go isn't as easy as I thought."

Real-life husbands also notice wives' possessive house-power attitudes. As one tired man said one rainy Thursday evening, "You keep referring to it as 'my kitchen.' If it really is your kitchen, not our kitchen, how come you expect me to mop the floor?"

Or as other perceptive men have said to their working wives, "If all this really is our family work instead of your work, how come you're in charge of methods?"

Now that women have added paid employment to domestic responsibilities, none of us can Do It All. To attempt it returns us to the pessimism of the 1980s when women decided "Superwoman is dead," and it seemed as if woman could not have it all.

But we *can* have it all if we will stop trying to do and control it all. And, instead, learn *comfortable* ways to Share not only the work but also the house-power.

10 Surefire Ways to Get to "He's Doing It Right"

Find Your Comfort Zones

Like the women in my survey who pinpointed the tasks they'd be glad never to do again, choose one or two responsibilities you dislike and start there. You won't be giving up your house-power in general, just in one or two experimental areas.

Why do you and not he choose where you'll start to Share power? Because the best way to make a start is where the transition is easiest for you. Of course, you'll also have to adapt as needed so he too is comfortable about his initial responsibilities.

Remember It's Reversible

By trying Sharing you can win a much pleasanter, less overburdened life and you have nothing to lose. If you don't like it, you can always change your mind. You can reclaim your power to set all the rules, standards, methods, and return to asking, pleading, for his "help." He's never going to object if you decide you want the work back.

So it's safe to try giving over house-power together with the task. You'll almost surely find that once you've begun, Overload-relief outweighs any disadvantages and nothing will persuade you to return to the old ways.

A woman frequently passes through the same attitude cycle when her oldest child first obtains a driver's license. While the teenager is practicing and preparing to take the driver's test, the nervous mother usually silently vows never to let the adolescent use the car to chauffeur the younger children.

Her resolve usually vanishes on the first hectic day after the teenager receives the license. Mother hears herself say, "Please go pick up your brother from his music lesson. Be careful how you drive. Make him buckle up and sit quiet . . ." Or "Please get me these things at the supermarket. Watch how you park and pull out . . ." Lots of worry on Mom's part about the teenager's driving. Nevertheless, with all the pressures on her, she rapidly sees the teenager's driving license as such a blessing that few overloaded working mothers would give up the relief it provides. Similarly, when her husband starts Sharing house-power and responsibility instead of just physically "helping," working wives find the benefits so outweigh the minuses that few would return to "helping."

See It as an Evolving System

Once you learn these techniques and you become comfortable about giving over authority for other tasks, the techniques can be used to shed more of your Overload.

For example, today you may have just one child. Perhaps the joy of having her look like a baby doll in perfectly matched outfits, including the right socks and hair barrette, makes it worthwhile to lay out all her clothes before you ask him to dress her. But the day the second baby arrives, increased family pressures may make you feel something has to give. Then you may decide to accept your husband's good-enough-match-of-tops-and-pants method of dressing her. You're ready to hand over the task with "This month (or from now on) it's your job to dress her, feed her, and take her to nursery school." You'll be able to say things like that because the next chapters provide the communication ideas & skills that will make him see that it's fair to move from "helping" you with *your* work to accepting home responsibilities as *his* work.

Or perhaps today it's worth it to you to take the towels out of the wash, fold them just so, and stack them neatly by color in your linen closet. Comes the day when life is busier, and you may decide you're ready to say, "I'll wash the clothes. But you launder the towels and sheets this month." (Or from now on, or whatever.)

When you understand that holding on to the *power* demands that you do it yourself and Sharing demands you let him do it his way, you won't be exasperated if he folds the towels unevenly or even leaves them permanently in the clean laundry basket for the family to take as needed. After all, lots of women also do it that way.

Look at His Methods as a Tradeoff

All mothers keep house and mother their children by accepting many tradeoffs. For instance, if you baked your own daily bread, you'd have that glorious oven aroma permeating your home and that crusty freshness to bite into. But we trade store-bought lesser bread for more time. And nobody loves or can care for children as their parents do. But practical pressures mean you accept some babysitting, or other paid childcare. These are samples of tradeoffs you probably make. Ease into Sharing with the same tradeoff mindset.

One woman who gave over food shopping to her husband as his permanent responsibility also stopped making food lists.

"Does he bring home all the brands you want?" a friend asked her. "No," the first woman admitted. "But it's a tradeoff. Because he does the shopping and the laundry, I was able to accept a promotion I was offered. I couldn't have taken this more interesting and better paying job otherwise. I'm happier at work, there's more money for the whole family's needs, and that combination is worth more to me than the satisfaction of having every grocery item exactly as I want it." Then she added, "I don't notice anymore. I don't think about it."

The tradeoff concept is one of your best aids for becoming comfortable with his methods. Are you gaining more in Overload-relief than you're losing by going along with his methods? Then it's a good tradeoff. You're coming out ahead.

Build in More Comfort by Allowing for Modifications

When you transfer the power and responsibility for a task to him, it's not etched in stone. You adapt as needed. The woman whose husband took over grocery shopping explained, "Though I stopped making lists, I realized I had to be flexible about unusual items. One day I wanted to combine some molasses with a bottled barbecue sauce to sharpen the flavor and we were out of molasses. I started to say he wasn't doing his grocery shopping job. He insisted that when I used up something offbeat like molasses, I had to add it to his list. I realized he was right. Now I do that and I also put down anything special I'd like to have, sometimes including the brand I want. But it's still his job to keep track of all the staples and provide a general range of food for meals.

"For instance, with the staples once I started to tell him we were out of dishwashing detergent. He walked to the closet, pulled out a new box, held it up triumphantly and said, 'Just where it belongs.' You could see he was proud of the fact that he'd mastered this new skill of keeping the larder stocked."

Evaluate the Difference between Your Results and His

A close look at the marginal differences between his results and yours can make you more comfortable about ceding house-power.

One woman I interviewed never mops her kitchen floor until she's vacuumed thoroughly, wiped down the kitchen chair legs, and carried the chairs out of the room; she then mops, rinses, and allows the floor to dry before replacing the chairs.

When she turned over the job and authority to her husband, she taught him that corners and under the counters must be done thoroughly lest food droppings breed bugs. That was an example of a family standard that she had a right to establish. She also taught him with their kind of vinyl floor, he couldn't drown the surface or the tiles would start coming loose. (Men insist on similar family standards in "their" domains: "If you use a garden tool, hang it back in its place in the garage. Don't just leave it lying around.")

Having established those standards, she then had to accept his methods. He doesn't see any point in vacuuming. "I just change the floor water more often," he says. He pushes the chairs around instead of removing them from the kitchen and he walks on the damp floor before it dries if he wants something from the refrigerator.

"Is his washed kitchen floor as clean as my washed kitchen floor?" asks his wife. She shrugs. "Probably not. But the marginal difference in cleanliness is worth it to me. I never have to think about or do the kitchen floor anymore. It's his job to do every week, and he does it. When the chair legs bother me, I do that detail myself. I wipe them down in two minutes."

That is the key. Is the marginal difference between your results and his results big enough to make it worthwhile to you to do the *whole* job yourself? Or can you come out ahead with his doing it using his methods—and you tending to details that matter to you that he will never see as necessary, such as the chair legs?

If you decide that having the job done from beginning to end with every detail just as you want it is absolutely necessary to you, then you'll have to do it yourself.

If, however, you decide the marginal difference isn't worth doing it yourself, then if he is going to have the responsibility to remember, plan, lay in supplies, and do the task, you have to treat him like an adult and let him do it his way.

Realize He'll Improve

It may be slow going for weeks or months. Patience. You had to learn. Encourage him. Just as you did, he'll learn and get better at it and you'll be rewarded with years of Overload-relief.

As one woman in my survey wrote in answer to why women often feel effort from him is "more trouble than it's worth," she said, "Initially they're not used to housework. It's very time consuming and they're not adept at it. If they could persist, it would become easier."

In his book *Househusbands: Men and Housework in American Families*, Brooklyn College sociologist Professor William Beer reports men tend to do one household job at a time while women often do several things at once, such as cleaning the floor, cooking, keeping an eye on the children. Beer speculates men's less productive methods may be the result of inexperience with the work. "When you first approach any job," says he, "you do it more systematically. Once you get more comfortable with it, you can handle lots of different jobs at the same time."

Allow Yourself Inflexible Areas

Though you'll expand Sharing as you go along and you both grow comfortable with it, there may be some parts of your house-power as mother and housekeeper that you will never be ready to part with. That's fine. But now you understand that the price of having a chore done exactly your way is doing it yourself.

Each woman's special areas will vary. One woman I interviewed cares passionately about the niceties of her own and her children's appearance. "I don't like shopping. But I care about my children looking 'right.' No matter what, I won't allow my husband, my mother, my mother-in-law, anyone to pick out their clothes."

Other women will shrug and see no reason why they personally must buy everything in the children's wardrobe. The exact cut, color, details of the garments don't matter that much to them.

That's why the system works for so many different kinds of women. You adapt it to your personality by giving over the responsibility and accompanying power only for those tasks where you yourself feel comfortable about tradeoffs, marginal differences, and living with his results. You keep the rest of the house-power—and the accompanying work— for yourself.

Let Him Make Mistakes

Nothing will imprint responsibility on his mind as well as a few failures. Columnist Richard Cohen, in an essay in Ms. magazine acknowledges that "like many (most?) men, I still was slow in appreciating the difference between sharing and helping . . . Sharing would mean carrying the concern around in your head when you are also trying to do a job (career!), raise children . . ."

If you keep reminding him and saving him from error, he'll never move to the stage of "carrying the concern" around in his head. He'll know he can depend on *you* to carry it in *your* head. Bite your tongue, leave the house, do what you must but let him find out some things for himself.

Say you've both agreed that this year he's in charge of your nine-year-old son's Little League activities. On the weekend morning of the first practice session your son asks, "Where's my uniform, and the new glove you promised me, and aren't we supposed to be at the game now? When are we going?" If your husband has not been carrying his Little League job around in his head, that man is going to be in a panic.

The resulting hullabaloo, the wailing and complaining because Dad didn't check out last year's uniform and it turns out to be too small, Dad hasn't got around to buying the promised new glove, and they're late for practice, will put the kind of dent in your husband's cortex that will last. Your child, who had to play in his own clothes without a uniform, minus the new glove, and late besides, will still be going on about it on the way home and tomorrow. "Taking care of Little League" will now be imprinted on your husband's mind in a way that your saving him from error would never accomplish.

Be sure not to undo the good. Weeks before you will have prepared your child to turn to Dad about Little League by emphasizing, "Daddy is taking care of Little League for you this year." Now if the child comes complaining to you about the disaster, do not apologize. Fatal! That just brings back responsibility to you together with the invisible 80–90% of Little League, the remembering, scheduling, preparing. When the child complains to you, you sympathize, remind him that "Daddy is taking care of Little League," and send the child back to Daddy for action.

Obviously, you're not going to let your husband make a mistake that costs your child too dearly. When you notice your husband hasn't checked and discovered that this year your town's Little League sign-up is first and third Tuesday evenings in February from 6–8 P.M. at the firehouse and your child will be shut out for the season, you'll have to speak. But why not tell the child instead of Dad? That way the pressure on Dad comes from your child who—if you're lucky—will actually say, "Dad, why don't you remember to find out these things by yourself?" At the very least, the prod from your impatient youngster will transfer mental responsibility to your husband more effectively than a reminder from you.

If your husband is in charge of drinks for your party, seal your mouth and do not point out to him that he's forgotten to lay in a bag of ice cubes and he's completely out of mixers. When your friends innocently keep requesting the missing items, he'll be surprised. He may never have had to think ahead and plan for his home efforts. You've always had it on your mind and your schedule. All he did was perform the physical task. Surprise, mild embarrassment, the bother of having to rush out for ice and mixers, will go far toward moving him along the transition from passively "helping" to actively carrying the planning, buying supplies, and scheduling for tasks he's taken on.

As always when he makes a mistake—in this case, the missing ice and mixers—guard against apologizing for the situation. Apologies from you always reinstate you as the person whose job it is and then you look and feel guilty.

Greet your friends' requests for ice and mixers with, "I'm doing the food for this party and Hank is in charge of the drinks. You have to ask Hank about it."

You are at that moment about to enter a glorious new personal era. In our new diversified culture, many people are ready to move from seeing the working wife as responsible for everything at home to seeing the husband as responsible for certain tasks—IF it is presented to people that way. So, when you stick to, "Ask Hank about the ice. He's in charge of drinks for this party," your friends will almost certainly glide into viewing it that way and you will be safe from criticism as a bad wife/housekeeper. In this new mood they may even stamp responsibility into his head by sending him some mild open criticism, "Hank, how come you invite us to a party and don't have ice or mixers?"

Allowing him to make mistakes will also improve his methods and his results. You know that if he fills the pot with that much water, it'll boil over and make a mess when he adds the pasta. Tell him to lower the water level before he adds the pasta and you're bossing and irritating him. Keep quiet. Let it boil over. If possible leave the room before it happens to avoid his being embarrassed in front of you. And do not gloat or comment. He'll learn and do it better next time.

Naturally, you use common sense and save him from mistakes that will hurt too much emotionally or physically.

Be Prepared to Accept His Competence

While learning to see his less than perfect performance in terms of tradeoffs and marginal differences, you must also ready your ego for tasks where he develops star qualities. One woman I interviewed told me, "If I say so myself, I'm a good cook. My husband took over our family dinner three nights a week. He did some take-out and frozen foods, but he also began turning out gourmet wonders that were in another league from my family cooking. It rattled me and I caught myself demanding regular congratulations on my routine meals.

"As meals turned into a weekly chore for him, he couldn't keep the gourmet pace and settled into less spectacular dinners. But now he's almost as good a basic cook as I am. I don't think I love the idea. Still, going back to being responsible for all the meals by myself is unthinkable. It's a different kind of tradeoff. Let him have his culinary reputation as long as I don't have to think about dinner three nights a week."

Realize You've Reached a New Freedom

Once you accept that different does not equal WRONG, you're free from "It's easier to do it myself" and "It takes too long to explain it to him."

It's only easier to do it yourself and it only takes too long to explain if you insist on imparting each detail of *your* method and insist he do it your way and only your way.

You're free too from the big one: "I can't let him do it because he doesn't do it right." Once you realize that if he accepts the responsibility for the task, he must be allowed to choose his own methods, then "doing it right" ceases to mean Do It My Way and My Way Only.

13

Your New Invincible Husband-Convincing Powers

*F*ORGET your past communication difficulties. Persuading your husband to accept a significant share of home and childcare will probably be much easier than you expect.

Previously you were captive to your belief that he was doing you a favor. You were asking, requesting, perhaps pleading for his "help" with what you both saw as your job. Now before you even open your mouth, your new feelings of Entitlement will send him powerful body language signals that *automatically* improve his attitude. Now as you talk about his assuming a fair share of family responsibilities, you'll have powerful new psychological allies that will help you. Here's how it works.

What You Think & Feel Affects His Reaction

Though percentages vary, communication experts agree that from 70–90+ percent of messages people receive when you talk come from your body language—your posture, gestures, facial expressions, clothing, and other aspects of your appearance. Viewed the other way, only a small 10–30% of the impression you make is produced by your words. Others take the rest of your message from your body.

You don't have to think about making your body say "I'm Entitled." Body language is beyond your control. If you believe something, all by itself your body will convey your attitude. And because people automatically and subconsciously read body language, your husband cannot help but recognize your new body language confidence and be moved to listen to you in a new way.

In the past when you discussed your overloaded life with him, your voice, your words, and your body language put you on the defensive with a Non-Entitled message of, "I know it's my job. But I just can't handle it all. Please be a good guy and do some of it for me." He read the message, "She knows this is her job, not my job." His reluctance was the natural reaction.

Now feeling Entitled causes your body to move in ways that send a very different message that says: "We have to straighten something out. This is not fair. We have to make it fair."

Body language cannot be faked successfully. Gerard I. Nierenberg, co-author with Henry H. Calero of the accepted classic guide, *How to Read a Person Like a Book,* believes only a superb actor or pathological liar can artificially direct what the body says. The rest of us have bodies that say exactly what we feel.

Nierenberg and Calero, business and government negotiation lawyers, built their landmark source book by videotaping 2500 real business negotiation sessions and obtaining participant feedback from those involved. "Participant feedback" means that after these business sessions they played the videos privately for participants and the participants told them, "Right there I was really worried the deal would fall through . . ." Or "Right there I felt we were in control at last." Or "There I was stalling for time while I tried to think." And on and on through the videos as participants confessed their emotions at different scenes.

From the negotiation sessions and the subsequent interviews, Nierenberg and Calero learned there are predictable body movements (a body language) that English-speaking members of Western civilization use unconsciously to express emotions they're feeling. As a child we learned to use and read the body-words from the adults around us just as we learned our spoken language. In other cultures not only the spoken language is different, but the body-words that accompany various emotions often are different.

Nierenberg and Calero's work is further substantiated by the research of Dr. Ray Birdwhistell, the renowned University of Pennsylvania professor of communication, who years ago moved reading body language from a vague "art" to a science.

When you feel Entitled and discuss Sharing household chores and house-power with your husband, your posture, the way you hold your head and shoulders, your gestures, your facial expressions, the way you walk will all deliver your new belief that your proposal about Sharing is fair and reasonable, something you will now be comfortable with, something that will also benefit him and the children.

Subconsciously his mind will read your sense of Entitlement. This time he'll receive your attitude as, "She thinks she's on strong ground. I'd better tune in." This message will not all by itself move him to Sharing. But it will change his listening attitude and the atmosphere between you. When you add the communication techniques in the next chapters, your body language will be an important force in producing a new kind of discussion and successful solution to your Overload.

Expecting Results Gets You Results

Because you now know you're Entitled, you set up—between you and your husband—another powerful psychological juggernaut that operates in your behalf: the self-fulfilling prophecy.

A self-fulfilling prophecy is a psychological term for what happens when you *believe* something will happen. Your belief that it will occur puts in motion psychological forces that affect your own behavior and the other person's behavior and often end by making things go the way you predict. In this case you expect (prophesy) that he should agree and he does.

This phenomenon is not wishful hocus pocus. The self-fulfilling prophecy occurs constantly in all our lives and is a proven human reaction. Psychiatrist Joseph T. Martorano and psychotherapist John P. Kildahl, authors of the book *Beyond Negative Thinking*, verbalize a belief among psychologists/psychiatrists and other motivation experts when they write, "Over the years we've discovered that when people *think* differently, they feel—and *act*—differently . . . If you think you can do something, you increase your chances of doing it." (All emphases are theirs.)

The self-fulfilling power of your expectation has been demonstrated many times by respected researchers. A very famous experiment was conducted by Dr. Robert Rosenthal of Harvard. He divided an elementary school class on a random basis with *no regard* for students' ability. Then he told the teacher that his testing showed the students in one group would reach unexpectedly high academic achievement but that nothing special could be expected from the youngsters in the other group.

At year end, the students in the group he labeled superstars showed more improvement on tests than did their classmates in the "average" group. Since the children were divided at random, this should not have happened.

As the experts explain it, because the teacher expected the first group to do better, the teacher must have subconsciously given those children extra effort, encouragement, and attention. As a result the children in the first group lived up to superstar expectations. Similarly, the children labeled "average" were expected to be average. They too lived up to the expectations.

In your case, your belief that you are Entitled to have him take over responsibility for parts of the family care load and that he should see it, adjust, and agree sets up a self-fulfilling prophecy. Because of your new sense of Entitlement you acquire the extra staying power and automatic body language power-movements that propel him toward agreement and making it happen.

In a study that directly shows how self-fulfilling prophecy can influence your husband to increase his home efforts, Pennsylvania State University sociologist Dr. Malcolm D. Hill worked with 150 wives chosen at random. He discovered that your attitudes toward marital roles do indeed make the difference. Two-thirds of the women in the study came from what the researcher calls "working class" families with very traditional male-female separate family roles. The remainder are described as from a "middle-class neighborhood." Among both types, there were some women who on their own developed non-traditional family attitudes. These women got their husbands to change and do what is traditionally thought of as women's work.

As Dr. Hill explains it, his results show that the women's own attitudes toward "conjugal role segregation"—"women's work" and "men's work"—have more of an effect on a husband's willingness to do a real share of family work than do the couple's initial family attitudes. The individual women's belief that he should accept the responsibility set up a self-fulfilling prophecy which produced results that matched her expectations and her views.

Trying to Influence Equals Results

Two Canadian family experts report that whether a woman is a full-time homemaker, part-time working wife, or full-time working wife does not affect her ability to influence her husband on family matters. In their research, psychiatrist Dr. Christine S. Sexton and sociologist Dr. Daniel S. Perlman found *the key difference* lies in *whether a wife tries to influence her husband.* They declare that it is her trying—your trying—that will produce results.

This proof that between wives and husbands TRYING TO INFLU-ENCE EQUALS RESULTS is confirmed in many other family investigations. One, supported by a National Science Foundation Grant, focused directly on men's beliefs that wives and husbands have "natural" and different sex roles. The researchers, sociologists John Mirowsky and Catherine E. Ross, point out that men are more likely to believe in natural sex roles because the traditional arrangement gives men more privileges. It is therefore to the men's "advantage" to hold onto those beliefs. Again in this investigation the researchers found that when a woman stopped accepting the situation and made an effort to convey her new views—made an effort to influence—her efforts succeeded and she *moved him* closer to her own attitudes of sexual equality.

This same research project shows that if he attempts it, a husband can also influence his wife toward his rigid sex roles ideas. However, other important work by Dr. Jay Belsky and Dr. Brenda L. Volling, two leaders in marriage and family research, reported in the book *Men's Transitions to Parenthood: Longitudinal Studies of Early Family Experience,* found that wherever you keep track of marital influencing over a long period of time, a wife's efforts to influence turn out to have more effect on changing her husband than vice versa! Isn't that a lovely bit of useful knowledge to remember and think about whenever you need an infusion of courage?

A last, very useful fact that can help you. In another experiment with 235 couples when wives succeeded in winning husbands' cooperation for two-paycheck family efforts, it "seemed to be the result of the wives' willingness to talk conflicts out rather than trying to work around the problems . . . the wives' belief (self-fulfilling power of expectancy) that their husbands should be willing to contribute seems to make the couple skillful at hammering out innovative relationships. And the husbands often respond with pride in their wives' accomplishments and individuality."

So go to it. You gotta talk up. Your silent power-allies—your sense of Entitlement, your body language, the self-fulfilling power of expectancy, and the fact that trying-to-influence-equals-results—will make your efforts successful.

14

*What to Say & Do When
You've Already Tried Everything*

*L*IZ Garvell, a successful Ohio real estate broker, can't remember exactly when or where she developed new ideas about more equality in her marriage. "Probably it was things I read in women's magazines, and that I heard other women saying. Suddenly I realized Jim's and my marriage was way out of balance. I was not only working to earn money we definitely needed but I was continually on the defensive apologizing to him if dinner, laundry, dusting, everything wasn't just so."

Liz recalls an incident that really triggered a change and that she now sees as the moment she started toward divorce. "I had two shelves in the kitchen where I kept my papers for my real estate work—which I was just beginning then. Jim had a desk and a whole small room upstairs for his use as a study, even though he had a 9–5 business office elsewhere. One evening he was in the kitchen and wanted a postage stamp. Instead of going up to his desk, he started rummaging on my shelves for my stamp envelope. When he couldn't find it, he got angry. 'Damn it. Why don't you keep this place in order? I can't even find a stamp!' "

Liz says she reacted with her usual instant sense of having failed at the housekeeping. She began apologizing, and rushed to her shelves to find a stamp for him. The incident passed.

Later, she recollects, "Something exploded in my head. I thought, 'They're my shelves. Why am I obliged to keep them in an order that suits him? If I went to his desk and began shouting about how he kept it, he'd be outraged and demand to know what I'm doing messing there and he'd say it's none of my business how he keeps his desk. Why isn't the same true of my business place?' Of course, I didn't say any of that to him."

But over the next 18 months Liz and Jim's marriage deteriorated. As Liz kept recognizing other parts of their life together that she felt were unfair, she brooded over them and cut back her home efforts. Jim responded with escalating complaints about the slapdash meals and housekeeping, their diminishing sex life, and what he called her new disinterest in him.

Liz struggled to save her marriage. She discussed her problems in changing him with two of her best friends who were having similar difficulties. Sometimes she worked hard at hints and pleasantly tried to get him to see that well, maybe, if he didn't like the way the house looked, she'd heard and read about other men with working wives who were starting to do some housework. Other times she lost her temper and told him straight out that he was a chauvinist and impossible to live with. Nothing she tried persuaded him to accept her new goals of a more egalitarian marriage. Eventually Liz gave up, moved out, and got a divorce.

❧❧❧

If you will go back and look at examples of the flood of 1980s and 1970s articles and books in which a woman discusses how her marriage broke up over her "new goals" and "his refusal to accept them," you will find repeated over and over exactly the pattern that Liz describes.

In these accounts, the wife experiences the same liberating "click." She suddenly perceives the unfairness of things in her marriage that she previously accepted without question. Liz's brand-new feeling that she should not have to earn needed family money and also singlehandedly keep house and meals in perfect full-time homemaker condition is a typical example.

As Liz did, in all these accounts the woman then talks to her women friends and/or her mother or sister about her struggles to change her husband. But just as consistently in these accounts, *nowhere* does the woman ever mount a constructive effort to plainly explain her grievances & goals to her husband and then try to work through with him to a new family pattern.

My own years of interviews with working wives, the evidence of these two decades of articles and books, and the many reported experiences of marriage counselors reveal that most wives sidestep direct speech when trying to communicate sensitive and/or potentially controversial ideas to their husbands. Instead the women use what might be labeled the "mind-reading method."

Like Liz, the women usually go on for hours with their female confidantes explaining their grievances and views in excruciating detail. Despite those protracted efforts, the angry wife frequently encounters strong disagreement from her female listeners about some of her new egalitarian views. Some of Liz's friends, for example, still had very traditional ideas. They argued with Liz that though she was employed, Jim still had the right to expect full-time housekeeping services.

Meanwhile between wife and husband there are no long hours of clear explanation of grievances and goals, or even a few minutes of straight talk. The wife may hint, recount what other husbands do, try to relay her thoughts through her moods or with barbed comments. But that is as close as many wives come to sharing new viewpoints with their husbands.

If she herself spent years *not* seeing the marital inequities, why does a woman expect her husband instantly to perceive what she herself for so long failed to understand? And if some of her female friends even after hours of discussion do not always understand her ideas, why does she expect her husband to grasp her new outlook through just a few hints?

There are many forces propelling women toward relying on mindreading. But first, it's essential to realize that men are usually heartbreakingly inept at these kinds of verbal nuances. Psychologist Ronald Levant expresses the consensus view of family experts when he says, "Men are not trained to be empathetic listeners. We're taught to listen to our opponents to discover their weaknesses." And when a woman uses male chauvinist accusations or hints about how "other men" are doing housework, her words turn on his "opponents" listening-mode. He doesn't look for common ground to solve her grievances; he looks for weaknesses in her position to decimate it.

So directing complaints and hints at a husband who is unskilled in verbal indirection and who, instead, is accustomed to seeing flaws in others' arguments, achieves nothing—except damage to a marriage. As the sessions continue, the wife's anger keeps rising because he "won't change." He reacts with mounting weariness and impatience because his wife keeps bitching on about her life and nothing seems to turn her off. Overall, she believes her hints and complaints have clearly conveyed why she's angry and what she wants him to do. But since she's never clearly told him what is on her mind—let alone discussed it—he usually hasn't a clue as to what her real complaints are or what she expects of him.

Under those circumstances, as a myriad of marital counseling and research files, articles, and books indicate, couples often spend months or years in masked verbal fencing, bickering, sniping, and battling over superficial symptoms without ever dealing with the core disagreement issues.

Examples abound as soon as you look at any of these marital relations sources. In an important family study reported in the *Journal of Marriage and the Family*, sociologists Benin and Agostinelli discovered that when couples were interviewed separately the women declared they were very dissatisfied and felt their husbands were not doing a fair share of home and childcare. The women said they were constantly "arguing," complaining and letting the men know how dissatisfied they were.

Yet when the men were interviewed, they were completely oblivious to their wives' anger. The men reported there were no fights at all about the men contributing more effort at home. Clearly the wives' methods of conveying their requests are so indirect that men don't even notice. Benin and Agostinelli cite another study, "Sex and Gender: The Human Experience," on the same problem that concludes, "It could be that the women perceive they are arguing by performing chores while slamming things around, sighing, or giving off other nonverbal signs of displeasure. Their husbands may not . . . attribute the wives' displeasure to disagreements over the division of labor. Perhaps if the wives stated their dissatisfaction more directly not only would husbands agree that arguments are occurring, but perhaps they would share a larger portion of the household tasks."

Marriage counselors agree. They report that well into a couple's sessions, a husband will burst out with, "Look, until now, you never mentioned all this. I can't read your mind, you know." One therapist's notes read: "Though Liza clearly felt a lack of intimacy in her relationship, though she was highly articulate and though she thought she'd told David how she felt, until they began counseling, she had never specifically expressed her wishes and needs to him."

Why Women Depend on Mindreading

Speaking up plainly may be seen as dangerous. Suppose her man gets very angry. Suppose he delivers a flat ultimatum, "NO!" As communication expert Dr. Paula Kurman puts it, "Women may fear that if they voice their desires clearly and he disagrees, they'll have to give up. That's especially true if the woman doesn't yet have a firm grasp on why she is Entitled to hold that view."

Dr. Kurman is a consultant to industry on the structure of human relationships and maintains a wide private practice. She explains that women also hesitate to speak up because of a misty feeling that "If he really loved me, he'd know." Or as the noted linguist Deborah Tannen, Ph.D., author of a bestselling book on differences in male-female communication styles, *You Just Don't Understand,* explains, "Many women feel, 'After all this time, you should know what I want without my telling you.' " At that point, the woman is truly reaching for the supernatural. No human being can read another person's mind, no matter how much love there is between them.

Psychologist Harriet Goldhor Lerner adds another important insight. Many of us "would rather keep our communication vague and fuzzy in order to preserve the peace and avoid bringing our conflicts and differences into bold relief. But, although keeping things fuzzy lowers our anxiety in the short run, in the long run it makes things worse."

Motivated by these reasons to depend on the mindreading method, intelligent, otherwise articulate women behave in self-defeating ways. An attractive 42-year-old public relations executive I interviewed has been divorced for twelve years and has never remarried. She told me that when she arrived at her new vision of a more equal marriage, she waited two full years for her husband to change before she gave up, moved out with her two young children, and got a divorce. Looking back, she acknowledges she never argued with him about her new goals. "I was brought up to believe that people in a good marriage never fought. So after I had the new views, I think I believed he'd just get the same ideas from what was going on in the country about women and equality or that he'd feel what I wanted. All I know is that I got a divorce without ever, ever telling him what I wanted. I expected him to know."

This woman is a successful public relations executive. Her business is communication. If someone in PR is depending on mindreading to convey a message, you can well believe other less articulate women are also doing so.

A working wife I met at a party offers another vivid example of how often and in how many ways women depend on mindreading. Her husband is an AT&T executive, she holds an executive civil service position. Their children are in college and her money is essential for their tuition. The talk turned to working wives' stressed lives and she volunteered that her "last straw" usually came at night after a long day at work, coming home, making dinner, and cleaning up. Then about 10:30–11:00 her husband walks into the clean kitchen, makes himself a late-night snack, and leaves all the fixings, dirty utensils, crumbs strewn around on counters and table.

With this book in mind, I ventured to inquire, "What does he say when you ask if he'd please clean up after himself?"

This woman, a college graduate, holder of a demanding executive job, paused before she answered and then said in what can only be described as a surprised, musing tone, "You mean you have to say something? They don't just know?"

50% Mindreading

Neither does loud and active complaining move you beyond the mindreading method. Yet women who rely on complaining to work out new marital patterns are usually sure they've already tried everything!

Complaining amounts to 50% mindreading. You know what's wrong. You have a good idea of what changes he should make to eliminate the problem. All you share with him is the problem. You keep possible solutions as your own private secrets. And you leave it to him to guess at the ideas you have in mind.

A young woman I interviewed told me a typical 50% mindreading story. "Though we commute to work in different directions, our child's nursery school is just as convenient to either of us. Stopping to pick up our three-year-old puts me way behind in making dinner and turns the whole evening with our child into an anxiety-scene. My husband will cook sometimes but certainly not all the time. For almost a year I've been going on about how hard it is. He keeps telling me to find a better, faster route to the nursery school, a faster route from there to home, or not to bother about a real dinner. What I want is for him to get our daughter so I can go straight home and start dinner. The whole evening will be better for all of us. He's a doting father who loves being with her. Yet he never offers to pick her up. I don't know why."

Again, I ventured to ask, "What does he say when you suggest he pick her up and you go start dinner?"

Again, the same surprise. "Well, I've never suggested it. Obviously, he must know what I want."

Not necessarily. Many people—both men and women—are not good at solution-thinking per se. Just because your logic tells you the solution is "obvious" doesn't mean it's clear to someone else. Or in situations like this people may drift into compartmentalized thinking and find it hard to break free. In this case the husband seems locked into the idea that his wife picks up the daughter. Maybe he believes she'd be angry if he tried to take away that private time in the car with their daughter. He's offered to give up having a real dinner. So, he's clearly interested in adapting to ease her stress. She should help him to help all of them by revealing her solutions to see if he finds them acceptable.

Fifty percent mindreading, where you know the possible way out and you supply only the complaint, and depend on the other person to learn your goals by reading your mind, is probably *the most popular communication method that working wives use in attempting to solve their Overload.*

Think about situations where you've known for a long time what he needs to do. Yet he shows no signs of doing it despite your frequent complaints. Have you depended on his arriving at the solution by reading your mind?

Consider that you've spent hours, days ruminating about the problem and devising various solution scenarios. He probably hasn't given the situation much or any thought. To him, it's something you are having a problem with. Chances are good that he thinks you're going to settle it. His generosity and love for you is not the point. Remember, men are not good at the verbal nuance hints you've been offering. Why play games waiting till the answers spring from your head to his?

One woman I interviewed whose marriage survived and rallied told what happened when the real cause of her fury accidentally burst from her and she moved beyond complaining and hinting.

"Our children's school bus comes very early," she said. "To get the children off to school, I always was the one who rose an hour earlier than our jobs require. For years I myself didn't see the unfairness. After all, mothers are 'supposed' to see their children fed, parented, properly dressed, and off to school.

"Then when I did see the unfairness, I dropped a number of hints and told him in detail about a relevant magazine article I'd read. Told him how I longed for a chance to sometimes have that extra hour's sleep in the morning. He didn't say anything connecting it to our situation. Nor did he change his behavior.

"One morning after several months of hinting and brooding about it when the alarm went off, something burst in me. I sat up, slammed my hand on the blankets, and shouted, 'It's not fair. It's not fair. I go to work. You go to work. Every morning when it's time to send them to school I want to sleep, you want to sleep. *Why is it always your turn to sleep and always my turn to get up?* They're your children too. It's not fair!!'"

"He turned his head and stared at me. It was obvious this was a brand new idea to him. My months of subtle suggestions and hints hadn't accomplished anything.

"He just lay there and stared while I went on screaming, 'It's not fair! Why isn't it ever my turn to sleep?' Finally he sat up and said, 'OK, we'll take turns getting up.' From that day on that's how it has worked. If I'd kept on with my subtle, vague hints I don't know how things would have turned out."

Certainly delivering your message plainly won't always result in so quick and equitable a solution. But saying it plain (starting more calmly, and continuing in as many ways and on as many occasions as necessary) will accomplish far more than complaining about the problem with him and other women, while expecting your man to come up with your solution by reading your mind.

Attitude Mindreading

Marital communication also fails because a wife develops a new sense of who she has grown to be. Then she depends on mindreading to transmit her updated self-image to her husband.

In her book *Sharing It All: The Rewards and Struggles of Two-Career Families*, counseling psychologist Dr. Lucia A. Gilbert describes this very common situation. In Dr. Gilbert's example a woman lawyer declares, "I complain about a bad day at the office and my husband says, 'Quit and take a different position.' That response makes me furious. It cuts off my conversation and shows little empathy and interest in me. I never say that to him. I expect him to have bad days and he expects to tell me about them in detail."

But that is as far as the lawyer goes. It makes her "furious." Yet she does not tell her husband that she is unhappy with his response. She does not explain what kind of reply would please her. She does not call his attention to the empathetic way she handles the same kinds of complaints from him. No, she just leaves him frozen in the wrong attitude and keeps getting "furious." As a lawyer she is well able to set forth her ideas. But she leaves her husband to discover the problem and solution— the way she would like him to react—by reading her mind.

A young manufacturing sales representative has done a better job of passing on her changing self-image to her husband. She told me, "When I first went back to work after the children reached school age, and I'd tell him I'd made a good sale, he'd always light up and say, 'How much commission did you make from it?' I was satisfied with that. Or, at least I didn't think much about it. Lately, that reaction has irritated me. Sure, we need my commission and it's exciting to earn it each time. But that's not what I want to hear. One night I told him so.

"I said, 'That's not the point I want you to concentrate on. I want you to see that I figured it out and made this big sale against stiff competition. I want you to say something that shows you know I'm getting to be an excellent sales strategist.' So I put the words in his mouth. And maybe I had to remind him a bunch of times and go into detail about what I meant about being a 'sales strategist and understanding the finer points of marketing.' And maybe he had a little personal trouble adapting to seeing me in that bigger light. But now he does see me that way, talks about me to others that way, which is the way I really am. And things are better, happier, and sexier between us."

By moving beyond mindreading and keeping his and her image of who she is congruent, this young wife strengthened her marriage. The more a husband or wife misperceives the other, the less core reality and strength there is to their relationship.

Dr. Alma Baron, University of Wisconsin-Extension's coordinator of Women in Management Programs, explains that women often fail to communicate their career goals to their spouses and children. And she says, "Without clear and shared goal-setting, it is difficult to manage all aspects of life effectively."

Usually, you are doing your husband a kind favor by abandoning the mindreading system and speaking plainly. Though no one is capable of mindreading solutions or the exact cause of your dissatisfactions, men are often well aware when their wife is angry, troubled, and resentful. Leaving him to guess both the problem and the solutions leads to the pointless and destructive rigamarole of battling over symptoms while making no progress at all toward eliminating the cause.

One of my interviews offered touching evidence that husbands of all ages respond well to undisguised talk. A 60ish, very traditional-minded husband gave me his version of what happened when his wife finally explained how she wanted his view of her to change. He told me that in the past when she'd come home tired and complained about her problems as a social worker, he'd tried to comfort her by saying they could live satisfactorily on his income and she shouldn't knock herself out. He told me, "I noticed she always got annoyed, or worse, looked sad and turned away. I didn't have any idea why. I didn't understand she saw her work as making a difference in the world and that it gave her a sense of pride and achievement; that what she wanted was for me to see she was changing and improving people's lives, people who might not otherwise have had meaningful help."

Later I asked the wife why she'd gone for years without telling him to stop suggesting she give up her work; and why she hadn't given him her view of the value of her work. She replied, "Well, I thought what I wanted was self-evident. It made me sad each time that he wouldn't say it and that I might have to spell it out for him. Why didn't he just know?"

He didn't just know because what's plain logic to you isn't necessarily plain logic to someone else. And because no one is good at reading someone else's mind—no matter how much love there is for that person!

You have to say it.

15

How to Say It So He Hears It— & Likes What He Hears

Maybe He'll Be Very Pleased

Your husband may react with open pleasure when you say you'll give over various family activities and no longer stand over him and give directions. As a male TV talk show producer told me when I mentioned I was writing this book, "Sounds great! My efforts at home get treated as if I were four years old."

Family researchers find that men derive as much satisfaction from their marital and parental roles as do women. The experts also report many men are very unsure of their housekeeping and childcare skills. Add your own obvious competence to his inner lack of confidence and many men hesitate to try. In the past you may even have contributed unintentionally to his sense of himself as a domestic klutz with your overburdened, impatient "Oh, give that to me. I'll do it. It takes you forever."

Build on your husband's initial pleasure at your offer to Share house-power by reminding him of his past successes. He's done this and that family task so well that you know he can take charge, learn, and be very competent in other family areas. If you acknowledge that you had to learn ("Remember how petrified I was when I had to go to that first parent-teacher conference," or "How did I ever figure out how to get the baby to stop pulling things off the shelves?") and if you reiterate your faith in his ability to learn, you open a whole new family world to him. A world he may see as very attractive. This is especially true when at appropriate intervals you rephrase your assurance that once he learns the ropes, you'll neither boss nor keep checking on him. Since he's probably had years of your telling him exactly how to "help," it'll take a while till your new offer sinks in and persuades him.

Of course, you'll have to be as good as your words about your faith in his ability. No little family jokes about his errors; no hilarious anecdotes for friends about his mishaps and misjudgments.

You'll know how to react in every situation if you remember that overall you're trying to help him raise what may be low home/childcare self-confidence. It's bare-bones human psychology. We all shy from activities that reveal us as inept. We're all happy to keep plugging at something we do well or where others praise our talent. So you're presenting the changeover and later living it as something he has human ability for. You'll comment only on his successes and shrug off whatever he bobbles.

You're setting up a self-fulfilling prophecy when you let him know you expect him to do well. Then he won't give up as he discovers how complicated many "ordinary" family life responsibilities are and how much effort it requires to fit them into his schedule. Instead, he'll live up to your mutual expectations that he will manage it and do well.

Important: Important: Important

This is "influencing," NOT "manipulating." All social and family life consists of interacting and thereby influencing, passive or active. To continue as you have and not act means you go on passively allowing him and inertia *to influence you* to stay with the status quo and continue to carry too much of the family responsibility.

Talking up and trying to influence your husband is the second part of the male-convincer. The experience of the team-couples and the psychological proof behind the invincible communication techniques indicate that wives (and husbands too) change family living patterns "by acting, by trying to influence" (chapter 13).

Well, how are you going to "try to influence?"

Hint? Delicately suggest?

Do it that way and you're back to mindreading. We already know that's hopeless. What are the other alternatives? Scream? Weep? Complain? Threaten?

Sensible "trying to influence" means saying it so it will be effective yet pleasant for the other person to hear. Kind hearted "trying to influence" means setting up supportive self-fulfilling prophecies that will aid him in making the transition. And remember, as his family skills and activities increase, he gets more from his family life.

So put the good news up front. As we've seen, a man longs for his wife's time and attention and is emotionally felled by her busyness, which he perceives as his own lack of importance.

Now tell him straight out that when he takes over parts of home life, you'll have more time and energy for him. More time to do things with him.

Then take care to follow through. If you are interested in strengthening your marriage, don't squander your new time and energy by saying "yes" to everyone else and taking on additional outside activities that keep your schedule just as hectic and leave him just as starved for your attention.

Man-Talk vs. Woman-Talk

Though many psychologists and communication specialists have noticed different male and female conversation styles, linguist Dr. Deborah Tannen with her recent best-seller, *You Just Don't Understand: Women and Men in Conversation,* has probably done more than anyone else to make people aware of the differences.

She explains most wives have sometimes felt their own husbands were unusually dense. But, she says, a husband's lack of understanding is not his or your fault or unique to your man. It's "neither idiosyncratic nor pathological but universal and explicable." So your husband is not "impossible" to talk to. Your feminine talk style (which may truly be clear, calm, and logical) is just very different from his.

Ignore the Man-Talk approach and insist on saying it in your Woman-Talk and you're back to a replay of what is probably a familiar scenario. You go to him and plainly explain your feelings about a situation. Let's assume you also offer the solution and tell him what it is that would make you feel happy.

The communication specialists report that most men sit through sessions like this silently, without a nod, without a sign that they're listening. No matter how lucidly you've said it, there's no response. "Stonewalling" and "withdrawing" are terms the experts use to describe his reaction.

If you insist on knowing how he feels about what you've said, he either continues his silence or bursts out with his version of, "For heaven's sake, what is it you want from me?"

You just told him. "I just told you!"

Mulish expression from him and more anger.

"You don't listen!" from you.

Silence, fury, withdrawal from him.

Dr. Tannen explains that the problem lies in the fact that women see discussion of personal problems as a helpful way to solve the situation. Women feel that if you're able to discuss a relationship, you're making progress toward improving it. But men usually believe that if you need to examine the relationship, it's a sign you're in big trouble. So men usually don't want to discuss relationships. Because of these differing male-female attitudes, you almost never see "how to improve a relationship" articles in a man's magazine while they are the central type in women's publications.

Yet communication specialists, both male and female, praise women's ability to handle the emotional base of interpersonal difficulties. John Gottman, professor of psychology at the University of Washington, who has been studying the psycho-physiological aspects of marital interaction for more than twenty years, offers a typical expert assessment of women's ability to deal with and solve emotional problems. He says, "Women tend to be better than men at managing conflicts . . . [the women] don't withdraw, they don't stonewall, they hang in there, express emotion and work things out."

Unfortunately, says Dr. Gottman, men see women's "expressions of emotion as whining, complaining, and nagging even if a woman is simply stating how she feels. The men come to marriage with a fear of negative emotions in themselves and in their wives. They don't know how to handle them and frequently react by withdrawing and stonewalling."

Furthermore, men listen differently and when it's their turn to talk, they would like you to react as they do. Women expect lots of listener responses such as the ones women offer like "Mmm," "Uhhuh," "Yes," head nods, changing facial expressions. Men object to all those little encouraging listener behaviors. They see them as interruptions. What he wants when he's speaking is what he's giving you: just look at him and listen.

So it's not that your Woman-Talk is of poor quality. You may be an excellent communicator. It's just that he's not equipped to discuss or listen that way. Since you're trying to convey the new Sharing ideas with a maximum of clarity *for him*, it's sensible to communicate it his way.

Saying It in Man-Talk

What do men feel comfortable discussing?

Solutions. Specifics of exactly "what you want me to do." For your Sharing purposes this is absolutely perfect. It means you don't pussyfoot around dwelling on the emotional part of the changeover to Sharing. You say you can't continue to carry both paid work and so much home and children responsibility with him just "helping." You're willing to give over authority in various areas. And how about if . . . here you name some specific tasks you're comfortable about passing over to him.

Take major encouragement from the fact that you have Man-Talk style specific solutions to offer. You'd like him to take over this and this task. In offering specific tasks, you've hit a Man-Talk jackpot.

In her research book *Love in America: Gender and Self-Development*, sociologist Francesca M. Cancian of the University of California, Irvine, highlights differences between how men and women express love. As everyone knows, women cherish romantic words, settings, and gestures. But she reports, "Men tend to have a distinctive style of love that focuses on practical help, shared physical activities, spending time together, and sex. . . ."

Dr. Cancian illustrates her point by giving us a typical example of how men act out their love with "practical help." She tells of a husband's reaction to his wife's complaint that he didn't love her because he didn't spend enough time talking to her. The man reacted with, "What does she want? Proof? She's got it, hasn't she? Would I be knocking myself out to get things for her—like to keep up this house—if I didn't love her. Why does a man do things like that if not because he loves his wife and kids? I swear, I can't figure what she wants."

Dr. Cancian provides another memorable vignette that captures men's method of expressing romance through practical actions. She recounts how researchers investigating the different male and female romantic styles asked a husband to increase his "affectionate behavior toward his wife."

The man went straight to it. He decided to wash his wife's car. Then the poor guy "was surprised" when neither his wife nor the researchers accepted his enthusiastic spit and polish as an "affectionate" act.

But great! This general male attitude is made to order for introducing a new system for family responsibilities. Since so many men see doing things for you as the best, most comfortable means of expressing his love, present your new family specifics to him, and he's primed to think Sharing is a workable, comfortable idea.

This Is Not a Monologue

You can't revolutionize your family life patterns with a short announcement from you and instant comprehension from him.

Just as saying it in Man-Talk greatly increases the chances he will be comfortable with your message, so it'll also help you if you use basic conversational mechanics which pass an idea from your head to someone else's. Psychologist Dr. Jesse S. Nirenberg has had a 30-year career as a communication-skills consultant to major corporations in the United States and abroad. He's the author of the communication classic *Getting Through to People.* As the subtitle indicates, he is a specialist in exactly the area we need: "The techniques of persuasion . . . how to break through the mental and emotional barriers that continually obstruct the flow of ideas from one person to another." The book has sold steadily for almost 30 years, in five languages around the world.

When you're trying to get someone to see something new, Nirenberg says, you must start the persuasion conversation by telling its purpose. You might use, "I want us to work out a different, fairer way of dividing our home and childcare work. I have *possible solutions* we can consider." It may be worth repeating that second phrase because it's the central Man-Talk approach: "I have possible solutions we can consider." Your up-front assurance that you're going to talk what-to-do specifics heads off his instant anxiety that you're about to embark on a feelings conversation. Dr. Nirenberg emphasizes there are no "right words." What you're trying to do is follow a *type* of conversation.

He explains there are three levels of hearing. First, where the person is not listening at all though he's gazing raptly into your eyes and even murmuring, "I see. You've got a point there." Second, where the listener remembers words you're saying but has really not absorbed the ideas. In this mode if you stopped suddenly and asked, "What did I just say?", he'd be able to say back to you the last sentence or two. But he won't be able to discuss any of the points you made.

Third, and the listening level you're after, is where the person *thinks* about what you're saying. Dr. Nirenberg warns this kind of thinking requires the mental effort of evaluating what you've said, comparing it with current conditions, looking at whether it's likely to work, whether the other person wants to do it, and making a decision based on all these considerations. "In order for you to be getting your ideas into the mind of your listener he has to be listening on this level . . . Your ideas will not be absorbed by him if he merely considers them in the abstract. He has to imagine these ideas in operation in some situation that involves him. He has to transform your ideas, shape them to fit his life pattern."

People—women and men alike—automatically resist all that mental effort. Yet unless you can stimulate the other person to think after you've presented an idea, it cannot pass into that person's view of the situation.

You must ask *appropriate* questions, says Nirenberg, in order to force the other person to think about your ideas.

"Keep in mind that telling of something is only the first step in getting it across. In order to absorb your ideas the listener has to mentally react to them; and you have to ask him to react."

Maybe you said, "If it's OK with you, what I'd like to give over are dinner preparation and cleanup two nights a week, keeping the bathroom clean, and the weekly grocery shopping." (Later, as you're both comfortable with the new family Sharing system, his list might expand.)

Now you use the technique of helping him absorb your ideas by asking questions to get him to think about the new ideas. You might ask, "Are there parts of [repeat the whole list distinctly] the dinners two nights a week, keeping bathrooms clean, and doing weekly grocery shopping that you think would be a problem for you?"

Listen; don't rush to interrupt. He's thinking and giving you a picture of what he sees as problems. By knowing his difficulties, you know what needs to be solved.

As he thinks about your question he might ask, "Are you going to give me a grocery list?"

It's your turn to talk it over and arrive at a solution that will work for you both. Maybe you want to keep control of the list. Or maybe you're satisfied to give that over also. If you do want him to keep the list, you might say, "We'll make a list together for the first 4–6 weeks. Then you'll know how.

"And remember, you're not going to have to shop my way. For dinners you're making, buy what you want. If it's more convenient to shop in stores on your commute route, go there."

Later when he's at ease about shopping, you'll find it congenial for you both if you sometimes ask for some special brands or items. After all, when you were in charge of food shopping, he used to ask for items. With Sharing you'll have the same normal family ability to ask the person in charge to accommodate you. The big difference will be that then the task—in this case grocery shopping—will not only be in his hands, it'll be on *his* mind and on *his* schedule.

He may react with alarm to the idea of your giving over the list. "How am I going to know what to buy?"

"Well, those 4–6 weeks we do it together, we'll check the freezer and food and cleaning supplies shelves, and you'll see what we need to keep on hand and the amounts we need. If you have a question, ask me. I had to learn. I made mistakes. Everybody who food shops learned at some time. You'll learn too."

If he lapses into silence, it's time to get him to think about the other tasks you're asking him to assume. Just saying, "Is cleaning the bathrooms OK?" is *not* a good question. Any question that can be answered with "Yes" or "No" does not force the other person to think it through! A much better query would be, "What parts of keeping bathrooms clean might be hardest for you?"

To answer that question, he has to engage in what Dr. Nirenberg says is the essential step: the point at which the person mentally reviews his picture of the situation and has to incorporate the new information. In this case in order to reply your husband has to review his idea of what "keeping bathrooms clean" involves. So he might respond, "What's there to it? When the sink is dirty and the mirror is hazy, it's time to wipe them down."

Now you need to admit, "You'll do your areas with your system but just the way you set standards about our cars—you fuss about my not parking close to the curb to protect the whitewalls, you insist on my warming the engine for 30 seconds every morning—there are some basic bathroom cleaning *standards* you have to learn. In a busy family like ours standards mean at least once a week—you pick the day and time— washing the floor including the corners and edges, cleaning the toilets inside and out (I'll show you), washing counters, bathtubs, mirrors."

Now you have him really thinking. He may say, "That sounds like a lot more than I thought cleaning bathrooms would be."

And you can respond, "Yes, maybe it is. But that's exactly one of the reasons I just can't go on doing it all myself anymore. With all of us using the bathrooms, they'll soon smell and look disgusting if they're not kept up."

At that point, you've scored a touchdown for Sharing. By getting him to think about it, you've put your major point through to him: You're overloaded. Many men truly do not realize how overburdened their working wives are. As a woman in my survey wrote, "The men just don't have any idea of what's involved in running a home." The working wives keep doing what the family needs and from his onlooker perch, he has no clear idea of how much she's carrying.

In this question and his thinking-and-answering exchange, he has learned that keeping bathrooms clean involves much more than he thought. He's received a practical nuts-and-bolts insight into your overloaded life.

Keep going. You said, "Two dinners a week." He nods, "OK. I've made dinner before. Don't make a big deal out of it."

But here too you need to ask "thinking" questions so that the words really pass through his mind and become edible weekly dinners. "Which nights would work best for you? If you could take Tuesday that would be good. It's my worst day at work and it'd be great to come home to a meal."

To which he may say, "Tuesday's bad for me too. I'll do Tuesday. But it'll always be take-out and maybe it'll be very late. I'll make a real meal Thursday."

OK. Now either you go with his way of Tuesday take-outs and maybe very late or you do Tuesday yourself. You may go the second route and decide that though you're stressed on Tuesday, you'd rather do Tuesday yourself. Fine. So then you might say, "No, I'll do Tuesday. You do Thursday. What other day could you do a real meal at a good time?"

Either way with these "thinking" questions, you've had a discussion, a meeting of minds, a working out of the situation in terms of task specifics. You've used the kind of Man-Talk expressions of practical help as a loving gesture that he's comfortable with.

These questions are also valuable for exploring tasks he rejects as "impossible." Of course, you do have to be flexible and substitute if necessary. But usually "impossible" can be solved with thinking questions such as, "Why wouldn't it work for you to drop Danny at nursery school in the mornings?"

Often the answer indicates his "It's impossible" decision is based *on inadequate facts* as in his reply which might be, "You know I don't leave here the same time every morning. It can vary from 7:45 to 8:30."

Once you've discovered what's worrying him about this task, you may be able to supply missing information that saves the situation. "You can vary the time of taking Danny there. It doesn't matter. If you go at 7:30, that's just ten minutes before I usually take him. And if it's later, Danny just gets a little more time home with you. It's fine. The school doesn't care."

Be sure to include questions about the whole new concept of Sharing such as, "What do you think of this whole new idea of Sharing versus when you 'help' me?"

Queries like these give you a pleasant way to pass on some essential reasons why two-paycheck families should forget one-paycheck family rules.

Left to themselves, most men jog along vaguely believing the one-paycheck notion that they're putting up with a lot by "letting" you work. His response to your "What do you think of this Sharing vs. 'helping' . . ." may evoke an answer of "I don't really see the big difference or the big need."

You now have the opportunity to use the persuasion technique of asking a question to get him to review the whole situation in his mind. "Well, suppose I gave up working and carrying both job and home, could we manage without my money? I often get so exhausted I think I'll have to cut back to part time and how will we manage without my money?" (Or if you're already part time, "give it up altogether.")

Family researchers find that calling it to his attention: "What would we do about the bills if I gave up bringing in money?" as a real question where you pause and make him come up with an answer can put his thinking and attitude change on fast forward.

Most men, say the researchers, especially those younger than 50, have moved from "allowing" a wife to work to "demanding" that she work. *But until forced to think it through in order to answer a question like this, many men do not realize they've decided they need and want her to work.*

Consequently, if you now present Sharing—his taking *responsibility* for some family tasks—as a new condition for your bringing in family money, he begins to take Sharing very seriously.

Other "What's the big deal about Sharing . . ." comments or questions allow you to pass on other proof that the one-paycheck rules can no longer apply to your family's' two-paycheck life. For example, "Since I'm now out there using up hours bringing in money for us, I can't continue doing full-time housework. We have to let me cut back and find money to pay for some of it. So I'm not going to do your shirts anymore. Find a place you like and you take care of them. Or you wash and iron them. I have my own wardrobe and the children's. That's more than enough."

"The laundry won't do shirts as well as you. They'll get worn out much faster."

"Carrying my job and the housework too is wearing me out fast. We can buy new shirts. We can't buy a new me. If you want full-time housewife service from me, then I have to stop earning money and be a full-timer here."

Or if you can live on his income, "Why do you have a right to career and family without killing yourself and I have to kill myself to have them both?" You've never dreamed of saying such things before because until now *you* also *believed* the one-paycheck rules.

This is a good approach because even the relatively few men who can support a family singlehandedly now often prefer the pizazz of a working wife. At this stage you may also be able to pass on your new and very relevant knowledge of how your job is making his life easier. Of course, all these sample conversations demonstrate ideas. They're not meant to be memorized. You adapt them to your particular circumstances and mate.

Dealing With a Closed Mind

Kim's husband, Ted, is one of those men who is very rigid about family roles. He sees himself as a good husband: he's faithful, he uses all his income for the family, he's considerate about anniversaries, birthdays. He takes care of the cars, the outdoor work and that's it. Everything else for the home and the couple's two children, ages ten and twelve, is Kim's responsibility. Though Kim has a demanding day as administrative assistant to a high-powered executive, Ted is firm about his free time being his own to use as he wishes. As a civil servant Ted has a generous amount of leisure. Work is strictly 9–5, no weekends. Ted uses his leisure for golf and for his hobby of playing bass in a string quartet.

In the past whenever Kim has tried to talk to Ted about his at least "helping" at home and with the children, Ted has cut her short with, "That's not the conditions and roles we had in mind when we got married. You can't change the rules on me now."

Each time Kim has retreated, defeated by what she felt was his "logic." Many women face variations of this same situation. Overload exhaustion for her; enough leisure for him to build an elaborate physical fitness regimen, or many hours in other activities such as a schedule of cultural activities, or sports, or hobbies, or interesting non-professional college courses, and, of course, TV.

If you're a wife like Kim, don't let your futile past experiences with him discourage you from trying again.

In the past when he said, "We can't change the rules from what they were when we married," or "What was good enough for my father and your father is good enough for me," or any version of the same traditional sex-roles view, you had no answer because back then *you too* still believed the three one-paycheck ideas. Now you know better. And you also know about the research that indicates even men with very traditional sex-role family ideas change their minds when their wives believe they are Entitled and the wives "try to influence" the men's thinking.

Now you're able to say, "But you yourself are not playing by those old rules. When we started the rules said house and children were my woman's responsibility and supporting us was all your masculine responsibility. I'm doing a significant part of bringing in money for us.—*In this economy most wives are working. You work hard and I'm proud of you. But nowadays most men need their wives' money too.*" You're helping him save his self-esteem as he absorbs the new recognition that "most men" are sharing breadwinning with wives. And that it's OK, you still think he's a success as a man.

You can continue, "I can't go on working and also doing almost everything for our home and children too. I've taken on a good share of your original job of making money. We've changed the rules in your behalf. It's time to adapt the old rules so I get a fair shake."

Somewhere in the discussion, be sure to call his attention to the fact that's true in every family, "Your outside work with the car is occasional. Home repairs and lawncare are occasional. Taking care of the children, meals, laundry, cleaning is every day morning and evening and all day on weekends."

With this approach when you call his attention to the fact you're doing some of "his" job, his natural reaction to keep his own self-respect is to show he's not a slacker who's going to take advantage of you. He'll try to make himself look and feel better by saying, "Yeah, well, I guess so. What did you say you wanted me to do?"

"Not 'do' . . . 'take over.' How about . . ."

As sociologist Peter Stein succinctly analyzes it in his chapter in the anthology *Women and the Family: Two Decades of Change*, "Changes in family roles are achieved through negotiation over 'emergent concerns.' " You can't get more "emergent" than the new oppressive Overload demands on working wives.

As part of negotiation, Nirenberg suggests you de-escalate a negative reaction by *rephrasing* what has been said into a question. For example, if he says he's not going to change no matter what, you might ask, "Are you saying you think it's fair for me to do a real part of your original family job of supporting us but you won't do the same for me by doing a real part of my original house and childcare?"

If you receive an irrelevant reply, hang in there. Repeat the question as often and in as many variations as necessary: "Do I have to do all my work and part of yours too? Is that what you're saying?"

Your rephrasing of what he's said in the form of a question is a perfect negotiation approach because in order to answer, it forces him to consider how his attitude will bear down on your life.

After your original comment and rephrasings point out you're doing a good part of his job, you should also reiterate the ego-saving acknowledgment that most husbands now need their wives' income.

As you stay with the questions, he's eventually forced to think about it in order to answer it. At that point any man who wants his marriage to last will realize he has to repudiate his old view. He's almost forced to say, "No, I don't mean you have to do everything at home and my job too. I'll do something. What do you want me to do?" Now you're ready for a Sharing discussion. To be followed by other Sharing discussions as needed.

You'd be back to mindreading if you expected an entire marriage arrangement to be completely, finally, totally revised in one discussion. There are lots of big new ideas involved. He may have to hear them more than once or twice to really take them in. What this first good discussion will do is begin your changeover from helping to Sharing. After that, it will be a matter of reviewing these ideas and covering them again as needed; and later again if it's needed, as you want to expand his role.

Changing Family Roles, Yes. Miracles, No!

You can win his cooperation for Sharing, but probably no one can transform a genuine Oscar Madison into a neatnik nor approximation. Don't worry. There are two levels of male indifference to household mess and the vast majority of men are fine potential family work partners.

Humorist Dave Barry says men don't notice household dirt till it's lying around in clumps. But as we now know, that's because the men take for granted that housecleaning is her job and on her mind. If a task becomes his, he'll usually be able to make the transition.

You'll know it's happening when your child carelessly lets the orange juice dribble down the carton side, over the counter, down the cabinet and onto the floor and you hear your husband who is now in charge of weekly kitchen cleanup react with, "Hey, stop that. I just did the floor. Juice is a mess to clean."

Or perhaps in all his years your husband has never before noticed when you're low on eggs, milk, dry cereal. After grocery shopping becomes his responsibility and he's reached in vain for eggs and milk a few times or the children have complained loudly *to him* about their missing dry cereal and milk, something will click in his brain and he'll learn to notice. (When they complained to you, you advised the children to tell their father: "Remember he's in charge of groceries now.")

That said, if your dearly beloved is one of the relatively rare true Oscar Madisons, you may not be able to bring yourself to let him do housework "his way." That's fine. It fits right in with the whole concept of this book. It takes us back to the original premise that you'll hand over house-power only for those tasks where it's comfortable for you. Perhaps you'd be happiest giving an Oscar Madison husband partnership in family care where neatness is not the central issue, such as making the children's lunches, taking charge of their dental appointments, lots of family chauffeuring and errands including taking everybody's clothes for cleaning, shoes for repairs, picking up the family's weekly take-out dinners, car-pooling for Sunday School, and perhaps doing occasional tasks where you can set minimum family standards like washing the shower stall and the windows.

Remember, throughout all this negotiation—as you avoid mindreading, say it in Man-Talk, use questions that stimulate his thinking—your invisible allies of feeling Entitled, body language, power of expectancy, trying to influence equals results, will also be at work sending him positive messages that strengthen your spoken words. The sum of your visible and invisible efforts will enable you to "SAY IT SO HE HEARS IT— AND SO HE LIKES WHAT HE HEARS."

16

How Sharing House-Power Makes Your Marriage Happier

Couples Who Try It

When you notice a successful behavior pattern every workday, year in, year out, you know you're on to something.

Janet Hill operates a day-care service used by middle-class parents in suburban New Jersey and she's now Northern Region Coordinator for the New Jersey Family Day Care Providers' Association. For years she's seen the happier marriages and happier children that Sharing can produce.

She says, "You see the difference among families. There's an easy camaraderie between parents when both carry family responsibilities. They work out arrangements that benefit the child the best. They're both in and out for class visits, health requirements, bringing and picking up the child. In homes where childcare is 'woman's work,' the child is often forced out of bed earlier than necessary so Mother can bring the youngster and still arrive at her job on time. At pickup in sharing families, the parent that can reach the child most easily comes and then starts dinner—rather than what happens in the other families where the child has to hang around waiting for Mother.

"It's clear from the parents' manner and comments that the marital relationship in the equal homes is much less stressed. The ones who have it 'together' in an equal sense love their careers, their children, and each other."

Everybody Resists Change

Psychologists have long known and long explained that we all feel "threatened" by suggestions that we alter our views and actions; that it's human nature to react with an instant negative mindset and then to hurl rejections. The new ways are "bad ideas," "aren't necessary," "won't work," and "just are not right for me!"

That's where we are now.

Every sensible woman at this point is saying, "Yes, but if I use the ideas this book has been discussing, will it really strengthen my marriage? Or will I win the battle of washing the kitchen floor and lose my husband? Even if he doesn't actually walk out, if I behave the way this book suggests, will he still love me?"

That is probably the most important question.

The facts that follow answer the question. The facts make it clear that going through the effort and yes, the adjustment of ideas and behavior that Sharing requires will not only solve your Overload, the change in your family life patterns is probably the surest way to make you, your husband, your children, and your marriage happier.

Marriage Pizazz

A Washington couple reports that after the birth of their first child, "Our worlds were slowly growing apart. After the second child, we decided to do shared parenting and providing. We have recaptured that feeling of mutual respect we had when first married and are closer . . . companions."

A New York woman I interviewed believes it is the effort to keep moving toward an egalitarian marriage that has kept their marriage exciting even though they've been married more than 30 years. They started traditionally where she did everything for home and children. As liberation ideas spread, she gradually talked up and pressed for changes. She says, "It's as if we've been in different and new marriages at each stage. I think it's *because* we keep evolving that our marriage has always been interesting."

Common sense tells you that sharing the central activities of your lives keeps the relationship fresh by injecting feelings of something happening, of problem solving together, and of being a "team." With mutual home plus job interests, daily life together becomes more interesting.

The formal family research confirms Janet Hill's observations and the Washington and New York couples' experiences. The anthology *Men's Changing Roles In the Family* features chapters by many of America's foremost family researchers and was edited by Marvin S. Sussman, Ph.D., Unidel Professor of Human Behavior at the University of Delaware, and Robert A. Lewis, Ph.D., department of Child Development and Family Studies, Purdue University. In the chapter "Effect of Paternal Involvement on Fathers and Mothers" the experts report, "Men who engagd in more family work reported better family adjustment" while working wives doing it all or too much reported "worsened family adjustment."

In her detailed close-up study of two-career families, Arlie Hochschild also found that though the couples who shared family care were few, they clearly had happier marriages. And during my 20+ years of interviews year after year I noticed that the relatively few couples who reported teamwork also evidenced the most contented relationships. Whereas a wife with an uncooperative husband usually admitted that his attitude caused serious marital tensions.

As for the effort and emotions you'll have to put into the changeover to Sharing, *see them for what they are, as signs of hope and success.* Dr. Lucia A. Gilbert, who did a book-length study of how two-career families live, decided "modifications in attitude and behavior may be necessary for the relationship to endure."

It's the marriage with no arguments, no alterations that should frighten you. At best, a marriage like that is a holding pattern for boredom. Worse, in its typical rigidity a static marriage reflects his or her sense of indifference or defeat so complete that the couple have stopped trying to work things out. With the loss of any real interaction and change between them, the marriage is imperiled or already dead.

A More Lovable You

Let's be completely honest with ourselves.

Overloaded working wives, as we've seen—and as you yourself may know firsthand—are usually disappointed in their husbands, overtired, discouraged, stressed, tense, impatient, and subject to many other corrosive emotions.

How lovable do you think that uptight woman is?

Burying your anger as so many women do by keeping the peaceful shell and seething or falling apart from Overload strain underneath is a turn-off, not a turn-on.

What you're feeling about him affects him. No matter how you cling to the popular practice of accepting the status quo as better than constant battles about "helping," your stress inevitably sends him irritated messages in your manner, voice, and body language. Will this everpresent tension between you make him more eager to rush home to you when work's over? Will it strengthen his love for you?

When you move from the frustrations of "helping" to the marital satisfactions of your husband accepting significant responsibilities for family care, you're bound to experience a leap of positive feelings *toward* him.

It's a human relations truism that people respond to you on the same emotional level as you project toward them. Project irritation, and even if you try to disguise it your irritation will be felt and stimulate a taut response. But relax and feel good about someone and your automatic signals from your manner, voice, body language that previously conveyed your dissatisfaction, now deliver your approval. As we've seen, everyone instinctively reads these body signals, and responds accordingly.

In this case when you start sending warmth, you're not dealing with a stranger. This man thought enough of you to marry you and he's still with you. You therefore have in him an already established affection base that's likely to respond well to your genuine new increase of affection for him.

So ingrained is this communication give-and-take that toddlers at the nursery rhyme stage of life already understand how emotions interplay:

> "What makes the lamb love Mary so?"
> the children all did cry.
> "Why Mary loves the lamb you know,"
> the teacher did reply.

As he shares more of the family workload, you'll stop being so uptight. The research indicates working wives don't need a 50–50 division of home labor to feel much better. What pleases women is his willingness to relieve her of portions of what was formerly her "women's" tasks. So with his new family role you'll have less work, less stress, more sleep, more leisure, an ebbing of your buried anger toward him.

He has to be aware of the melting of tensions between you. As your attitude toward him thaws, he's bound to react by seeing the new pleasanter, warmer you as a helluva lot more approachable and lovable. All by itself, a more lovable you is the most powerful reason for making the effort to move to Sharing.

And there are delightful extras. With Sharing you're attracting many other marriage boosters.

Your Disappearing Battlegrounds

There are no fights among the experts on this subject. The marital surveys reveal couples argue most about family chores and money with accompanying heavy losses in marital happiness and a noticeable rise in marital breakdowns.

As you move into Sharing house-power and he does more for home and children, you solve and neutralize the Chore Wars hostilities. You also neutralize many money fights because there are surprising angles to how your new family arrangements can increase the family dollars you can comfortably earn.

Did you seek and accept a job in the immediate neighborhood even though you might have done better economically and professionally with an ordinary commute? If so, you're typical. Two geographers who received $122,000 in grant funds to investigate the geographic perspectives of women's career patterns find working wives routinely ignore(!!) better pay, better job opportunities because they're carrying so much of the home load and therefore must locate a no-commute job a very few minutes from the children's school and home.

When Dad takes on house-power and responsibilities, he can take over some school visits, some family errands, start or make some dinners. The shift of more family life to him frees her to search for and accept the better jobs that probably aren't in the immediate home area. As she seeks and accepts the better positions within an ordinary commute, she often significantly raises the family income with no significant increase in the time that she devotes to her work. And with no extra drain on her energy because Dad is carrying some of the family responsibilities that used that portion of her strength.

So there you have it. His new family responsibilities eliminated most or all of your chore wars. Your stronger paycheck raises the family income and you and your husband are less likely to fight about money. With many, many fewer chore fights and money fights, you're enjoying a much happier marriage.

Your Happy New Daily Opportunities

It's not unusual for working wives to somehow cope with children, home, and job. What frequently gives is time for herself and for her husband. A perceptive lifestyle reporter notes his interviews have taught him that even supportive husbands lose interest in wife and marriage when the man feels she's too busy to allow him a prime place in her life. By Sharing you gain time to spend relaxing with your husband and children. As you do, you tap into what marriage researchers dub healthy "joint leisure patterns."

The phrase "joint leisure patterns" is sociological and family research jargon for spending evening and weekend time sitting around relaxing with your husband and children and/or in sports, hobbies, and other family activities. It's also jargon for enough leisure for a relaxed date and romance with your husband. As women in a *Working Mother* magazine survey of readers' Overload problems put it, "Tell the men they'd see a lot more action in the bedroom if they did their share at home." So consider how moving to Sharing can give you time—and inclination—for a more enthusiastic sex life. And there you'll have a marital happiness builder with the most glittering of proven credentials.

"The more time together in activities such as eating, playing and conversing, the more satisfying the marriage," say two University of Virginia sociologists who studied how 321 couples spent their time and how they rated their marriages.

And after interviewing 459 married women of all ages for his book, *Dating, Mating and Marriage*, University of Michigan sociology professor Martin K. Whyte found that "shared leisure activities" (together with shared financial control and family values) "were associated with marital success."

Great Extra Marriage-Builders

Besides the many obvious happiness enhancements that accompany Overload-relief, expect numerous hidden marriage boosters:

With Sharing and four adult hands and maybe effort from little hands too, the family dinner and its potential for marital contentment can make a comeback in your home. Demise of family dinner as a regular event in two-paycheck homes has been widely documented. Yet psychologists say the family meal feeds your family's soul as well as bodies. It gives participants a sense of well-being and provides a setting to pass on your family values and really get to know each other. In short, the family dinner table is a proven setting for more marital pleasures.

Another and a truly hidden marital benefit of Sharing lies in its frequent ability to *shorten* a man's work day and bring him straight home *without cutting into his income.*

Two nationwide employment time-use surveys found that bosses and coworkers generally believe many male employees are accomplished procrastinators. The surveys were conducted independently by the public opinion Gallup Organization and by Priority Management, an international management training and development organization.

The summary of The Gallup Organization, Inc. poll slammed its news with the title "Brace Yourself Men . . . Women Work Harder Than You" and the subtitle "National Survey of American Workers Finds That Women Are Significantly More Productive On The Job." The president of Priority commented on his organization's poll by pointing out that women get more done on the job and get it done faster because women are "much more goal oriented than men tend to be, with a better feel for priorities. They are much more likely than men to do the right things first."

Well, of course. With Overload, if working women didn't figure things out and keep moving how would they and their families ever manage?

Priority's president unintentionally reaches the core of how Sharing can bring your man home earlier each day with his next remark. The president points out that men are not necessarily more productive in those extra hours. He explains, "Since the men tend to have fewer responsibilities at home, they feel free to procrastinate, knowing they can catch up by putting in more time at the other end of the day."

So before you shrug off the idea of Sharing because you believe your husband "has to" work long hours, try it. See if his having more responsibilities at home doesn't cure his workday procrastination and his unpaid overtime and give the two of you more time together in the evenings to build and enjoy family life.

Other Ways Sharing Makes Him a Happier Man

OK. You put your message across. Slowly your marriage evolves toward a fairer division of family work and a better relationship between you. What's going on in his internal feelings about himself?

Upbeat. As men gain more of the family closeness that comes with true involvement in family life and that is now so powerful a male goal, their self-image rises. With the new arrangements, they're freed to indulge the interpersonal warmth part of their personality that the old sex roles repress. This fits nature's rhythms. Psychologists tell us that once past first youth, men become more nurturing; women become more assertive. With Sharing you're both empowered to go with nature's flow.

There are also pleasant, even amusing male ego advantages from the new egalitarian arrangement at home.

Some family experts see turning over food shopping to your husband as a means of gratifying men's primitive joy in food hunting and returning home with a catch. Whatever the basis for their pleasure, interviews with male food shoppers reveal them as more achievement-oriented than other men, as having a "more contemporary image of themselves," and as feeling "calm," "efficient," and "competent" while they push those supermarket carts.

Also consider the health benefits your husband may derive from doing housework. A report at the 1989 annual meeting of the American Association of Marriage and Family Therapy revealed that seventy-nine couples were followed during four years and men who did housework were "far healthier than men who didn't."

John Gottman, Ph.D., who reported this bombshell, suggested that the health reward probably is not the cardiovascular effect of wielding mop, vacuum cleaner, and toilet brush. Instead it seems that when a man works through to seeing why it's fair to do his share—and then does it—it's an indication that these men have resolved marital conflicts and are in happier marriages. The men's increased marital pleasure then improves their mental and physical health.

So What Does the Evidence Add up To?

There are people who can consider all the above multifaceted marital benefits of Sharing and still demur. If we both do everything, what then of the sexual charge of marriage—what then of La Difference?

The New York Times editorial board which worries about everything has not solved how to arrive at Sharing. But it has devoted an editorial to providing us with a measured, literate summary of why it's desirable.

Responding to the question, "Even if both men and women can succeed in playing all roles, what then will they need each other for?" they say, "For partnership, memories, intimacy, discoveries, hopes, love. That's what for—the same old song, really, with a new twist."

17

Why Your Children Will Love Mother More

*G*UILT.

GUILT about the children.

It is the universal emotion that working wives mention.

There's nothing wrong with guilt, anxiety, concern that keeps you constantly aware of the children's physical and emotional, visible and invisible needs. It's good and it's essential for your children's welfare.

This book advocates no diminution there!

What it does advocate is dividing the worry, thinking, attention, anxieties and GUILT *with the other parent*. When there are two of you doing, attending to, actively thinking, foreseeing, and parenting, you will be carrying much less. Your guilt will then serve only to keep you on track. It will no longer overstrain you.

What this book champions is the end of the current omnipresent attitude that shapes every working mother discussion in private life, in print, TV, radio, government, business and turns out endless updates on how Mom agonizes over job vs. children without any comparable angst for Dad. Headlines such as "Moms' Jobs Said to Hurt Kids . . . says a nationwide survey of pediatricians" and "Distance Makes the Heart Skip for Commuter Moms" are still frequently used in the 90s without apparent embarrassment—as if the stork really had conceived the youngsters. Why not "Dads' Jobs Said to Hurt Kids" or "Distance Makes the Heart Skip for Commuter Dads"? Both parents are away supporting the family. Both parents have equal human rights to all three of life's core rewards: marriage, children, paid accomplishment. Why is it only she who must be emotionally savaged by job-children conflicts?

Though we know it's the irrelevant one-paycheck rule that says home and children are her jobs, we also know the rule shouldn't apply to two-paycheck families. In the majority of cases he wants her family paycheck and he wanted the children too. Indeed, because young wives are vastly more aware than young husbands of the problems of juggling family and career, it is often she who hesitates and he who is hellbent on having a baby right now!

Moving Up

All very well, the cynic may say. But how is *he* to climb in his career to his total potential, maybe to the top, if we transfer a real portion of parenting to him?

True.

And how is she to achieve her career goals if she carries so lopsided a load of the parenting?

The last question is relevant *even for women who have no great career ambitions* but who nevertheless suffer from the universal working mother child-guilt. Neither kind of woman will ever solve her Overload if we go on as we do now where every job-family conflict means she must twist her life around: call in sick, arrive late, leave work early, antagonize boss/coworkers by shirking her full job load, and/or under hideous time pressures phone frantically around for someone to cover the children today.

All working wives suffer too many of these job-family crises because of still another hidden assumption. This one says, "Though she's carrying a job and her husband has all the male advantages of her second family income, he still has total one-paycheck freedom to devote himself to his personal career goals."

On a scale of 1–10, we've gone on assuming the husband of a working wife retains the one-paycheck prerogative to try for a "10" in his career (or at least an 8 or 9). And it's therefore her role to sacrifice in whatever way needed to clear the path for him. This view gives him the edge in almost every job-family conflict. When a family need might interfere with his career, it then falls on her to cope. No wonder she feels over-loaded and overwhelmed.

To permit him to aim at an 8, 9, 10 level career, the couple tacitly expects her to parent and make do with a 4, 3, 2 work life. Trouble is that holding on to a 4, 3, 2 job still means her body must be at the work station and she must produce results. The combination of the demands of her 4, 3, 2 employment, turning herself inside out to solve all their family-job conflicts, and attempting her own and his share of conscientious parenting are exactly what make her feel so overwhelmed. These are three full jobs without even considering the homecare. More than anyone can do.

❧❧❧

You cannot solve your Overload or ameliorate your sense of guilt if you continue to hold down a job, accept absolute career ambition for him while you continue to cope with all the resulting job-family conflicts, and also attempt his share of daily parenting.

Only when you remember that women have the same right as men to have it all and that you therefore are Entitled to have him assume his share of parenting and job-family sacrifices, can you free yourself from the crushing burdens of this *wrong* kind of guilt created by your trying to carry both parents' share of everything.

Shared parenting & shared family-job conflict sacrifices may very well mean—though not necessarily—that all he can manage is a 5, 6, 7 career.

Shocked? Unrealistic in terms of family income?

Don't say no till you consider the pleasant and practical family ramifications.

With Shared parenthood as well as Shared home responsibilities, you'll then have increased time and mobility to seek the better pay and better opportunities beyond your immediate neighborhood. You'll be rid too of the grinding pressure to solve every job-family conflict through your own personal sacrifices. Buoyed by these massive reductions in your physical and emotional Overload, *even if you're not "ambitious,"* you'll probably find it comfortable to raise your career to 5, 6, 7—and still be well ahead with far less stress and guilt. Thus yours and his dual 5, 6, 7 careers and joint 5, 6, 7 family incomes will be as high or higher than under the current unjust his 8–10 vs. your 2–4 arrangement.

And what of the fact that his career pressures will be complicated by putting him on 5, 6, 7 Daddy Track? As we've seen in chapter nine, many men are voluntarily choosing the Daddy Track. For the others, an unfair status quo is not a justification for continuing the inequity.

The fact that these men have never before been inconvenienced by the fatherhood so many of them lobbied for is not a reason to continue loading it all on her. It's his turn to grow up and make the adjustments that parenthood and two family paychecks require. When he does, the greatly improved climate of his marriage and family life will be exciting compensation for most 90s men who yearn for these strong family relationships.

If we turn muddleheaded and insist it's not nice to thrust these new parenting responsibilities on the poor man, we're also saying it's perfectly nice to leave his poor working wife staggering under both his and her parenting jobs.

Mothers' Special Problems with Shared Parenting

What's your reflex reaction to these phrases: "school visits," "booster shots," "after-school child's activities," "finding out about swimming lessons for the children," "back to school and which of last year's clothes still fit?"

Mothers have a variety of automatic responses. They range from "I'll get to it this weekend . . ." "I have to arrange for . . ." "I'll call and make an appointment . . ." "I'll run out and do it on my lunch . . ." to "How am I going to fit this in? Let's see if I . . ."

The answers are really all the same. The mother's invariable attitude is "*I have to take care of this.*"

When he Shares parenting, your reflex reply can change for the better. As you start translating "children's needs" and "parent should" to "something he *or* I can attend to," your feelings of being overwhelmed diminish and the whole family profits.

For starters even with your conscientious straining, you may be among the majority of parents (54%) with children under age 18 who give yourself only a "B" for the job you feel you're doing in bringing up your children. (13% rated themselves "C"; 1% didn't know; and only 31% feel they merited an A—but these 31% were *not* asked what it was costing them in mother's Overload and resulting strain on the marriage.) Yet almost all the parents in this Gallup survey admit stress—81% say it is more difficult to raise children now than it was when their parents raised them.

So if you believe your parenting is "B" or "C" level or if "A" is costing you heavily in exhaustion and tension with your husband, it's worth considering the real price of doing too much of the parenting alone. It's worth realizing that semi-solo parenting is costing you dearly in the loss of your children's affections!

To put it positively, consider how Sharing the parenting and doing less of it yourself can increase your children's love for Mother as it also strengthens your marriage.

Yet the transition to joint parenting involves problems beyond house-power. Anyone who looks into the family research discovers widespread ambivalence *among women* about sharing parenting-control. Women have hundreds of thousands of years of socialization passed down to them and all their hormones telling them that raising the children is their job. Until a nanosecond ago in time motherhood was a woman's sole claim to self-worth. She carried the fetus, bore the baby, raised the child. In a world where he alone supported the family, both society and she believed she alone was responsible for child rearing.

The research makes it clear that the vast majority of working wives have not separated themselves from the one-paycheck view of mother-hood. As a result:

Women Feel His Parenting Efforts Mean "I'm a Failure"

Because women are so exhausted and overburdened, they may ask or pressure him to parent. *But then they go on seeing it as "my job" and often see his parenting efforts as a source of increased guilt.*

Research reports in the *Journal of Marriage and the Family*, published quarterly by the National Council on Family Relations, reveals that work-ing wives who are forced by circumstances to give over a real portion of parenting often see it as a sign that "I have failed in my job as a mother."

In turn, this attitude of hers that "It's my job" creates the famous vicious circle where he resists taking on much of this "women's work."

As she continues to make clear that she believes hands-on parenting and parenting decisions are really her responsibility, the young father typically moves from initial parental joy to seeing the child as a rival for his wife's attention. He concludes that "our" child is only technically true. In reality, it's "her" baby. Often, that's an accurate appraisal. Many mothers admit they come to view themselves primarily as mothers, only marginally as wives. Sexual activity in the first year after the first baby arrives often plummets as she loses interest. Within 18 months of the birth of the first child, his satisfaction with the marriage typically takes a serious drop. Hers, the family research indicates, sank dramatically within six months when he refused to do the amount of childcare—under her command—that she had expected. The researchers report the pattern of strain and dissatisfaction with the marriage usually is aggravated further with the birth of each additional child and the escalating parenting demands riveting her attention on the children.

When babies and young children are present and necessity forces her to pressure him to "help," he may go beyond the twenty minutes or so of "fun" chores like story time or baths that most two-career fathers willingly do. As he accepts more of the childcare that both he and wife continue to see as *her* job, his self-esteem sinks, his resentment rises, and the marriage and children too are ill served as the children sense his displeasure.

Getting to His Parenting as Your Success

When, however, you at last understand that just as he is a success as a breadwinner even though you are sharing the breadwinning, so you are a success as a mother when he shares the childcare responsibility. With that change in *your* view and *his* view of childcare, you're finally free of the one-paycheck stricture, Rule #3, that said home and children were exclusively a wife's responsibility. You're now ready to explore the many ways the family work of Shared parenting is great for you *both*.

And this is an essential new idea to keep in mind. *His and your new view of the work make a complete difference in his reaction to doing the work!!* When you *and he* stop seeing childcare as women's work and instead regard it as family work *that is appropriate for men*, the research proves his added childcare responsibilities raise his self-esteem (instead of threatening it). His Shared parenting then builds your marriage instead of stressing it.

Where We Were

When women were full-time homemakers, we had plenty of time and energy for pleasant interaction with our children. We had time to listen with full attention to childish tales over breakfast and school day lunches that we prepared and shared with them five days a week. After school we baked together, talked and joked as we drove together to and from such activities as scouts, dance, religion, and music lessons. There were plenty of opportunities in the morning to search together for Show & Tell objects; to help with school or hobby projects after school, watch children's TV together before dinner; be available at home every day so children could play freely without schedules with neighborhood friends in suburban backyards or with all of them popping in and out for treats and indoor playtime.

Now as mothers cling to the idea that "child raising is still my job and I'm a failure as a mother if my husband has to do a significant part of it" we're at the sad stage where all we've kept is the work. By and large in our overextended schedule, we don't have that many chances for happy times with our children.

As mothers I've interviewed have acknowledged, "I'm too tired; too busy. Don't have patience, time, or energy to play and hang out with them." Neither is it a matter of women choosing spotless housecleaning over children. The minimum demands of job and family survival-chores leave her few moments for spontaneous companionship with her children.

Our home work-patterns themselves are also now skewed toward reducing loving episodes with our children. When we were full-time homemakers, we had time to stop and enjoy some childish interruptions; patience to allow little hands to slow us with their help. Now we're so tightly scheduled that as we scurry around attending to everything, we're often pushed into impatience, "Oh, just go watch TV or do something. Let me get done with this."

In essence, we've ceded many of the daily pleasurable moments of parenting to Daddy as he does his parenting through story time, excursions, baths, etc. while you're in the basement with the laundry, or trudging around tending to other family necessities.

Where We Are Now & Thanksgiving Shock

A look at what we might call Thanksgiving Shock can dramatize working mothers' current everyday predicament with their children.

Let's go through an ordinary four-day Thanksgiving weekend and see how it plays in your children's eyes—and what it tells us about your mother-child relationship every day all year long.

You've been gearing up for Thanksgiving all week. By Wednesday evening you're into the cooking. That takes all Thursday morning together with setting the table and tidying for company. The food turns out well and you're happy as you scurry back and forth from kitchen to dining room serving, clearing, seeing that everybody's fed and content. Dad may join you for cleanup and that makes you feel good about your family life and marriage. Friday after Thanksgiving, as everyone knows, is the largest dollar-volume shopping day of the American year. You're out there getting a head start on Christmas or Chanukah. You shop nonstop and attend to other pre-holiday errands on Friday and maybe Saturday as you try to make the most of these last few free days before the holidays. Sunday perhaps you or Dad make a pancake brunch and you use the rest of the afternoon to get ahead of the upcoming week with the children's needs, cooking for the freezer, and the whole family goes out for fast-food dinner together.

That night when you tuck the children in, if you happen to say to them, "Didn't we have a nice Thanksgiving?" you will discover your child's loving view of the weekend you've all just lived together.

"Yes, Daddy took us to the parade on Thanksgiving and this afternoon he took us to the movies." (That was when you were cooking Thanksgiving dinner and doing the Sunday pre-week family survival chores.)

If you press them with, "And Mommy made a nice Thanksgiving dinner, didn't she? And we had fun at other meals?" they will look at you with childish interest trying to fathom what you're talking about. Meals are just meals, even if they're extra good. You don't love the cook for being the cook. Most children, as they automatically try to please, will go along and mumble agreement. Then "And in the movie today that Daddy took us to . . ." and off they go again with what in their minds were the real parental efforts of the weekend.

You have succeeded in making the entire two-paycheck family machinery of this weekend function by giving over to Dad his usual fun childcare jobs. You have done all the rest of parenting. The arrangement has added to the children's special memories and love for Dad while for all intents and purposes you have been to the children nothing but a BUSY BLUR. Even the Thanksgiving dinner that you produced saw Dad sitting there most of the time chatting with the children while you went busily between kitchen and dining room fetching, clearing, attending to everything.

Thanksgiving Shock is a prototype for what is happening between you and your children every busy day all year round.

With Shared parenting as he assumes his fair portion of the routines of parenting—not just the fun jobs—you can reclaim your fair portion of the parent-child experiences that help build happy memories and strong parent-child ties.

If he takes over the chore of making their school lunches and finding last-minute morning needs, you have those extra morning minutes to really listen and talk with them instead of responding on automatic busy pilot with "Oh good. Oh, too bad."

If he takes them for medical checkups or regular allergy shots, you have time to take them ice skating. (You did home or personal chores while they were at the doctor. If you'd taken them to the doctor, you'd have returned to the chores with no time for ice skating.)

If he takes charge of the older children while they pick up toys from the recreation room floor and then he instead of you mops it down, you have time to spend taking the little one for a haircut-and-ice-cream outing.

None of these examples are especially important tradeoffs. They merely suggest patterns to help you reclaim your portion of happy parent-child occasions while he takes on his portion of everyday necessities.

Will such Shared parenting make them love you more than under working mothers' current usual tense BUSY BLUR lifestyle?

What do you think?

But How Competent Is He?

As recently as ten years ago this was a topic for serious debate. Today attitudes toward men's parental rights and their ability to parent have changed both legally and in the average person's mind. Just as women have proved they can function well in every kind of career, men have spent the past few decades making it clear they can parent.

The Census Bureau reports nearly twice as many fathers raising children alone today as compared to ten years ago. With their new paternal confidence men have sued, won, and forced airports across the country to install diaper changing facilities especially for Dad or to add unisex changing areas open to both parents. The idea of men choosing the househusband life and becoming the "primary" at-home parent has moved from a freak notion to an accepted mainstream lifestyle choice. The National Father's Organization and its newspaper *American Fatherhood*, supported by divorced fathers who are passionately devoted to being an active part in their children's lives, work to expand childraising rights of divorced fathers. Researchers who probe father-child relationships find fathers can parent as successfully as mothers. They say dads can be as protective, giving, and stimulating as mothers. Dr. James Herzog, M.D., a psychiatrist at Harvard, sums up the new findings about men's parenting abilities. "It's settled. We no longer have to prove that men can father well."

Winning His Cooperation for Shared Parenting

All the communication facts and techniques in chapter fifteen for putting across the fairness of Sharing housework and house-power apply as much to Sharing the responsibilities and power of parenting.

One team-couple mother gave me a useful general strategy. She started her system the first week home after childbirth. "Neither of us knew how to bathe or diaper the baby. I purposely drew him into learning. We were both clumsy and scared to death. We learned together. And I made sure I didn't become an instant expert and leave him behind as a bumbler. I've tried to continue that attitude as the children grow and we have new roles and skills to learn."

Another woman told me she encouraged her husband into increased and more confident parenting by suppressing her urge to decide every-thing. Children's personality needs can change with bewildering speed. Each stage is as much a surprise to Mom as to Dad. But typically, Dad will say, "What do I do if . . ."

Sometimes she knows from reading, mother-talk, or experience. Very often she doesn't really know. Like all mothers she just muddles through, coping with necessity as best she can. This woman explained she now says, "I don't know. I'm in the same boat as you. I've never had an eleven-year-old with a situation like this. Let's figure it out. What could we do?" By allowing him to share the decision process, she is allowing him to be a parenting partner instead of the old-style "helping" underling.

This dual parental relationship with your children will serve you well throughout their adolescence as well as their childhood. Martin Gold, professor of psychology and research scientist at the University of Mich-igan's Research Center for Group Dynamics, has discovered that the popular idea of children maturing through rebellion is flat wrong. He finds that adolescents who have good relations with their parents mature "by working through conflicts with their parents and by establishing close relationships with them." These lucky teenagers go on to learn trust and warmth and enjoy better peer and friendship relationships than the rebellious ones.

As you do shift from him "helping" with childcare to both of you Sharing childcare, you aid not only your children but your marriage. University of Pennsylvania family research tells us that when men willingly do their portion of childcare, you reduce the risk of divorce. The researchers find that fathers who are deeply involved in parenting are simultaneously willing to put more effort into maintaining the marriage. "The more the father does . . . the stronger the attachment [to the child] and the less likely he is to give up that relationship" through divorce.

Here then is very significant encouragement. Should you shrink from making the transition to Shared parenting on the grounds that it will provoke changeover tensions in your marriage, he's doing less for and with the children and consequently you're loosening his ties with his children. You're therefore increasing the risk of the ultimate family battle of separation or divorce.

Do It for the Children

Besides creating a happier marriage, making you a more lovable wife and mother, and solving your Overload, Shared parenting will probably bless your children with a happier mother. A survey of 600 couples found that women who carried most of parenting had depression rates double men's. When fathers shouldered more of the daily parenting, women's depression subsided. And the new childcare responsibilities did not create emotional problems for the fathers if the men understood that childcare for Dad was a fair arrangement in a two-paycheck marriage.

The conclusion comes through clearly in the family research. Children who have two involved parents develop high self-esteem. They internalize realistic concepts of modern male-female lifestyles to aspire to. With quantities of active attention from both their parents they see themselves as human beings who matter.

What greater treasures can you give your children?

18

Emotions vs. Logic:
Figuring It Out

Secrets

"The choices aren't really black and white," says Jerri Missingill, a 37-year-old working wife. "Last Sunday I encouraged my husband to take the children swimming and barbecuing at the lake. I stayed home and spent six hours—can you believe six hours—waxing the dining room furniture with a beeswax compound. Don't tell me I could have hired someone, or that it's heavy work I should have suggested my husband do, or we could have done without it altogether, or that I passed up a wonderful afternoon with my family for housework that nobody but me cares about. It was buffing the wax into the carving on the chairs and breakfront that really took time. My arms ached. My back ached. And I was happy anyway."

Nancy Fischer remembers being unhappy. On the surface nothing could have been less controversial and more useful than transferring to her husband Brad and her 10- and 13-year-olds the task of cleaning the kitchen and stacking the dishwasher after weeknight dinners and week-end meals. Yet as she recalls, "I found myself insisting on me 'helping' them, hovering in and out of the kitchen, making them feel supervised and getting no real relief for myself."

Acknowledging that when it comes to home and childcare, logic goes just so far, can help you. We're all a mixture of secret pleasures, goals, and rebellions. Admitting this to yourself can make your Sharing choices and transitions vastly easier.

Many women have a strong nesting instinct. Among older women, some household tasks provide a familiar comfortable structure for their hours at home. Among younger women there's an attractive novelty to some home tasks. A woman may never before have furnished a home, arranged a closet full of her very own linens, polished her own silver. Yet many working wives are so overwhelmed they've fallen into the habit of bemoaning all domestic tasks without sorting out which have some private appeal for them. Furthermore, widespread working wife Overload has made it rather unfashionable to admit—except perhaps for cooking— that you actually enjoy some housework. Forget whether it's a stylish view or not. Before you can comfortably move to new family life patterns, you must know which tasks offer you pleasures you enjoy.

Someday Jerri may tire of waxing the family's dining room furniture. But now the pieces are only a year old. It's taken Jerri and her husband almost fourteen years of marriage to save enough to discard the battered hand-me-downs they've been using. That Sunday as Jerri polished, the feel of the wood under her hands, the sight of the burnished glow after she finished buffing filled her with contentment. It wasn't drudgery. Her mood wasn't complicated. She just plain couldn't think of anything else that she wanted to do that afternoon.

With no way to think through what was troubling her about kitchen cleanup, Nancy supervised the family for months provoking not a few roaring arguments from Brad. "What is it with you? All this talk about giving me control and here you are watching every move?"

Nancy finally realized the dishes themselves were generating her anxiety. She explains, "They're not that expensive. But my grandmother, who was already very ill when Brad and I got engaged, made my mother help her up from her sickbed and take her to buy the dishes for us for a wedding present. I loved my grandmother dearly. She died before our wedding and now that I've worked it out I realize I've always felt that the dishes were not only her present but also her loving presence in our home. The kids and Brad aren't as careful stacking the dishwasher as I am. It's inevitable some dishes will chip. I now understand that was what was making me so jumpy."

With her new insights Nancy was finally in control of her Sharing transitions. She could have decided it was worth it to her to return to doing cleanup herself in order to continue using her grandmother's dishes daily; or she could have decided she'd keep the dishes safe for special meals when she herself cleaned and buy an inexpensive set for Brad and the children's cleanup days. She chose the second solution and then was at ease about disappearing after meals and leaving them to their own systems.

Ways to Think It Through

You can make your own Sharing transitions much easier by applying three self-knowledge questions to tasks you're considering handing over to your husband.

For jobs you think you "ought" to feel happy about giving over but somehow don't want to, try:

1. What is there about this routine job that I enjoy?

2. What is the worst thing that could happen if *they* (someone other than you) do it?

3. What will *I* lose if I don't do it any more?

With these questions, Jerri would have found her answers immediately with question #1: "What is there about this routine job that I enjoy?" Jerri's reflex reaction would have been: "Routine job, maybe. But at last we have this gorgeous dining room furniture. Every time I see it sitting there I'm happy. I just want to use this special wax they recommended and see it glow and be happy as I do it."

Nancy would not have been helped by the first question. She could dredge up nothing especially enjoyable about cleaning the kitchen after a day at work. If she'd moved on to the next question, "What is the worst thing . . ." her mind would instantly have flashed, "They're going to chip and break some of the dishes. You can't expect 10- and 13-year-olds to be as careful as you are."

Then she could have consciously worked it through with, "So what if some dishes chip? They're not bone china. They're just an ordinary set of dishes."

"No, they're not ordinary!! They're from Grandma!" her indignant mind would have bellowed back at her. And there she would quickly have had her answer.

Another woman I interviewed, Danielle Kinsley, would have to move through to question three before she understood her Sharing confusions.

She knew she "ought" to give over laundry to her husband. It was an ideal family job for him. He had been a bachelor till age 31, raised by a divorced mother who had taught him when he was 12 to use washer and dryer. By the time they'd married, he'd had 19 years of careful laundering experience. Danielle was well aware that her husband was as good or better than she at turning out wrinkle-free permanent press, bright colors, neatly folded piles of linens and underwear and blouses and shirts on hangers. So what made her uncomfortable about passing laundry to him?

With question #3, "What will I lose if I don't do it anymore?" she knew.

Danielle works as a hotel catering-convention sales executive meeting people in person and phoning, talking all day. When she does the laundry, she escapes for an hour or so to the basement and her husband cares for the children. If he laundered, she'd lose her few hours a week when she's conscientiously producing for the family but has some quiet time for herself.

Understanding your secret pleasures and goals requires you to accept your personal needs as Danielle finally did. She knew that mothers who are away working all day are "supposed" to want to spend every free minute with husband and children. Yet Danielle needed those few quiet hours. They made her a better, more patient mother and wife. And the children were doing fine with Daddy's attention during that period. So forget what the lore and media tell you mothers are supposed to desire. Use these questions to discover what really motivates you and what you personally need. Then with your new self-knowledge, you're ready to work out with your husband a comfortable new division of family responsibilities.

19

. . . .

Hiring Help When You Can't Afford It, They Won't Do a Good Job, & There's No Help Available in Your Area

. . . .

*P*OPULAR folklore to the contrary, money can buy some kinds of happiness. It doesn't take that many dollars spent on home services for you and your husband to have more time, more energy, more joie de vivre.

To stop feeling overwhelmed, you want to ditch your children's view of you as a BUSY BLUR, return yourself from a hard-driving uptight woman to the lovable person your husband married, and allow your husband in from the periphery to a central Sharing part of family life.

You can accomplish all that much faster and more easily if you lighten the pressures on you and your husband by paying others to take over some family chores.

From interviewing so many women, I know that at this point too many women don't even consider purchasing family services. My observations are confirmed by similar research findings by the government and other experts cited throughout this book.

The women flatly reject the idea of hiring some help with a reflex "Oh no!" My interviews have taught me that nationwide, if you probe, women reveal the same five fears about why it's impractical or hopeless to consider paying for Overload-relief.

1) It's Wrong: I Should Do My Own Work

We've taken care of this objection throughout the book. We now know "I should do my own work" may have had some validity for a full-time one-paycheck housewife. But it does not apply to the two-paycheck working wife, whether employed part- or full-time.

You're Entitled.

2) We Can't Afford It

"We can't afford it" shows up just as regularly for women with family incomes of $100,000+, $80,000, $60,000, $45,000 as for those with less funds. This is true because "We can't afford it" covers many convoluted hidden meanings.

Till now women have felt it acceptable to spend family money on all kinds of luxuries. For instance, family time management surveys reveal working wives often cope with Overload by purchasing weekly restaurant dinners and/or multiple weekly meals of take-out prepared foods, or supermarket convenience foods. These purchases are always much more expensive than supermarket basics. Similarly, because it's acceptable, working wives will lay out $10–$15 for casual family treats of ice cream cones and fixings at the shopping mall. They'll spend on impulse purchases: $3.50, $6.95, $25.95+ for cute junk and gimmick gadgets that you see people standing on line to pay for in drug stores, greeting card stores, mall novelty shops, and even at budget discounters like Woolworth's, K-Mart, and Wal-Mart.

However, though you can go down to the middle-income mall or discount store any evening of the week and watch average wage earners tossing money away on expensive snacks and ephemeral gadgets/signs/cutesie stuffed items, etc., the women in the families will tell you they "can't afford" household services.

After surveying 291 working parents in thirty states, University of California women's studies professor Dr. Gayle Kimball explains what she's learned about this widespread working wife contradiction. Though the women feel comfortable about handing over money for cute odds and ends, they resist using the dollars for valuable home help because "buying home services has always violated the women's sense of how a good spouse behaves."

With that taboo guiding them, working women have arranged their family expenditures with no effort to include home services.

Yet once women feel Entitled to lighten their responsibilities with some household help, even women with a very modest budget often discover they *can* afford some services.

The magical difference lies in the fact that with her new sense of Entitlement she now feels it's OK to rearrange some spending choices.

Previously money spent for impulse family junk was socially acceptable; chore relief was indecent. Now that she feels Entitled and chore relief is respectable, it's not that hard to pass up the impulse junk and put that money into buying bi-weekly home cleaning service that frees evenings and weekend hours for both her & him. And now it's not difficult to choose three family home parties of supermarket ice cream and toppings at about half the mall price of one cone apiece—with saved money put to buying an entire week's family freedom from laundering Dad's shirts.

Sharing where Dad takes over a few workday dinners can be a regular source of big bucks' worth of chore relief. With Dad producing a few workday meals from simple supermarket ingredients, the pressure is off her to resort so heavily to costly convenience dinners, and the family's weekly food money savings can be substantial. The significant amount of saved money is then available for regular home cleaning and/or other family services.

Whether or not you spend money on mall ice cream or the other extras mentioned above is irrelevant. Except for the very, very tightest of budgets, there is some family discretionary money. Once you make the mental breakthrough and recognize how much some paid help will reduce your whole family's stress level and increase your relaxed pleasure in each other's company, you can usually find some chore funds by rearranging other spending priorities.

Though affluent families—once she feels Entitled—can often handle both impulse purchases and services, they do need to protect their services money from big purchase pressures. Unless thought of and safeguarded in the budget as a necessity, even their chore relief cash can melt as they take on too many costly good-life trinkets.

You also add to your ability to afford help by restructuring your own view of family money and your own contributions to it. Family specialists find that many working wives see their income as "our money" or as part of "his" money. They hand over their paycheck and go right on asking permission for every purchase. When a wife does retain some or all of her income as her own, she frequently then uses it for family needs: college tuition, car payments, family vacation. It becomes a matter of semantics: really family money but under another name. When a woman uses her paycheck in these ways, she often ends up feeling she has no personal money of her own to spend.

Another popular and mistaken view subtracts all the childcare costs literally or in the family's mind from her paycheck. Usually they're his children too. Subtracting childcare from her dollars made sense under one-paycheck rules that said she was responsible for the children. No more. Now that childcare is family work, a two-paycheck responsibility, presenting Mom with the childcare bill is obsolete.

Therefore, whether childcare money is really coming straight from your income or only subtracted in your and his minds, give up that view. See your childcare costs as divided between both your family incomes. Or, how about making up for all the past years when the money was literally or figuratively (and mistakenly) lopped from your income alone? From now on draw it all from his income. That new allocation system will certainly pump up your family dollar contributions in both your minds.

Here's another big chore fund source: If family income is buying him all that relief from *male* chores—lawn care, car washing, indoor room painting, etc. (our chapter five), put his male chore money back into the general house chores funds and reparcel.

Before you dismiss all these reallocations as just a game of mentally shifting family dollars around in your mind, remember the other abstract situation where the mental game of feeling Non-Entitled caused your whole Overload dilemma. Now any mental revisions that further strengthen the family's view of your economic contributions are worth cherishing.

3) There's No One Around Here to Hire

Maybe once, but no more.

There's money to be made offering convenience. This, after all, is the land of capitalism and ingenuity.

One-third of Americans now say they *always* feel rushed. (Among working mothers the proportion is higher.) The other two-thirds of Americans aren't swinging lazily in the hammock on the porch. They merely have escaped from *always* feeling overscheduled.

So no one to hire?

Look again.

Check your telephone Yellow Pages, service ads in your town's freebie shopper newspapers; bring up the topic with friends. Family services aren't a local maybe anymore; they're a national trend.

For instance, *Business Week* did a cover picture story, "PRESTO! The Convenience Industry: Making Life A Little Simpler," and ran through samples of home services you can buy *either* regularly or for those special tired days when dollars allow you more leisure time and the prerogative to go straight home after work instead of two more shopping stops in the winter rain.

A family chore fund and a phone call buys you everything from dogs walked to packages wrapped and mailed; children's birthday parties arranged and supervised; children chauffeured to and from after school activities; grocery orders assembled at supermarkets and delivered; local and franchised home cleaning services. Elsewhere there are reports of the reappearance of home milk delivery, errand runners who drive your car to and from repairs, attend to everything from arguing with companies about billing errors, to sending holiday greeting cards. Growing in number are old standbys like drug store deliveries and service laundromats where your husband or you drop off big bundles of ten days' worth of dirty stuff and that evening pick up neat, washed, bleached, blued, dried, folded bundles of ready to be put away clean clothes & linens.

To Your Specifications

Creating the services you need may be the simplest and cheapest way to buy the high-quality relief most valuable to you.

Instead of starting with what is available, turn it around. Begin with what you want. For example, many women recoil from using a cleaning service because they say the services have a routine of certain things they clean "and I'm left to do all the extras that are really bothering me."

One woman I interviewed explained how she solved this problem. She checked the Yellow Pages, phoned the cleaning service listed, and asked if they'd quote her not a job rate but an hourly rate and then let her schedule the tasks she wanted done during each visit. The first agency wasn't interested. The second was. She arranged for two hours' worth of work apiece for a team of two, or four work hours weekly. Each time she leaves a note telling the workers her priorities. They do some basics and all her specials. "It's perfect," she says, "and the same price as four hours of routine service would be."

Another woman told me how she usesd service customizing to rid herself and her husband of a twice-monthly difficult errand. Their local suburban dry cleaner/shirt service/shoe repair opens after they leave for work and it closes before they return. Attending to it weekends was just one more drag.

One weekend the wife stopped in and asked a clerk at the shop if she would be interested in $5.00 for herself for a round trip of picking up and returning the items as she came and went from work. The clerk drove through the woman's neighborhood anyway to and from her job and she was delighted with the customer's suggestion. To the clerk, each pickup meant found money. And for the couple, no more dragging armloads of shirts, cleaning, and shoes back and forth on weekends was well worth the cost. The woman left the cleaning et al. inside the house storm door; she paid the bills and clerk with checks left in the pickup. On that suburban street the arrangement was inconspicuous and safe.

The point of this detailed anecdote lies in the fact that you can probably create any kind of specialized service you need on the same independent contracting basis with one of the employees at any of your neighborhood businesses.

Home cleaning too can lend itself to many types of customizing. Beyond what the first woman arranged with time purchase is the discomfort many women feel at having an impersonal team working in their homes when they themselves are away at work. Several women told me how customizing had given them not just personalized cleaning help but a real friend. They advertised in their local papers or their church bulletins for a housewife or college student "With your own transportation; make your own hours."

One located a college student who worked out splendidly. When he graduated, he passed the job on to another student. Several other women's ads drew calls from local housewives who were home with preschool children and were looking for a few hours of income. One woman's experience was typical. The woman she chose is a homeowner in her own town. "We're real friends now," she says. "And, of course, I'm 100% comfortable about her being in the house when I'm not there."

Another woman found the same kind of personal comfortable help by asking at her hair salon. An operator had a friend, a young mother with small children, who worked part-time as a sales clerk and was finding the sales hours too rigid. The young mother was happy to take on the housework once a week while a neighbor watched her children and she mentioned the pay for cleaning was far better than her sales clerk rates.

4) It's Not Right to Exploit Other People

The admission that home cleaning rates often far surpass sales clerk per hour income leads us to pleasant truths that detonate the exploitation notions.

Rates vary by communities. But nowadays, they are almost always dollars well above the minimum wage. In some suburban centers, home cleaning brings as high as $8, $10, $12, $15, even $20+ per worker hour. So if you go the custom route, consider that while cleaning services in your area may be charging $10–$20 or more per worker hour, the worker doesn't see that much money as the agency takes its share for insurance, overhead, profit. With that in mind, if you advertise a few dollars less than the going service company rate in your area, or better yet close to it, money to pass directly into the hand of the person working for you, your ad will sound very attractive.

Cleaning is an essential part of making a home. The work is intrinsically valuable. Nothing could be further from exploitation. You're offering an excellent paying job for work that matters in the pleasant surroundings of your home. Those who choose to accept do so because the hours meet their own needs and the pay scale is more than they could otherwise earn. An honorable win-win situation for them and for you.

5) They Won't Do as Good a Job as I/We Do

There are many reassuring answers to this worry. How about:
"So what?"

"At least neither you nor your husband have to come home from a day of your own work or use your weekends to do it."

"You can always do the corners and spit and polish details yourself but the main part is done."

"Talk up and take time to explain how and what you want done better." And "Try another cleaning person/service. As with anything you purchase, quality among suppliers varies."

Essentially here you have the same problem as with your husband's Sharing efforts and your learning to accept tradeoffs and marginal differences. Is relief from the house chores you're paying for worth living with the margin of difference between their results and yours? Or are the differences in results so big that you're willing to give up hiring help and take back all the work for your husband and you to do?

Judged in that way, people usually decide that purchasing some chore relief and then sitting down together with the family to watch the two rented movies in peace—with no feeling that you and your husband ought to be catching up on housework—is a tradeoff that is worth every penny in family contentment.

20

Conclusion: Should You or Shouldn't You Use This System?

*Y*OU can play it any way that suits you and still come out ahead.

You can decide on a little Sharing, a lot, or none. Whichever way you go, you're much better off than you were when you began reading.

In *Wait a Minute, You Can Have It All*, we've examined each of our feminine possessive attitudes toward our home and children. We've discovered how media, business, society, pound at us to continue our possessive attitudes; to continue living by one-paycheck family rules that are irrelevant for two-paycheck marriages.

In revealing why one-paycheck rules don't apply to two-paycheck couples, we've seen how your income vastly improves your husband's life, why he's a success even though your family needs your money, how your job can add thirty to forty years to your youth and middle age, and why you're Entitled to purchase chore help and to expect him to Share childcare and homecare.

There is no right or wrong answer. It doesn't matter how many or how few responsibilities and accompanying *control* you now decide to Share. With the insights from this book, all your choices will now be knowledgeable. You'll be able to *foresee the consequences* of your choices.

If to you the psychological satisfactions of being in charge of certain tasks are worth the burdens, you may decide to retain control of them.

But now you'll know *beforehand* that if you keep the power, you'll end up doing most of the work including 80–90% of the hidden parts of tasks he "helps" with. You'll be aware that as you keep the power, you're saying, "This is still my women's work"—and therefore not really suitable for a man.

But since at that point you'll choose power with the knowledge of its Overload costs, you'll no longer continually be frustrated by your heavy work load and his inadequate contributions.

Conversely, when you decide the costs of house-power are too high—in your own stress, in marital strain, and in BUSY BLUR mothering—you now know you must accept the alternative. You must permit him to be an equal home partner with control of tasks he takes over and the right to do them his way. Only by conveying your new sense of Entitlement and ceding power do you transform it from your women's work to our family work.

It is this transformation in *your* behavior as you transmit your sense of Entitlement and cede house-power to him, that makes him view the tasks as worthy of masculine cooperation.

Whatever the personal equation you arrive at, it's a good decision. That's the whole point of this book. To enjoy its benefits you don't need any crash effort to remake your routines. You pick and choose.

Begin by using only as many of the solutions as you're comfortable with.

Tomorrow is another day.

As you gain experience with Sharing, as your life moves along, your desires and priorities may alter. As that happens, you now understand why you're Entitled, and the way to talk to your husband about Sharing, the way to keep moving toward a fairer distribution of family responsibilities.

Though individual unreachable Macho-Neanderthal men do exist, the vast majority of married men are reachable.

So when you're ready and you use this book's ideas and methods to eliminate your working wife Overload by changing to Sharing the work and the house-power,

you'll succeed.

You now know you can Have It All—& enjoy it too!
And you know how to make it happen.

Backgrounder

. . . .

How Media, Business, Government, Society Generate Working Wife Guilt & Prevent You from Solving Your Overload

. . . .

*D*O you remember the old story about the newspaperman and his drinking buddy? Seems that during one mellow bout, the newsman remarks, "There are 10,000,000 llamas in Peru." The buddy declares that cannot possibly be true. A few weeks later the newsman needs a filler at the bottom of a column and he inserts, "There are 10,000,000 llamas in Peru." That evening as soon as their first drink arrives, the buddy shoves a newspaper across the table and admits, "You know, you're right. There *are* 10,000,000 llamas in Peru. Says so right here in the paper."

The anecdote has survived these many years because we instinctively know it illustrates a truth about human nature. We tend to believe it if we see it in print.

Social psychologists Marvin E. Shaw and Stephen T. Margulis conducted experiments testing the truth of this instinct and found the written word does indeed have an awesome "mystique." Put something in print and people frequently accept it as fact.

In the respected publication *Journal of Social Psychology*, Shaw and Margulis tell us why we behave that way. They say people deal with complex issues by *conforming* to the view they find in the written word. Print, they find, gives people the feeling the matter has been investigated and here are the facts. Hence, they say, print is often believed regardless of the quality of the communication.

Al Neuharth, that shrewd student of human psychology who created *USA Today,* illuminates another powerful effect print and other media have on us when he writes that media are the glue that pulls the globe together. He points out that more than politicians, academicians, or economists, the media decide what's important in the world by what they choose to cover. They are "the agenda setters." Then the slant that media assign a subject teaches us how to think about it. And by and large we then move to "conformity" and accept that opinion.

Because of this tidal wave power of the printed word (supplemented by TV/radio media power), you and all working wives/mothers would have to be superhuman to resist "conforming" to the constant multimedia message that tells you working wives are Not Entitled to deviate from one-paycheck family rules.

How Media Pressure You to Try to Do It All

Henry David Thoreau dismissed newspaper reading as a waste of time because, he said, there are just the same few basic stories over and over: wars, murders, accidents, fires, money made & lost, sad fate of an innocent, etc.—the same tales endlessly repeated with only names, dates, and details varied.

With the publication and enormous impact of *The Feminine Mystique* in 1963 and its indictment of the full-time housewife life as too narrow and hence destructive of women's mental health and self-esteem, women began moving en masse out of full-time homemaking. At that time *the media adopted one basic angle for discussing women in the workplace. —They have never deviated from nor updated their original angle.* It may only be an accidental conspiracy, an invisible sexist assumption that they themselves don't see. But they tell the same working wife/working mother story over and over; only the names, dates, and details vary.

The slant of the media's entire treatment of working wives/mothers is how she's gaining a wider, freer life and how he's losing out at home in eroding patriarchal authority and diminished home services from her.

They tell the working wife/working mother story from the husband/male worker's viewpoint; how her "new life" is "disrupting," "making it difficult" or "still making it possible" for women to fulfill their wifely roles under the three one-paycheck family rules.

The examples of these media views are in every newspaper, magazine, TV/radio news report about working wives/working mothers that you read, see, and hear.

A particularly naked instance appeared in a 1990s *Fortune* as it pounded home the three one-paycheck rules in a coverline article, "How Dual-Income Couples Cope." The initial theme of the article is Rule #2: A Man Is the Family's Real Breadwinner or He Is a Failure as a Man.

You don't need to read between the lines to arrive at this conclusion. It's right there in their own lead that sets the focus of the piece: "Men's identities as *the* [their emphasis] family provider have become threatened by wives who are providers too." Notice "threatened."

Why present your useful family income as a "threat" to him, as something you should feel guilty about? Why aren't you praised for your family efforts? And why in the 1990s, when women comprise about half the workforce, are they still agonizing over whether almost 50% of the working populace has a right to high income and career success?

They're doing so because of their underlying invisible belief in the one-paycheck rule, His Masculinity Depends on Being the Family Breadwinner. (This belief may be invisible even to themselves.) By labeling and discussing your career success as a "threat," their formidable printed authority reteaches two-paycheck wives (and husbands too!) that you as a working wife are Not Entitled to behave in any way that violates the rule. Hence the pressure on you both to create family fictions about how your income is for extras and he is supporting the family.

The next lead sentence reminds us of what your job is "costing" him (one-paycheck Rule #1). More guilt is laid on you when we're told that an employed wife means a man "loses her full-time services as nurturer and builder of his ego." Of course, because this article, like most media pieces, is from the husband's viewpoint, there's not a word about *your* need for *his* full-time services as nurturer and builder of *your* ego. In these discussions his success is success; her success is a "problem."

Here and there in these stories they often include a few comments about what he's getting out of it. They may mention that she is saving him from the need to work two jobs or that she's raised the family's living standard from tight budget to good life. But these are just a few sentences or paragraphs in pages of the original slant. They're not the focus, just asides adding journalistic balance.

Don't make the mistake of believing this male slant is due to *Fortune* being a man's magazine. Maybe once, but no longer. *Fortune* is trying to attract subscribers from both sexes, the one-third of post-1970s MBAs who are female, the female entrepreneurs who are going into business at twice the rate of men, the 30% of managers who are female.

No, this *Fortune* article is worth examining in detail because it is so *commonplace*, so typical of the working wife/mother angle thrust at us daily in newspapers, magazines, TV, radio, advertisements, corporate policy, product directions, government rulings and legislation.

So total is the slant when dealing with working wives that sadly it has even influenced women's best champions, their own women's magazines.

Because I have worked so long for the women's magazines, I have great respect for what they have been able to accomplish for women. I believe the magazines are doing the best they can to achieve equality for women and to serve their readers. However, the general overall larger media focus is so powerfully in favor of the three one-paycheck rules for two-paycheck marriages that even women's magazines are able to move away only marginally.

For instance, they run stories like:

> CHECKMATE: In one out of every five dual-income couples the woman earns more than her mate. Is she the one who has it all or is she left holding the bag?

Then they discuss her career success, her effort toward equality, as a problem. The focus is his feelings, his life, what her working success and accompanying good income is "costing."

One of the very best of the women's magazines runs a permanent section for working mothers titled "Guilt" in which they feature first-person reader articles like "I'm a Good Mother, But a Lousy Wife" and "I'm a Lousy Housekeeper—So Sue Me."

In all these confessionals the women relate they're pushing themselves to the limit doing the best they can at home and carrying demanding paid jobs that bring in needed family income. Nevertheless they are guilt-ridden. They're not perfect housekeepers, nightly sirens, perfect patient listening supports for their husband's career problems.

Nowhere does the magazine suggest that being a working wife/mother changes the rules. The reader is left to understand that guilt is the correct reaction; that the old one-paycheck standards should be obeyed by two-paycheck wives.

Business, Government, Society: Sure You're Entitled to a Career Just as Long as You Still Do Everything at Home

There's a perfect example of how business thinks and pushes one-paycheck rules at us for our two-paycheck lives in a news release of a prestigious nationwide business research group. It reports "working moms" can feel better about childcare's "income eroding expense" in these lower cost cities.

They say "working moms" though the text throughout indicates they mean two-paycheck couples. So why not "working parents"?

Clearly this respected business research group and probably most of the businesses they serve present childcare as a "working mom" issue because they still see home and children as her job (Rule #3). By directing news of childcare costs to "working moms" they're saying that if she wants all this new freedom to have a job and flout her real Rule #3 duties to home and children, let her pick up the childcare tab directly from her paycheck. They're making it clear businesses don't expect child-care money from Dad because childcare is not his job!

This view of childcare as still a feminine responsibility is massively disseminated in corporate ads, newspaper editorials, business news, politicians' speeches, government debates, even in women's organizations' agendas and publications. All of these institutions keep referring to child-care as a "major working woman's issue!"—not, as it should be, a working parents' issue.

The result: As you and your husband constantly meet that working mom view set forth in the influential printed word and on TV and radio, you both are continually influenced to remember that you are Not Entitled to shift significant childcare responsibilities to your husband—that paid job or not, childcare is a mother's job, *not* his.

Individually, some women see through it. *Newsweek* runs a cover story on "Mommy Wars," alleged divisions between employed mothers and at-home mothers. Then it admits several weeks later in a special high-lighted section of its letters page, "Many writers [of letters] felt *Newsweek* missed the point, saying the problem is not warfare among mothers, but rather a sexist society. 'Men and women alike will be liberated when both genders share equally in parenting,' wrote one mother."

Business Week runs a cover story on the Mommy Track and reports similar objections from some readers. *The New York Times* does a major feature on "Barriers to Sexual Equality Seen as Eroding, But Slowly" with a caption that tells you how their editors see and slant working woman stories. The caption reports that the working mother in the photo juggles her job and caring for their year-old twins with the "help" of her husband. Some readers heatedly write to ask why in the 1990s the *Times* is still offering as their example of progress a husband who "helps" his employed wife care for the couple's infants instead of taking on a full parent's share of the work.

The very fact that individuals have to write to contradict the basic media slant leaves those women who see through it as individual dissenters. It leaves those women as outsiders against the perceived common belief in the one-paycheck rules which media, business, society keep drilling into two-paycheck couples.

The pressure in favor of one-paycheck rules also comes from government. In fact, a shocking example of government's one-paycheck attitude to your two-paycheck life was written into the federal job bias laws. Not until after the Clarence Thomas hearings did Congress feel pressured to at last grant women job bias rights that had long ago been granted to those who suffer race or nationality discrimination. And even now, there is a two-tier arrangement. If someone sues on racial grounds, there is no limit to damages that can be won. Women who sue on sexual grounds have a limited ceiling on damages they can obtain.

Until this late 1991 law change, women who were victims of employment discrimination were permitted to sue to reacquire their jobs and back pay, but they had no right to recover damages for medical and emotional discrimination injuries. Neither were they permitted to sue to punish offenders.

Yet civil rights job legislation has always allowed blacks and other racial minorities to sue for all facets of discrimination including medical and emotional damages and for the right to punish offenders. That means if you sued for job discrimination on racial grounds (as a male or female), you had these rights. But if a woman (of any color) sued on *sexual* discrimination grounds, she did not have the right to recover damages for medical and emotional injuries or to sue to punish offenders.

This was true even in such blatant circumstances as a case described in *The Wall Street Journal.* A woman suffered what the judge himself characterized as "sustained, malicious, and brutal harassment" by male workers "resulting in physical and mental debilitation" and still she had no right to sue for medical or emotional injuries.

The two-track government legislation for racial and sexual job discrimination indicated that bias on racial grounds is rightly seen by the government as unjust—and the court system must cope as best it can with the possibly large number of cases that may be brought. The government's refusal until so late in 1991 to extend similar rights to women (on the grounds that the courts might be overburdened with the number of cases brought) sent the message that the government sees the one-paycheck family rules as applying to working mothers. In the government's eyes apparently she should be home and it therefore will not extend the same on-the-job-bias damages to her as ethnics have. Another heavy reminder that home is *her* Job. No wonder women internalize so much Non-Entitlement.

Have You Ever Read an Interview that Sympathized with a White Supremacist?

These continual media, business, government features, reports, policies dealing with women's equality in terms of what it's "costing" her, him, the family, and society are a travesty.

They're upside down.

The media has—correctly—reported the black civil rights effort as people seeking their rightful equal place in society. Just as with women in the workforce, in each black civil rights story only names, dates, details vary and the focus remains the same. Only this time the media's basic slant is correct and very different. The slant says: Blacks are entitled to equality; here is today's news story on some aspect of that theme.

Nowhere do media, business, government, society consider black equality with a focus sympathetic to the former slave owner or modern white supremacist racist with a slant on what black equality is "costing" the slave owner or racist.

When was the last time you read a feature on how difficult it is for white southerners who were born into a segregated world to adapt to a non-segregated life? Nor have you ever read a feature on how tough it is for the supremacist to sit next to a black person on a bus, in a restaurant, at work, complete with sympathetic discussion and quotes from psychologists trying to ease the bigots' discomforts.

When and where do you ever see media features focusing on and sympathetically discussing the psychological stress of the white employee who has to take orders from a black boss?

Just mentioning these hypothetical feature topics gives many people unpleasant shivers.

The attitude of the media—correctly—is that black people were formerly treated with injustice and are now entitled to have their equality acknowledged. As for any sympathetic discussions of segregationists' feelings and problems with integration, the media/social attitude is that it's the business of the bigot to straighten out his thinking by himself.

Why don't they treat women's move from inequality to equality in the same way? Why do they report each equality effort for women in terms of what it is "costing" him?

For instance, when blacks join a previously all-white country club or move into some other formerly all-white area, you'll never find a print or electronic media feature built around the bigot's viewpoint—

> "And how do you feel today sitting down next to a black in your formerly all-white club dining room?"

> "How does it affect your self-esteem to be taking orders and working for a black boss?"

Yet every time a barrier falls for women, you can take for granted that tomorrow's newspapers and TV/radio news will deliver a jolly bunch of features reporting the event from the bigoted viewpoint:

> "And how does he feel today sitting down next to a woman in his formerly all-male dining room?"

> "And how does it affect his self-esteem taking orders and working for a woman boss?"

Worse, the what-it's-costing view becomes accepted and permanent. For example, in late 1991, twenty years after women moved seriously into careers, respected organizations like Gallup were still accepting assignments to run polls on how both women and men feel about female bosses. And TV, radio, newspapers, magazines report the results of surveys like these without apparent embarrassment. When did you see a respectable poll conducted among whites and blacks on how they feel about having a black boss?

In these media features and reports about women's progress because it's the same old story, you know beforehand they'll balance the central focus of how he feels about women in "his territory" with brave "he's putting up with it" and "he's a good guy who's supportive" copy. In the end the sum slant and effect of the article loads women with working wife guilt & Non-Entitlement. As it dwells on his reactions to what they frequently still term her "invasion" of his former male preserve, it hammers home the message to all working wives and their husbands: Look. Even if he's brave about it, just see how women's equality battles are costing him!

"Her battles for equality," the oft-reiterated media phrase, reinforces women's sense of Non-Entitlement. In the word "battles" used to describe her legislative and individual efforts for equality, we come to the ever-present danger that she may be seen as abrasive or pushy.

Blacks who with justice demonstrate, speak out, demand, march and shout for equality are never labeled abrasive, nor are they warned they should promote their cause nicely, softly, politely. They are seen as right, entitled to say what needs to be said to win that equality—*because the media and other social institutions at least publicly believe in their right to equality.*

By contrast, women are continually warned off about hurrying or asserting their equality rights too energetically lest they appear "abrasive." In other words, the women are being told it's all right for the institutions to lag in enforcing sexual equality. But it's not all right for the women to forcefully call attention to the lag. "Feminist Issues Tend to Turn Off Some Businesses," says a typical newspaper headline discussing the topic.

It is because all the engines of society still appear to believe and, in fact, do deal with women's equality with the invisible assumptions that her real job is in the home; her real job is to support his ego and to look to him as the real family breadwinner that the institutions are quick to see her strivings toward equality as "abrasive," "pushy," "shrill"; as something she is Not Entitled to put forward with vigor.

It is this endless inverse reaction of seeing women's progress in terms of how it meshes with the old sexual inequality one-paycheck rules and as a problem for *him,* that convinces two-paycheck couples they must continue to obey those rules that say:

1. She must carry all or most of the work at home to make up for what her job is "costing" him.

2. She must never point out that she's now sharing the family breadwinner burdens and that it therefore would be fair for him to share the family care. To do so would rob him of his "I am the Family Breadwinner" status and mark him as a failure as a man.

3. She must not attempt to shift any significant portion of home/childcare to her husband, children, paid help. To do so would doom her femininity and mark her as a failure as a woman.

The institutions teach working wives to feel guilty when job-home energy and time pressures force her to deviate from these rules. They reach her Non-Entitlement for others' efforts.

The solution lies in the institutions at last recognizing that one-paycheck family rules simply do not fit the facts and therefore are irrelevant to two-paycheck family life.

The solution lies in media, business, government, society at last looking at two-paycheck life right side up—not in terms of what it's "costing," but as progress toward her inherent right to equality. The solution lies in the institutions at last accepting women's human right to the same full life men have always been "entitled" to and then presenting the working wife/working mother story from that same Entitlement angle.

Research Notes

. . . .

CHAPTER TWO
Overload Impact: How It Crushes Wives, Husbands, & Marriages

Time magazine cover story . . . "Women Face the 90s," 12/4/89.

Working Mother . . . "The Weekend Squeeze: Survey Results on Our Readers' Hectic 2 Days 'Off,' " by Pamela Redmond Satran. *Working Mother*, October 1987.

Professor Cynthia Fuchs Epstein . . . Her expertise in this area is demonstrated by the book noted in the text. This quote is from her contribution to the anthology *Spouse, Parent, Worker* (Yale University Press, 1987).

Also, a *New York Daily News* cover story, 9/24/89, titled "Taking Him to Task," quotes Matti Gershefeld, psychologist and president of Couples Learning Center, Jenkintown PA. "We see it all the time, whether a woman is a high-powered lawyer or a filing clerk, in addition to her paid employment she continues to do the major housework as well. And even when the man does some of it, he is 'helping her out.' That expression explains whose job it really is . . ."

In a *Savvy* magazine Editor's Column, "Close Up," January 1989, Annalyn Swan writes, "No matter what their jobs, wives do it all, or most (don't even ask about working mothers with small children)."

Most Women Who Work at Jobs . . . *The Second Shift: Working Parents and the Revolution at Home*, by Arlie Hochschild with Anne Machung (New York: Viking Press, 1989).

Ann Landers letter to & her reply, 4/23/90. Creators Syndicate Inc. Used with permission.

Today's Woman Is Fed Up . . . *The Record*, Hackensack NJ, Peggy O'Crowley,

Lifestyle Reporter, 5/14/90, writing on the Roper Organization's study of women and time conducted for Prodigy Services. Prodigy study based on ten surveys comprising 20,000 adults, half & half men & women. The article also reported Roper's Virginia Slims study of women, also released in that month.

Nor are the women doing "just" homework . . . from The Conference Board, a staid, respected non-profit business research organization, in their *Information for the Press*, 6/4/85.

"Men Volunteer for the Fun Jobs," . . . *The Wall Street Journal*, 2/12/85.

Also supporting the fact that men do only the "fun" jobs: "2nd Shift Has Low Morale," Knight-Ridder News Service, 3/2/85. The article quotes Beth Anne Shelton, assistant professor of sociology at SUNY-Buffalo, who notes that men aren't really doing that much more. "All this media hype about this big change is really in a sense just that [hype]. There hasn't been that much change. Men tend to do discretionary things that can be put off like painting a room but women do tasks like making dinner, things that must be done every night."

declined swiftly the dirtier . . . noted by Hochschild in her book, op. cit., and in Roper studies, op. cit.

A survey among a cross-section of 1594 Americans 18 and older conducted for *Family Circle* magazine by the National Opinion Research Center at the University of Chicago found that men greatly exaggerate—even in their own minds—how involved they are in household tasks. The survey appeared in *Family Circle*, 10/25/85, under the title "What's Become of the American Family?"

They speak about sleep "the way a hungry person talks about food" . . . "How His Chores Are Different from Her Chores," by Dr. Arlie Hochschild. *Glamour*, July 1989.

Even . . . fortunate wives . . . cleaning help and good childcare . . . *More Equal than Others: Women and Men in Dual Career Marriages* by Rosanna Hertz (Berkeley: University of California Press, 1986). "Still, the presence of children in dual-career marriages is found to lead to asymmetrical division of labor between husbands and wives, with mothers assuming the role of household manager."

His Risk of Losing You . . . *New Woman*, November 1990. "The American Gender Evolution: Getting What We Want," by Carin Rubenstein, Ph.D. Based on a telephone survey of 1,201 adults supervised by the polling firm of Yankelovich Clancy Shulman, conducted during March 1990. Commenting on the results reported in Dr. Rubenstein's survey, Dr. Ethel Klein, author of *Gender Politics*, says that marriage is probably better overall for men than women because wives provide the empathy and psychological support men need and can't get from other men, whereas women are adept at finding intimacy in friendships with other women. Elsewhere the survey revealed that "when he doesn't help [do his share at home], his behavior can steadily erode his wife's feelings of goodwill and tenderness toward him."

Also, 73% of women, 81% of working mothers, said in a national *Woman's Day* survey that they felt their husbands expect too much housework from them . . . based on 60,000 written responses reported by Martha Weinman Lear, 11/11/86.

In a *Family Circle* magazine survey (op. cit.) 46% of wives who have "seriously considered divorce" cite their husbands' inadequate home contributions as a major cause of their marital dissatisfaction.

as a major *New York Times* feature reports . . . "Left at the Altar: Modern Tale of Woe," by Keith Bradsher, 3/7/90. Also mentioned in *Family Circle*, "What's Become of the American Family?" op. cit.

Vernal Brown, who makes auto bumpers . . . used as an example of this new feminine attitude toward marriage in a survey article about women's 1990s attitudes, *Time*, op. cit., p. 82.

the men suffer deeper emotional wounds over . . . Dr. Zick Rubin, Dr. Charles T. Hill, and Dr. Letitia Peplau (at Brandeis University at the time of the research) spent two years in the 1970s analyzing 103 dating couples who had broken off their relationships. Contrary to what most people would expect, the research revealed that the men had been quicker to fall in love, were more anxious to turn acquaintanceship into love, *and were more depressed, lonely, unhappy, and guilty after the breakup* than were the women.

Where the man caused the split, the woman was often able to adjust and say, "OK, let's be friends." But when the couple parted at the woman's suggestion, the rejected man was usually unable to accept a new role. "Impossible," was his reaction to the idea that they remain friends.

My report is based on a phone interview I conducted with Dr. Rubin.

Blind to the interpersonal nuances that are so important . . . Sources are cited at length in research notes for chapters fourteen and fifteen.

As one separated wife explains it . . . *Family Circle* survey, 10/25/85, op. cit.

His Risk of Losing Touch with His Children . . . "The Role of Divorce in Men's Relations with Their Adult Children after Mid-life," by Teresa M. Cooney, University of Delaware, and Peter Uhlenberg, University of North Carolina at Chapel Hill. *Journal of Marriage and the Family*, August 1990.

His Risk of Living within an Unhappy Marriage . . . "domestic chores" ranks second only to money as the principal cause of conflict . . . Roper/Virginia Slims survey, op. cit. above under "Today's Woman Is Fed Up."

"Women Find Men Mean, Oversexed, Lazy" . . . by Gary Langer. The Associated Press report appeared in *The Record*, 4/26/90, account of a Roper Organization poll of 3,000 women.

Less Sex & Less Ardent Sex . . . **Dr. Merle S. Kroop** . . . **Dr. Sharon Na-**

than . . . Ms., April 1987, "The Guilt That Drives Working Mothers Crazy," by Barbara Berg. Its subhead is "What Sex Life?" "[The] . . . overwhelming majority of women interviewed for [Berg's] book *The Crisis of the Working Mother* confided a loss of sexual spontaneity and closeness in their relationships. 'What romance? What sex life?' asked one, while another quipped, 'At this rate, we will never have to use birth control again.' And a third admitted, 'I wish it weren't so, but my love life is a fond memory relegated to my fantasies.' "

Less Money . . . Jeanne Stanton, an assistant professor at Simmons College Graduate School of Management, found that two-thirds of women interviewed were unable to combine full-time career with motherhood, especially after their second child was born. "It becomes untenable. So they reduce the amount of energy they give to the job, either by working part-time or stopping altogether." Quoted in the article "I Don't Want to Work Anymore," by Liz Roman Gallese, author of *Women Like Us* (NAL, 1985) a study of the women of the Harvard Business School class of 1975, published in *Mademoiselle*, 1987.

"Putting a Career on Hold" . . . *The New York Times Magazine*, 12/7/86, by Barbara Basler, a *Times* business reporter.

Los Angeles Times survey . . . "Working Parents Crave More Time Home," by Lynn Smith and Bob Dipchen, Los Angeles Times News Service, 8/12/90. Yet, though men in surveys such as the one above say they want more time for fathering, when given the chance fathers spend surprisingly little time with children—approximately 20 minutes a day—whether or not their wives are employed. "Women's Employment and Family Relations," by Glenna Spitze, Department of Sociology, State University of New York. *Journal of Marriage and the Family*, August 1988, p. 607.

the two-thirds of American couples who are dual wage earners . . . Bureau of Labor Statistics says 65% of American wives under age 65 are working outside of the home; they put it at 27 million couples. The latest government statistics available are from 1987–88. And it is realistic to assume that with the many marriages since then among people in their twenties and the return of many working mothers to the workforce, that the number is still higher now, hence 27–30 million couples.

CHAPTER THREE
Found: The Mysterious, Missing Male-Convincer You Need

The Search So Far . . . How can it be that not age, nor education, occupation, residence, socialization, nor any other seemingly meaningful personal factor in and of itself enables women to solve their Overload?

There have been so many distinguished research efforts funded and carried out during the last few decades seeking the "Male-Convincer" that they cannot possibly be listed. *Herewith some distinguished summary comments:*

"Husbands' and Wives' Satisfaction with the Division of Labor," by Drs. Mary Holland Benin and Joan Agostinelli, Arizona State University, in *Journal of Marriage and the Family*, May 1988: "The variables that fail to affect satisfaction with the division of household labor are important by their absence. Of particular interest is the finding that paid work hours are not important to either spouse in determining satisfaction with division of household labor. [Division of household labor] is not affected by overall work commitments. Likewise, education, age, salary difference between husbands and wives, and status difference between husbands and wives all fail to affect satisfaction with the division of labor."

"Finding Time and Making Do: Distribution of Household Labor in Non-metropolitan Marriages," by Drs. Constance Hardesty and Janet Bokemeier, Department of Sociology, University of Kentucky. *Journal of Marriage and the Family*, February 1989: "Women continue to bear almost sole responsibility for housework and child care, regardless of their employment status . . . women's increased participation in the labor force has not been accompanied by a renegotiation of the traditional division of household labor between husbands and wives. In housework, a clear pattern of gender differentiation persists. Men tend to take responsibility for the mechanical and sporadic tasks such as mowing the lawn and making household repairs when necessary. However, their contribution to the most time-consuming tasks of tedious routine housework and child care is negligible." They then cite various other research sources as the basis for the above.

"Gender, Parenthood, and Work Hours of Physicians," by Grant, Simpson, Xue Lan Rong, and Peters-Golden. *Journal of Marriage and the Family*, February 1990. "Women physicians are still carrying the domestic load just as their less educated sisters are."

"Implications of Men's Provider Role Attitudes for Household Work and Marital Satisfaction": paper by Drs. Maureen Perry-Jenkins, University of Illinois, and Ann C. Crouter, Pennsylvania State University. They report: ". . . Research to date on family work indicates that dual-earner husbands do considerably less family work than their wives." They sum up the various research into the effectiveness of characteristics such as age, education, etc. that we've discussed: "This literature, however, does little to explain *why* [their emphasis] this is the case. A number of research hypotheses have been proposed to explain the inequity in household labor in families including: power relations, relative wages, time availability, and perceived responsibility (Spitze, 1988). Current research suggests that one of the most promising routes to understanding 'why' focuses on people's attitudes, their deeply held notions, about work and family roles."

"the first X-rated dissertation" . . . description coined by Dr. Romberger's adviser, who said it was "the first X-rated dissertation I ever reviewed." From the article "Some Beliefs Women Share About Men," by Darrell Sifford, distributed to U.S. newspapers in the week of 10/6/85.

It all comes together in a study . . . "A Typology of Working Women," by Judith Langer. *Management Review*, 10/82.

A man who owns a personal service business . . . "Business Trends: Delegating Household Responsibilities," *Working Woman*, 11/88, p. 113.

. . . she requests and receives less efforts from teenagers . . . "Adolescents' Chores: The Difference Between Dual and Single-Earner Families," by Mary Holland Benin and Debra A. Edwards, Arizona State University. *Journal of Marriage and the Family*, May 1990.

shouts a *Working Mother* coverline . . . prominently displayed on the cover above the magazine title, July 1990.

This Is the Two-Part Male-Convincer . . . Other corroborative research: "Negotiating Household Rules and Responsibilities: Resistance, Conflict and Change," research paper presented by sociologist Dr. Myra Marx Feree, University of Connecticut, to the conference "Gender Roles Through the Life Course," Ball State University, October 1988, and as a "Distinguished Lecture" at the Annual Conference of the National Council on Family Relations, Philadelphia, November 1988. Also by Dr. Feree is "Gender, Conflict and Change: Family Roles in Biographical Perspective," a research paper delivered at the conference "Statuspassagen and soziale Risiken im Lebensverlauf," University of Bremen, October 1989. Very similar to the first paper, with small variations.

Though Dr. Feree definitely makes the connection between a change in a working wife's expectations and her feelings of Entitlement and then her actively attempting to renegotiate household labor roles with her husband, Dr. Feree believes that income equality (or near equality) may be necessary to give the wife the leverage to renegotiate; and she also says she is open to and looking for other leverage. She says in her papers that we need to know how both spouses conceptualize provider and homemaker role responsibilities in the family, as well as examine the entitlements implicit in certain roles. Then we will be able to learn "under what circumstances paid jobs can create the conditions that empower women to attempt to change the household division of labor, and sometimes to succeed in this attempt."

This book's thesis diverges completely. Based on my years of research among working wives wherein I've observed, interviewed, and analyzed the attitudes and communication styles of team-couples I find that working wives already are in possession of all the power they need to renegotiate household labor division with their husbands—and I find that there are two reasons why women do not use that power. The first is one-paycheck guilt heaped on two-paycheck wives (discussed in this chapter, and in chapter four and the Backgrounder chapter) that robs women of their sense of Entitlement. The second is women's legitimate fears and anxieties about giving up house-power (discussed throughout Part Four) that are preventing working wives from acting. This book therefore is devoted to exposing and negating those two barriers which prevent working wives from recognizing and using the power they already have to effectively seek and arrange with their husbands a new, fairer division of family labor.

Elsewhere quantities of family and general communication research have found . . . See entire text and notes of chapter thirteen.

Dr. Myra Marx Feree . . . interviewed 103 employed married mothers . . . op. cit.

CHAPTER FOUR
The Three Real Reasons Most Husbands Scorn Housework

Are You Running Your Life This Way? . . . *New York Daily News* poll, 9/4/ 89, found "in many masculine minds the traditional views of what is 'men's' and 'women's' work not only survive, but seemingly flourish."

The New York Times front-page story, "Women: Out of the House But Not Out of the Kitchen," 2/24/88. ". . . *Times* survey . . . shows that the idea of equality at home is an illlusion . . ."

"Why Don't Dads Do More?" by Carin Rubenstein, Ph.D., *Working Mother*, June 1990. The article's sub-headline: "American men are changing, but many still don't do their fair share. Want to hear their excuses?" ". . . Our poll shows that Americans certainly believe fathers should help out with children . . . Most recent research shows that the amount of time fathers spend with their children has not changed much over the past 20 years. Results of a recent national study, for instance, reveal that fathers spend only about two and a half hours a week with their young children, taking on less than one-third of the childcare. This is true even in families in which the mother has a full-time job.

". . . What reasons do men give for not spending more time with their children? . . . For men the main reason [they give] is simple: they 'have to work too hard making a living.' But the women surveyed believe that the reason is more personal, and one that men can control: They 'just don't want to be involved.' "

But here for clarity are two quick examples . . . A good illlustration is a full-page American automobile company ad in *Self* magazine, January 1990, "How to Get Ahead of Time, Part of a Series on Time Management Brought to You by Ford Division," is directed only at women, as indicated by the first sentence, which reads: "Take a look at yourself. If you're like most women, anxious to achieve, trying to make the most of every minute, you're facing one of the greatest shortages today—time . . .

"In the coming months, *Self,* in conjunction with Ford Division, Ford Motor Company, will take a look at the dilemmas facing women right now and offer solutions for getting ahead of time . . . Women who have a fulfilling job, a happy home life and manage to live relatively stress-free are looked at as the exception now rather than the rule . . ."

And that is why the family research . . . see notes for chapters two & three.

Monthly Labor Report . . . published by U.S. Department of Labor, February 1989. "Families of working wives spending more on services, nondurables." Subtitle: "When a wife becomes a second earner, families spend more on work-related and time-saving items, such as child care and food away from home." Eva Jacobs, Stephanie Shipp, and Gregory Brown. Ms. Jacobs is Chief of the Division of Consumer Expenditure Surveys, Bureau of Labor Statistics; Stephanie Shipp is chief of the Branch of Information and Analysis in the Division. Gregory Brown is an economist formerly with the Division.

In a chart on page 17 of the article they list the services *the working wives are buying* such as "Food away from home"; "child care." The chart makes it clear that the women and their families are not paying for anything remotely connected with domestic services.

As one working wife vividly sums it up . . . "Men Trouble," by Nina Keilin. *Ladies' Home Journal,* August 1990.

by continuing to use breadwinning to measure your husband's masculinity . . . "How Dual-Income Couples Cope," by Julie Connelly. *Fortune,* 9/24/90. "Men's identities as *the* [author's emphasis] family provider have become threatened by wives who are providers too . . ." This concept & example discussed in detail in text of Backgrounder chapter immediately before Research Notes.

Though working wives weighed down . . . the average one-third of the family's income that women contribute is big. . . . The U.S. Government's high-visibility *Monthly Labor Review* reports in February 1990 in an article titled, "Compensation trends into the 21st century," by George L. Stelluto and Deborah P. Klein, using the latest available government labor statistics: "In 1988, in traditional married-couple families where the husband worked but the wife was not a labor force participant, median weekly family earnings were $489; in families where both the husband and wife worked, earnings average $824. On average, working wives contribute about 30 percent of family income. This ranges from 13 percent for wives who work only at part-time or part-year jobs to 40 percent for those who work year round, full time."

This has been a pattern for some time. A 1981 government report in the *Monthly Labor Review* of nine years before, February 1981, "Husbands and wives: As earners: an analysis of family data," by Howard Hayghe, used 1978 government data as the latest data then available. Averaging out all working wives in 1978, including the part-time and part-year, revealed the wife was producing an impressive 26% of family income back then. Full-time working wives of 1978 contributed on average 37% of the family income (or more than a third).

So nationwide, couples create family fictions with each other . . . "The Provider Role: Its Meaning and Measurement," by Dr. Jane C. Hood. *Journal of Marriage and the Family*, May 1986. Also *The Second Shift*, op. cit.

The *It's Costing Him* Farce & You . . . *Backlash, The Undeclared War Against American Women*, by Susan Faludi (New York: Crown, 1991), documents this situation. *Kirkus Review* says this book deals with this working woman myth and many others wherein through "deliberate action or passive collusion, the government, media, and popular culture have ensured [the myth's] overpowering influence on the public."

CHAPTER FIVE
10 Big Ways Your Job Makes Your Husband's Life Easier, Better, Happier

Wives now provide . . . U.S. Census Bureau data and *Monthly Labor Review* report, op. cit., chapter four.

As for housing . . . American Association of Home Builders, phone interview with their Washington, D.C., national headquarters. Jay Shackford, VP of Public Affairs, 10/26/86.

The results of the Chicago Title & Trust Company survey are from "Higher Home Prices Force Buyers to Tap Two Incomes," by Kirstin Downey. Washington Post News Service, 2/18/90.

president of the largest personnel society . . . Ronald C. Pilenzo, president, retired in the fall of 1990 after approximately eleven years as president. Quotes are from a telephone interview conducted November 1986.

Research by a Fordham University . . . Professor Marta Mooney at Fordham University . . . *The Wall Street Journal*, 5/19/81, p. 1.

Your Family Purchasing Power . . . economist Eliot Janeway . . . "Reviving the Economy, If Women Can't Do It, No One Can." *Working Woman*, 1977.

Your Income Builds Your Husband's health . . . by Dr. Sheldon Cohen, professor of psychology, reported in *The New York Times*, 9/12/89. *Careers*, "More Stress Found in the Workplace," by Elizabeth M. Fowler.

More than . . . 70% of the time . . . Conference Board press release, October 1984.

The income she brings in also permits him to follow new knowledge of what constitutes a healthy diet . . . with the two incomes he can afford tasty, quick cooking menus of white meat poultry, veal, out-of-season fruits and vegetables. Lest we forget, it is the very poor in America and abroad who are often significantly *over*weight as they're forced to choose what is cheap. Everywhere, "cheap" usually means sugar, starch, grease. *The Wall Street Journal*, 12/18/90, "Amid Ghetto Hunger Many More Suffer Eating Wrong Foods: High-Fat, Salty, Sugary Fare Exerts a Powerful Draw for Poor and Uneducated."

Your Income Eliminates His Unemployment Desperation . . . eased for your husband if you have a job: Today women have the ability to earn not an old-fashioned woman's pittance, but real money in what used to be "men's" professional, executive, white-collar, sales, technical and high paying blue-collar jobs. For example, 25–53% of students in the major professions are now women, according to the research work of economist John B. Parrish of the University of Illinois, reported in *Business Week*, 2/15/85.

When a man was the only family breadwinner . . ." from a telephone interview with John Crystal in 1986.

Your Paycheck Frees Him to Follow . . . annually at least 10 million Americans . . . *American Demographics*, November 1991, "Doing the Career Changing Shuffle," by Paula Mergenbagen.

columnist Barbara Roessner . . . *The Hartford Courant*, "Changing Life's Goals in the '90s," 4/1/90.

James E. Challenger, president of Challenger, Gray & Christmas, Inc., 150 South Wacker Drive, Chicago, IL., in press release 8/7/89, "Working Spouses May Increase Lure of Entrepreneurship."

As a *New York Times* critic points out . . . "Year of the (Sort of Strange) Family," by Caryl Rivers: "On the plus side of this family TV sitcom trend, we see men dealing with children and their problems; fatherhood comes out ahead of careerism."

"Family Time Is More Important . . ." Robert Half International press release headline, 6/28/89.

As *Life, Texas Monthly* . . . *Reader's Guide to Periodical Literature*.

Good Morning, Merry Sunshine . . . Publishing history obtained in phone interview with Jessica B. Miller, Publicity Department, Viking Penguin Inc. Hardcover version of book is published by Atheneum, paperback by Penguin.

A Gallup Poll . . . reported in *USA Today,* 11/7/84.

Your Income Buys Him Freedom . . . **Most working wives agree** . . . overview of the situation from the U.S. Department of Labor, op. cit., chapter four.

more than four billion dollars annually . . . data from phone interview with Ron Hall 12/2/90.

Ms. Sandy Marting, Public Relations Director for the Professional Lawn Care Association of America, with headquarters in Marietta, Georgia, estimates from the data that there are between 25,000–30,000 of these lawn care services now. However, she cautions that *there really are many more* than that number indicates because huge companies like Chemlawn, which has hundreds of local branches, are listed as *one* company. She explains, "It's as if you asked how many retail grocery companies there are in the United States, and A&P was listed as one company."

CHAPTER SIX
Your Man Is a Success! Even If Your Family Needs Your Paycheck Too

Three women's lives . . . Eventhorpes, Kosnicks, Jensenns . . . All families are composites.

Many working wives say . . . Major psychological research reveals that *both wives & husbands are afraid to admit out loud* that Dad needs Mom's paycheck to pay for middle-class family bills because the culture says his manhood is built on being *the* breadwinner. Consequently, couples work out rationalizations of how her money is for extras even when it's plainly paying for necessities and they believe he's a failure as a man if they admit it.

From a review of more than 200 serious research papers, reports, books: "Gender in Families: Women and Men in Marriage, Work, and Parenthood," by Drs. Linda Thompson, University of Wisconsin-Madison, and Alexis J. Walker, Oregon State University. *Journal of Marriage and the Family,* November 1989. ". . . Partners (wives & husbands) collude to sustain belief that men are primary providers but parenting is shared . . ." Discussion of and many details about this study in text of chapter eleven.

Jobs that pay enough to support a family are disappearing . . . "The Declining Middle," by Bob Kuttner. *The Atlantic Monthly,* July 1983.

"Making a Living Is Now a Family Enterprise," by Louis Uchitelle. Only story and headline on front page of *The New York Times* Sunday supplement "Careers," 10/11/87. Article lead says flatly that "Pursuing a livelihood in America is increasingly a family enterprise, where success is no longer measured by the earning power of a single job . . . Family income, rather than the particular achievement of a husband or wife, then, is becoming the key to making a living and to job success."

Fortune 500 industrial companies . . . "Tomorrow's Jobs: Plentiful, But . . . ," by Louis S. Richman. *Fortune,* 4/11/88. Between 5/90–5/91 another two million jobs vanished. *Business Week* 5/6/91.

U.S. Labor Department data shows . . . *The New York Times,* 9/26/88.

And though both husband and wife work . . . "What It Takes to Get Along?" by William O'Hare. May 1990.

flat as pancakes . . . *The Wall Street Journal,* "When Firms Cut Out Middle Managers," by Carol Hymowitz. Under their "Management" section banner, 4/5/90.

Two million middle-management positions . . . *Business Week* cover story "Downward Mobility," 3/23/92.

As the conservative *New York Times* . . . 6/19/88.

Despite their problems . . . many other American working wives (75– 85%) . . . May 1989 *Working Mother* poll of their readers; Gallup poll for *Newsweek,* March 1986.

Family research . . . This information comes from many sources. For example, Dr. Harold Voth, chief of staff at Colmery O'Neal Medical Center, Topeka, KS, is quoted in *Boardroom Reports* 7/1/5, saying, "Most women still think it's the man's job to support the family . . . Many resent it when their salary checks are needed for basics such as paying the rent."

Gregg's pay cuts and benefit losses . . . a new, near-universal . . . "A Cutback Looms in Health Insurance . . . Employers are getting the green light to trim reimbursements for working couples with separate plans . . ." *The New York Times,* 10/4/87.

Also, "As Jobs Increase, So Does Insecurity," by Louis Uchitelle. Lead article in *The New York Times* Sunday "Careers" section, 5/1/88. "Cutbacks in pension plans and health insurance are also making jobholders uneasy. Employees are increasingly being required to pay part of the premium for their health insurance policies said . . . a Bureau of Labor Statistics economist who gathers data on corporate benefit plans."

Gregg's employment history is a composite of cases cited in *The New York Times,* "Price of Freedom and Budget Cuts: Retraining on L.I.," by Eric Schmitt, 4/20/90.

American Demographics . . . September 1988, Editor's Note by Martha Farnsworth Riche, "Back to the 50s." "In the 1950s, the U.S. economy dominated the world, and American workers had extraordinary buying power. For the first and probably *the only time in history, a man with less than average education could afford a house, two cars in the garage, three or four kids, and a non-working wife.* But the rest of the world has caught up. *It now takes*

two earners to attain the family lifestyle Americans have come to take for granted.''
[Emphasis added]

Since the economy requires Marie . . . "Women's Income Makes Ends Meet,"
by John E. Yang. *The Washington Post,* 6/12/90.

"Why Good Economic Times Don't Feel So Good: Prosperity Without Security," by Kathleen Lynn. *The Record,* Hackensack, NJ, 2/8/87. "Many
young mothers do not have the choice of being stay-at-home moms, like
their own mothers in the 1950s. Buying a house and supporting a family
on one income is impossible for many couples."

Business Week **magazine researches** . . . "Breadwinners Are Still Running to
Stay in Place," 6/23/86.

"U.S. Living Standards Are Slipping" . . . *The Wall Street Journal,* 6/27/91; lead
front-page story by Alfred L. Malabre, Jr. Subhead says: "Taking account
of inflation and taxes, people find they have less to spend."

Median weekly family . . . "Not Getting Ahead? Better Get Used to It," by
Louis Uchitelle. *The New York Times,* lead story from "News of the Week
in Review," 12/16/90.

Only the top 20% . . . *ibid.*

Sixty percent of American husbands . . . "Longer hours, not pay rises, boost
most families' income." *The Wall Street Journal,* 1/21/92.

". . . Lowest Income Group Grew," by Jason Deparle. *The New York Times,*
5/12/92, "Census Bureau Report released today . . ." says that in 1972 12.1
percent of all full-time employees earned below "equivalent of $12,195
which was then $6,905. By 1990 that figure had risen to 18 percent." The
likelihood of earning that low sum or less is "shared by a broad range of
Americans: men and women, whites and minority members . . . with and
without a high school education . . . also occurred among people with a
year or more of college."

"The Incredible Shrinking Middle Class," by Greg J. Duncan, Timothy M.
Smeeding, and Willard Rogers. *American Demographics,* May 1992. "In the
1980s, the rich got richer, the poor got poorer, and the middle class got
smaller . . ."

Washington Post News Service, 6/21/92: "After long and bumpy ride, Greyhound making strides," by Martha M. Hamilton. Industry analyst Jan Loeb
of Legg Mason Inc. in Baltimore predicts bright future for Greyhound
because of "the growing number of families earning less than $25,000 a
year . . ."

Lately economists have noticed . . . "unequal pay" . . . "Unequal Pay Widespread in U.S.," by Louis Uchitelle. *New York Times,* 7/14/91. Article
quotes Harvard economist Richard Freeman to illustrate serious implications of "unequal pay": ". . . The wage spread means [many people] no

longer make it into the middle class. And they are working just as hard as people did 30 years ago."

when your family went to a fast food place like McDonald's . . . "Let's Do Lunch," by Thomas Exter. *American Demographics*, April 1990. For example, besides dinner, even brown-bagging lunch is now on the wane. "The typical wage earner spends $6.79 a week on lunches eaten away from home . . . the average household spends $473 a year on lunches eaten away from home but in the local area. Households [like the Jensenns] with annual incomes of $50,000 or more spend an average of $970.00 a year on lunch."

"Feeding Frenzy," by Thomas Exter. *American Demographics*, January 1990: "Couples with children under age 6 spend 36% of their food budget on restaurant meals; couples with children 18 or older spend 43% of food purchases on restaurants; couples with no children spend 45% of food purchases on restaurant meals."

In 1954 we spent . . . U.S. census figures from Census of Retail Trade, supplied by Jennifer Nelson, Survey Statistician, and National Restaurant Association statistics supplied by Diane Byler, Information Specialist.

Today giant hotel chains target . . . For example, an expensive full-page ad in *The New York Times*, 4/27/90, touted "Marriott's Two for Breakfast Weekend," which includes a complete breakfast for two. And, if you bring the kids, their breakfast is only $1.95.

Yet an article on the electronics industry . . . "Electronics: It's Not Home Without It." *The New York Times* "Home" section, 3/29/90.

It now takes two earners to attain the family lifestyle . . . "Back to the 50s," *American Demographics*, September 1988.

CHAPTER SEVEN
Why Wanting a Career Is So UNselfish—
Even If Your Family Can Live Well on His Income!

PROBLEM: "The accusation of selfishness" . . . "Reflections on Guilt, Women and Gender," by Grace K. Baruch. 1988 Working Paper #176, published by Wellesley College Center for Research on Women.

DEFINITION OF NEW TRADITIONALIST WOMAN . . . *The Wall Street Journal* reports in a column on "Advertising," "Grappling with Women's Evolving Roles," by Kathleen Deveny, fall 1990: "Good Housekeeping thought it had found the key to the woman of the 1990s with its well known [sic] 'new traditionalist' campaign . . . All the women in the first three ads—photographs of women and their children accompanied by a text exalting the traditional values of home and family—stayed home full-time. One had never worked.

"The striking black and white visuals got the attention of the [advertising] trade but the message drew the ire of women nationwide who resented the implication that professional success was no longer an appropriate goal."

Newsweek poll by The Gallup Organization, Inc., reported in *Newsweek*, March 1986, with coverline: "America's Mothers Making It Work: How Women Balance the Demands of Jobs and Children." Cover picture shows baby playing in an open briefcase.

Working Mother survey reported in *The Wall Street Journal*, 4/25/89, published in *Working Mother*, May 1989.

Spouse, Parent, Worker: On Gender and Multiple Roles, edited by Faye J. Crosby (New Haven: Yale University Press, 1987), p. 147.

"The best mental and physical health occurred when it was complemented by other roles. In general, the triple role configuration of employment, marriage, and parenthood appeared to be the most consistently and positively related to health and well-being, especially for women."

On p. 127: "Mental health has come to be defined as including happiness, life satisfaction, and self-esteem." . . . "Women who are both employed and married are the healthiest, and those who have children are just as healthy as those who don't . . . though multiple roles can cause stress, the stress of inactivity may be more damaging to health than the stress of many activities.

"While jobs bring certain pressures, they also bring benefits; the use of one's skills and education, social contacts, access to ideas, and information, and of course, income . . . they stretch your scope."

On p. 152: "Not working for pay outside the home appears to be stressful for both women and men . . . In this culture, working is not only linked to a person's identity and primary role (breadwinner) but lack of employment appears to have serious negative implications for all other aspects of life."

The proof in favor of family plus career . . . Patricia A. McBroom and Maria A. Guarnaschelli, *The Third Sex* (New York: William Morrow & Co., Inc., 1986).

when a woman wants a paid job . . . "Happiness in Single and Dual-earner Families: The Effects of Marital Happiness, Job Satisfaction, and Life Cycle," by Mary Holland Benin and Barbara Cable Nienstedt. *Journal of Marriage and the Family*, November 1985.

Dr. Barnett explains, "There are two ways to look . . ." Rosalind Barnett and the late Grace Baruch, both psychologists, studied 238 white women—never married, married with and without children, divorced, working and nonworking—in the Boston area. The results were reported as "Examining Women's Work and Family Roles: Expanding the Stress Research Paradigm." Wellesley College Center for Research on Women, fall 1989.

Additional research by experts at the National Center for Health Statistics . . . Lois M. Verbrugge, Ph.D., research scientist at University of Michigan, & Jennifer M. Madans of the National Center for Health Statistics, quoted in *Self*, May 1985.

Also, from the National Institutes of Health and Ohio State Medical Center . . . "The Mind/Body Link," by S. P. Policoff. *Ladies' Home Journal*, October 1990. "Now we know what tribal healers have always known— that there is a unity between brain and body," says Novera H. Spector, Ph.D., a neurophysiologist with the National Institutes of Health in Bethesda, Maryland.

. . . you struggle to teach practical and moral life codes . . . "Mother's Employment and Parent-Youth Similarity," by Alan C. Acock, Virginia Polytechnic Institute and State University; Deborah Barker, Southern Methodist University; and Vern L. Bengtson, University of Southern California. *Journal of Marriage and the Family*, May 1982.

Children's school performance too seems to benefit . . . Reported in *Woman's Day*, 2/10/87, p. 21. Ellen Greenberger study of 283 middle-class families reported in "Women at Work," *Graduating Engineer*, January 1990.

As children mature and leave home . . . *University of Michigan News*, 1982.

Also aiding working women as they move into the empty nest stage, says Dr. David Gutmann, psychologist at Northwestern University, is the fact that women seem to become more assertive as they move toward and into midlife (similar to the views of Jung). Unfortunately, some women have been conditioned to fear and resist their new drive and abilities . . . think they're "wrong" and try to suppress them. This can lead to feelings of depression . . . but if these attributes are used, as in employment, women find their developing competence and ambition often leads to their lives growing more interesting and satisfying.

Sexually, because of your job . . . "Sex and the Working Mother . . . The surprising—and sensational—results of our ground-breaking survey," by Carin Rubenstein, Ph.D. *Working Mother*, May 1990.

Occupation Housewife . . . The next to last line in the poem, "She diets. And with Contract she delays . . ." refers to days whiled away playing the card game Contract Bridge.

CHAPTER NINE
1990s' Disappearing Macho Man:
16 Big Reasons Why He's Ready to Share the Housework

60% of fathers 35 years and younger . . . Study cited in *The Wall Street Journal*, 11/1/88.

Many 35-and-older fathers . . . An "Invisible Daddy Track" . . . "Moving Beyond the Mommy Track," by Douglas T. Hall. *Personnel,* December 1989.

what *The New York Times* calls the "myth" . . . 88% of the men . . . "Fleeing the Office and Its Distractions" by Deirdre Fanning, 8/12/90.

Knowledge-banks like *Fortune* and . . . *"Layoff Victims Tell of Trials and Fulfillment,"* by Amanda Bennett. *The Wall Street Journal,* 9/11/90.

are not transitory blips . . . persist throughout the 1990s . . . "A White Collar Guide to Job Security," by Amanda Bennett. *The Wall Street Journal,* 9/11/90.

How His Working at Home Can Make Him More Cooperative . . . There are 38 million homeworkers, male and female, in the U.S. The number has been growing at about 13% a year since 1985, *American Demographics* Editor's Note, November 1991. "Most are part of a dual-income household . . . and forecast is for substantial increase throughout the decade." "The Homing of America," by Valerie Free. *Marketing Insights,* Spring Issue, 1990.

says Harris L. Sussman . . . "Roundtable on Jobs in the 90's," *The New York Times,* 4/16/90.

says Dr. Rosabeth Moss Kanter . . . Ibid.

Also, in *Marketing Insights,* spring 1990, "Recession Psychology," by John P. Shields, Jr. "However, the most devastating blow has come from the flattening of the corporate pyramid . . . suddenly thrust into economic limbo."

Tomorrow's Bosses . . . "Spousal Employment Assistance Needed," *Personnel Journal,* March 1989. Employee Relocation Council, Washington, D.C.

Male Baby Boomers . . . "Baby Boomers Are Bringing Back the Nuclear Family," *Business Week,* 2/2/87. Also, *Marketing Insights,* "The Homing of America," op. cit.

The Olsten Corporation (this is Olsten Temporaries) press release June 22, 1992, "Employee Attitudes Shift Toward More Family/Leisure Time." Release states that according to a new Olsten Corporation survey, "Employees are less willing than five years ago to sacrifice family or leisure time for more opportunity on the job . . . Unpaid leaves of absence are now commonplace at most companies, and . . . four out of ten companies (41 percent) will grant paternity leave time (paid and unpaid) . . ."

The Wall Street Journal, 6/23/92, "Work & Family," by Sue Shellenbarger, reports a Federal Express policy that forbids middle managers to turn down employee requests for family leave. Only executives at vice president or above can do so. They explain that middle managers may be less likely to grant the leave whereas those at upper level may be more likely to see the value of the leave to Federal Express. They report, "A Federal Express executive says, employees who ask for family leave often 'perceive the situation to be a crisis. If that means they have to quit (to get time off), they'll quit.' "

Close-to-the-Hearth College Students . . . "In Focus," by Norma R. Fritz; from surveys conducted by Emhart, Incorporated, with Foundation for Student Communication and Research Strategies Corporation of Princeton, NJ.

Fatherhood Today: Men's Changing Role in the Family, edited by Phyllis Bronstein and Carolyn Pape Cowan (New York: John Wiley & Sons, 1988).

Fortune, 2/16/87 cover picture, main coverline story: "The No. 1 cause of Executive Guilt: Who's Taking Care of the Children—and How Will They Turn Out?" The article quotes a "recent Stanford University study . . . husbands of dual-MBA couples have more anxiety about the children than their wives do."

His New Desire for Emotional Closeness . . . *The Wall Street Journal*, 3/31/92. "Men Claim Desire to Become Less Macho." According to an "in-depth survey of 1,000 men conducted by the Roper Organization for *Playboy* magazine, nearly five times as many would rather be seen as 'sensitive and caring' than as 'rugged and masculine.' . . . 'The 1990s will clearly be a time of transition for American men,' says Roper's Thomas Miller."

Family Circle, "What's Become of the American Family?" op. cit.

Changed Male Definition of Success . . . **63% of 90s men** . . . *Men's Life* survey reported *USA Today*, 9/4/90, "Before sex, career, fame or fortune."

Also, *Glamour*, May 1989: "Men: What Do They Expect from Marriage?" by Nicholas Dawidoff. "More and more men expect to shape their careers around their family, as opposed to the more customary process, whereby the family shapes itself around Daddy's work . . ."

"Careers Start Giving in to Family Needs," by Cathy Trost and Carol Hymowitz. *The Wall Street Journal*, 8/19/90.

"New Trend in Business: Husbands Following Wives to New Jobs." Press release of executive search company Goodrich & Sherwood NYC, 11/13/89.

Women accounted for 20% of transfers in 1989, according to the Employee Relocation Council, in *The Wall Street Journal*, 9/18/90.

Avoiding Housework No Longer Part of "Masculinity" . . . "Happy Father's Day: Now help out around the house, please," reporting a *Working Mother* poll done at Walt Disney's Epcot Center: "America's view of a father's role . . . has shifted dramatically, says social psychologist Carin Rubenstein, on poll of 2,962 adults and children . . ." Appeared in *Working Mother*, June 1990.

Seeing Each Other Eye-to-Eye . . . *American Demographics*, March 1987. Also, "No More Mrs. Degree," reporting a study sponsored by *Cosmopolitan* titled "The Changing Life Course of American Women," in *American Demographics*, January 1990.

M magazine, May 1992, "Fathering of the Nest," by Aaron Latham. "As women have redefined the workplace, men are redefining the home and trying to find their place there."

Househusband: From Scorn to Cheers . . . says Robert Coulombe . . . "The Daddy Track," by Aimee Lee Ball. *New York* magazine, 10/12/89.

At Last, Parental Job Leave Is Expected . . . "Paid Parental Leave gains a foothold and may spread," *The Wall Street Journal*, 9/4/90. "U.S. Cedes Lead to States on Family Leave Politics," *The New York Times*, 9/21/91.

Women's 1990s Sex Ratio Advantage . . . "Coming Soon: More Men Than Women," U.S. government demographic data, from the Census Bureau, reported in *The New York Times*, June 1988.

"Economic Power, and Women's Roles: A Theoretical Extension and Empirical Test," by Scott J. South. *Journal of Marriage and the Family*, February 1988.

Men's Attitude & Behavior Change Constantly . . . *Men's Changing Roles in the Family*, edited by Lewis & Sussman (New York & London: The Haworth Press Inc., 1986).

CHAPTER TEN
How & Why Working Wives Prevent
Husbands from Doing More at Home

"The Adventure of the Blue Carbuncle," from *Adventures of Sherlock Holmes*, by Arthur Conan Doyle.

As late as the 1970s, house-power was women's only source of prestige . . . A career added nothing to your social status. In fact, it diminished it . . . There are innumerable sources that can testify to the fact that until the 1980s men were ashamed to have their wives work because it was seen by others as proof that the man could not support his family. Millions of these sources are alive and well and living in the United States. They are all the people who were adults in the 1970s and before and who remember.

One of the numerous printed sources is found in *The Good Life: The Meaning of Success for the American Middle Class*, by Loren Baritz (hardcover, Alfred A. Knopf, Inc., 1989, trade paperback, Perennial Library, 1990), p. 115: "Opinion polls revealed that three-quarters of the women and 80% of the men did not approve of employment for a married woman whose husband was capable of supporting her, for fear that she would displace a man and because, of course, her place was in the home . . ."

Pp. 164–165 "The middle-class separation of life into distinct spheres—public and private—continued and deepened with the man in charge of the public,

if he had a job, and the woman reigning over the home, even if she had
a job."

Pp. 217 ". . . Fearful of slipping, believed that his manhood would be com-
promised if he had to 'send his wife to work' because he could not 'provide
for the family' on his own."

**it's reasonable that women feel ambivalent and sometimes angry when
men . . .** Many psychologists, journalists, family experts have commented
on women's reluctance to let go of their power in the home. These com-
mentators have confirmed women's desire to insist on their own methods
and standards for all housework/childcare—but except for a bland comment
that women "should let go" *have not explained the roots* of women's attitudes
nor offered plans that would make it comfortable and practical for women
to "let go."

Some of the diverse sources that have commented on women's disinclination
to "let go" include:

Ellen Goodman, 6/19/88, "A Day for New Fathers . . . and New Mothers
Too": "It turns out that sharing the work of raising children also means
sharing the power over children's lives. Sharing the power—even the kind
you didn't fully recognize—is harder than expected. It doesn't sound like
a dramatic struggle. But it can come with a sudden, internal wrench."

The New York Times, 4/23/late 80s, "De Gustibus" column, "Anyone Who
Can Read Can Cook, Right? Five Men Find Out," by Marian Burros. "In
an interview with a psychologist a few years ago about women's roles [the
psychologist] suggested that men still don't do their share of the housework
because many women don't feel they will do it as well and won't give up
their roles."

"When My Husband Became Mr. Mom," by Prudence Kay Poppink as told
to Gretchen P. Alday. *Woman's Day,* 5/9/89. "In fact, I found it extremely
difficult to let go of those small details of mothering for which I'd automatically taken responsibility—and enjoyed! One day, when Bill called
me at work and mentioned that he'd bought new shoes for the girls, I burst
into tears. That was always *my* job!"

Parenting Together: Men and Women Sharing the Care of Their Children, by
psychologist Diane Ehrensaft, discussed by Jill Goetz in *Psychology Today,*
September 1987. She references the book as saying, "Some women feel
jealous when their husbands fall head-over-heels in love with their kids,
while others are surprised to discover they're reluctant to give up the jobs
of mothering to their husbands."

"Home is where the heart is for house-husband," by Mark Finston. *The Sunday
Star-Ledger,* Newark NJ, 3/24/85. "He [the house-husband] has suspected
that one reason men aren't interested in nurturing is that women don't

want them to be. It's a power struggle. She who can accomplish the task better than anyone is in control."

"Coming Clean About Our Housework," by Dan Sperling. USA Today, 10/4/84. Catherine Berheid, head of the sociology department at Skidmore College, Saratoga Springs NY, recently completed a 10-year study on housework among married couples. Most women, she says, have been raised to think of housework as their domain and responsibility, and tend to be evaluated by society on how clean they keep their houses. "We're finding that some women are reluctant to give men, as they see it, power over what has traditionally been the woman's sphere. They're afraid of losing what little has been their territory.

". . . Then too, some women regard the male's help as a mixed blessing . . . Many women feel that it's almost as hard—or even harder—for them if their husbands help them than if they do it all by themselves. And that's because most husbands aren't as efficient and effective at housecleaning because they aren't as experienced at it."

Anne Fischer, director of parenting at Booth Maternity Center, Philadelphia, in "Working Solutions for Working Parents," by Phyllis K. Bonfield, Management World, 2/86, is quoted as saying, "Women are possessive of parenting and want things done their way. Also women have traditionally been responsible for the private domain called 'home and family,' and challenging this domain creates a difficult social issue."

"The 4 Percent Solution: Confessions of a Husband Who Does His Fair Share of Housework," by Anthony Brandt. Savvy Woman, April 1989. "But whose house is it? Where is it written that her [his emphasis] standards of cleanliness must prevail?"

"Dust bunnies, disappearing dinners, and wage hikes for women: welcome to the '90s," by Tim Appelo. Savvy Woman, January 1989. "Ironically, as men show an increased interest in domestic affairs they are horning in on a woman's historic power in the home. She may not have been the boss outside of the house, but she got to call the shots inside."

CHAPTER ELEVEN
Sharing vs. Helping: What's in It for You & Your Family?

In an awe-inspiring project . . . "Gender in Families: Women and Men in Marriage, Work, and Parenthood," by Linda Thompson, University of Wisconsin-Madison, and Alexis J. Walker, Oregon State University. *Journal of Marriage and the Family*, November 1989. From the above source: "Researchers have devoted a lot of attention to the drop in marital satisfaction, especially among wives, when partners become parents." (Staines and Libby 1986) "Mothers end up doing most of the child care and house-work regardless of what pattern was established or expected before children arrived." (Cowan et al. 1985; LaRossa and LaRossa 1981; Ruble, Fleming, Hackel, and Stangor 1988) "The more the division of labor changes toward the traditional with the birth of the first child, the greater the plunge in marital happiness, especially among nontraditional wives." (Belsky, Lang, and Huston 1986) "Cowan and her colleagues (1985) found that conflict increases after children arrive, *and disagreement over who does what domestic work is at the top of the list.* [My emphasis.] Many mothers experience the husbands' new devotion to providing as pulling away from home at a time when they are needed most and promised they would be around." (Cowan et al. 1985) "Partners *seem to collaborate to sustain the belief that fathers are intimately involved with their children and 'fairly' sharing child care when mothers actually are doing the daily parenting* [emphasis added]." (Backett, 1987; LaRossa and LaRossa 1981) . . . "Backett (1987) found that couples sustain belief in father involvement in the face of contradictory evidence in three ways . . ."

In the section Conclusion and Recommendations, "Gender specialization in families persists across the domains of marriage, work, and parenthood. Everyday and ultimate responsibility for marriage, housework, and parent-hood usually remains with women . . . *although partners collude to sustain belief that men are primary providers but parenting is shared.*

Partners tend to view men's minimal help with raising children as substantial, and women's substantial help with provision as minimal. A growing number of women are bothered by this lopsided arrangement, but for the most part, women and men do not consider family life unfair." [Emphases added.]

Other research on the drop in happiness with the birth of children:

Joe F. Pittman and Sally A. Lloyd, University of Utah. "Quality of Family Life, Social Support, and Stress," *Journal of Marriage and the Family*, February, 1988: "Abbott and Brody (1985) have found that couples with children in the home report lower marital satisfaction than couples without children in the home." "Most parents report high levels of satisfaction with the parenting role . . . parents recognize simultaneous existence of satis-factions and stresses in the role . . . well educated mothers report the early years of parenting to be the most difficult."

Woman's Day magazine survey . . . "How Working Wives Cope," 9/20/77. It would be safe to assume that the percentage of overloaded working wives who've given up the tasks has risen considerably since then.

"Americans have reordered their priorities." . . . Laura Lein, director of the Center for Research on Women at Wellesley College, quoted in *The New York Times*, page 1 of "Home" section, 4/11/85, in article "In Busy Lives, Housework Is No Longer a Top Priority," by Lisa Belkin.

Selling Areas Marketing . . . *Ibid.*

"Changing Attitudes Toward Family Issues" . . . by Dr. Arland Thornton of the Institute for Social Research. *Journal of Marriage and the Family,* November 1989.

This is the kind of third eye and ear that is beyond . . . Dr. Frank Pittman, psychiatrist and family therapist, and author: "Parenting cannot be done efficiently in your spare time. The old concept of 'quality time' is a cruel cop-out. You have to hang out with your children, interacting spontaneously in uptime and downtime, for the parent-child bond to form." *New Woman,* November 1991.

"Middle-class mothers know considerably less about their teen-agers' friends than they may think . . . two psychologists find . . . 'We were surprised at the lack of knowledge even in cohesive households.' " *The Wall Street Journal,* 10/1/91.

"School administrators and teachers are increasingly troubled by many parents' lack of involvement in their children's schooling." *Executive Summary:* "Schools Have Key Role to Play in Nurturing Parent Involvement . . . The growing number of two wage-earner . . . educators are growing increasingly familiar with the new form of disadvantage in the family—one that exists when well-educated parents (typically middle class . . .) remain unavailable to their children's learning and provide few social and psychological resources in the home." Office of Educational Research and Improvement, U.S. Department of Education, September 1991.

"Teenagers need adults. Cries for independence represent part of adolescence. Needs for support, time and attention also are strong. Home is haven . . . Research has revealed parents actually do remain teens' number one influence." Professor Vivian Center Seltzer, professor of human development and behavior, University of Pennsylvania, quoted in *The Philadelphia Inquirer,* 4/12/91.

Dr. Morton H. Shaevitz . . . *The Superwoman Syndrome with Men's Responses,* by Marjorie Hansen Shaevitz with "responses" by Dr. Morton H. Shaevitz (New York: Warner Books, 1984), pp. 48–50. She is the director of the Institute for Family and Work Relationships; he is a practicing clinical psychologist.

You gain the time and energy you need . . . While you're giving him the gift of the time and attention he craves, how will his new childcare tasks affect his stress level? This was answered by sociologists Catherine E. Ross and John Mirowsky, University of Illinois, from a national telephone survey of more than 600 couples, reported in *Psychology Today,* April 1989.

"When child care was solely the women's responsibility and help hard to obtain women were depressed twice as often as men. But if the husband shouldered some of the work, women were depressed much less often, even when child care posed problems. And sharing the care burden didn't cause men any greater emotional distress. The researchers found that if working men and women have similar child care responsibilities, their mental health is the same on average."

"How will your children turn out?" . . . Three of our foremost family experts, Michael E. Lamb, Joseph H. Pleck, and James A. Levine, answer in their "Effects of Paternal Involvement on Fathers and Mothers" chapter in the book *Men's Changing Roles in the Family*, edited by Robert A. Lewis and Marvin B. Sussman (New York & London: The Haworth Press, Inc., 1986). On p. 81, they say, "If there is one general truism in developmental psychology, it is that contented, adjusted parents tend to have contented, adjusted children."

CHAPTER TWELVE
How to Get Him to Do It "Right"

As management consultant Nancy Lee . . . *Targeting the Top* (New York: Doubleday & Company 1980).
Dr. Myra Marx Feree . . . op. cit., chapter three.
Househusbands: Men and Housework in American Families . . . William Beer (Granby, MA: Bergin & Garvey, 1982).
Columnist Richard Cohen . . . "Sharing," *Ms.*, August 1984. "Sharing would mean carrying this concern around in your head when you are also trying to do a job (career!), raise children, and have the requisite number of daily sexual fantasies. Sharing means shouldering some of the anxieties. That's heroic."

CHAPTER THIRTEEN
Your New Invincible Husband-Convincing Powers

. . . **communication experts agree that anywhere from 70–90+ percent** . . . The extreme 90+% ascribed to body language influence is found in work of Dr. Albert Mehrabian, author of the book *Non Verbal Communication* (Chicago: Aldine Publishing company, 1972) and "Communication Without Words," in *Psychology Today* 9/68.
Dr. Paula Kurman, formerly professor of communication at Hunter College, now a consultant to industry, believes it's about 80%. Other experts put it at 70–80%.
How to Read a Person Like a Book . . . Because this book is a classic, there

are various editions. The one I used is published by Cornerstone Library, New York, 1971.

Body language cannot be faked . . . further substantiated by . . . Dr. Ray Birdwhistell . . . Both are from a phone interview I conducted with Gerard I. Nierenberg.

Psychiatrist Dr. Joseph T. Martorano and . . . Martorano and Kildahl, *Beyond Negative Thinking* (New York: Insight Books, division of Plenum Publishing Corporation, 1989).

Also, "How to Get Out of Your Own Way," subtitled "Things We Do to Hurt Our Chances for Success," by Dr. Daniel G. Amen. *Parade*, 9/24/89.

A very famous experiment . . . discussed in "Potential & Expectancy," by C. R. Spicer. *Personnel Journal*, September 1979.

In a study that directly shows how self-fulfilling prophecy . . . "Class, Kinship Density and Conjugal Role Segregation," by Malcolm D. Hill. *Journal of Marriage and the Family*, August 1988. "Results show that respondents' attitudes toward marital roles . . . are more powerful predictors of conjugal role segregation."

Two Canadian family experts . . . "Couples' Career Orientation, Gender Role Orientation and Perceived Equity as Determinants of Marital Power," by Christine S. Sexton, University of Manitoba, and Daniel S. Perlman, University of British Columbia. *Journal of Marriage and the Family*, November 1989.

One supported by a National Science Foundation grant . . . "Belief in Innate Sex Roles: Sex Stratification Versus Interpersonal Influence in Marriage," by John Mirowsky and Catherine E. Ross. *Journal of Marriage and the Family*, November 1987.

Also, *Journal of Marriage and the Family*, November 1989: "Couple Consensus During Marital Joint Decision-Making: A Context, Process, Outcome Model," by Deborah D. Godwin and John Scanzoni.

whenever you keep track of marital influencing over a long period . . . The book *Men's Transitions to Parenthood: Longitudinal Studies of Early Family Experience*, edited by Phyllis W. Berman and Frank A. Pedersen (Hillsdale NJ: Lawrence Erlbaum, 1987) quotes studies by professors Jay Belsky and Brenda L. Volling. "Their most significant finding perhaps is that wherever longitudinal (longterm) pathways of influence were uncovered, they involved the father rather than the mother being influenced." Dr. Belsky is acknowledged in the field as one of the top experts on the effect of parenthood on marriage and the effect of various types of childcare on the child.

In another experiment with 235 couples . . . "Husbands' Attitude and Wives'

Commitment to Employment," by Catherine C. Arnott. *Journal of Marriage and the Family*, November 1972.

CHAPTER FOURTEEN
What to Say & Do When You've Already Tried Everything

But just as consistently in these accounts, *nowhere* does the woman ever mount a constructive effort . . . "Husbands' and Wives' Satisfaction with the Division of Labor," by Benin and Joan Agostinelli, in *Journal of Marriage and the Family*, May 1988, found that in general when wives are dissatisfied with the division of family labor, the men are completely oblivious to the wives' dissatisfaction.

The authors . . . cite another study . . . James A. Doyle, 1985: "Sex and Gender: The Human Experience."

Psychologist Ronald Levant . . . Rutgers University psychologist and author of *Between Father and Child.* This same idea of his is also quoted in *Fortune*, 1/1/90, "Why Grade 'A' Executives Get an 'F' as Parents," by Brian O'Reilly.

Examples abound . . . There are many sources for marriage counselors' experiences with women who appear to be relying on mindreading with their husbands as the women shy from discussing what exactly is bothering them. Some examples include:

"Tired of Same Old Fights," by Linda Chion-Kenney, *Working Mother*, 2/19/90, includes the advice in large letters in the article's callout section: "Say what you mean. Your spouse can't read your mind."

"Can This Marriage Be Saved?" section in segment titled "My Husband Wanted the Perfect Housewife," by Sondra Forsyth Enos, *Ladies' Home Journal*, January 1989, as reported from marriage counselor files of Robert L. Barker, M.S.W., Ph.D., of National Catholic School of Social Services in Washington, D.C., and a private practice in Maryland includes the husband's complaint *as reported and noted by Dr. Barker:* "Look, until now, you never mentioned all this. I can't read your mind, you know."

"Can This Marriage Be Saved?" section in segment titled "My Husband Doesn't Want to Make Love," by Margery D. Rosen, January 1990, reported from marriage counselor files of Evelyn Moschetta, D.S.W. and Paul Moschetta, D.S.W. includes *the counselors' explanation of the problem as* "Though Liza clearly felt a lack of intimacy in her relationship, though she was highly articulate and though she thought she'd told David how she felt, until they began counseling, she had *never specifically expressed her wishes and needs to him."* [Emphasis added.]

Dr. Paula Kurman . . . She is the president of Metamorphosis Inc., Teaneck, NJ, corporate consultant to industry on the structure of human relationships and private practice. The quote is from a telephone interview.

Dr. Deborah Tannen . . . *That's Not What I Meant: How Conversational Style Makes or Breaks Your Relations with Others* (New York: William Morrow & Co., Inc., 1986).

Psychologist Harriet Goldhor Lerner . . . "I Don't Need Anything from Anybody: A Psychologist Talks about Why So Many Women Can't Bring Themselves to Ask for Help." In *Working Mother*, November 1984.

Dr. Lucia A. Gilbert describes . . . *Sharing It All: The Rewards and Struggles of Two-Career Families* (New York: Plenum Publishing Corp., 1988), p. 77.

Dr. Alma Baron . . . *The University of Alabama News*, 1990. "Set Goals, Priorities, Working Mothers Told."

CHAPTER FIFTEEN
How to Say It So He Hears It—& Likes What He Hears

Family researchers find that men get as much satisfaction from their marital and parental roles as do women . . . Peter J. Stein in his chapter "Men in Families" in the book *Women and the Family: Two Decades of Change*, edited by Beth B. Hess & Marvin B. Sussman (New York: The Haworth Press, Inc., 1984).

Dr. Joseph Pleck, acknowledged by other experts as one of the top national authorities on men's behavior in families, believes that because men do take so much pleasure in their marriage roles, increasing their housework and childcare efforts should be much easier than many people think.

unsure of their housekeeping and childcare skills . . . many sources, including Stein op. cit., p. 158: "Pleck offers . . . many men who want to be more involved in child care and housework may feel limited by their lack of skills and supports. They might experience low self confidence stemming from the . . . above or lack peer group support or encouragement from their own wives."

This is "influencing," NOT "manipulating" . . . As we saw in chapter three, men's non-sexist beliefs do not in and of themselves in any way cause them to *behave* that way. We saw that a man is influenced to change his home efforts behavior only when his wife 1) believed she was Entitled to his efforts, 2) spoke up and attempted to influence him to change. In addition, as we saw in chapter thirteen, even when a husband holds a firm belief in innate sex roles, his attitude and behavior *can* be altered if his wife tries to do so.

Dr. Deborah Tannen . . . *You Just Don't Understand: Women and Men in Conversation* (New York: William Morrow, Co., Inc., 1990).

women see discussion of personal problems as helpful . . . Ibid.

Also on this topic, *Why Men Don't Get Enough Sex and Women Don't Get Enough Love,* by Dr. Jonathan Kramer, Ph.D., and Diane Dunaway (New York: Pocket Books, 1990). "Men tend to avoid discussion of personal problems because it reveals weakness. Consequently, when women want to talk to solve an issue, men would rather get to the point, not discuss the emotions but focus on coming up with a rational solution. His style of few words also allows him to maintain his armored distance and emotional anesthesia. The limited talking lets him avoid emotion while simply conveying information and logic."

Dr. John Gottman . . . "Why Men Withdraw," by Glenn Gollins. *Self,* March 1990.

Dr. Francesca M. Cancian . . . *Love in America: Gender and Self-Development* (New York: Cambridge University Press, 1987). In the chapter "Feminine and Masculine Love," pp. 75, 76 in book section titled "Evidence on the Masculine Style of Love."

Dr. Jesse S. Nirenberg, Ph.D. . . . *Getting Through to People,* subtitled: "The techniques of persuasion—how to break through the mental and emotional barriers that continually obstruct the flow of ideas from one person to another." Notably chapters 2, 8, 9.

Most men, say the researchers . . . **have moved from "allowing"** . . . Stein, op. cit., p. 149.

Dave Barry says men . . . From his column "It's All a Matter of Genes," distributed by Knight-Ridder News Service, February 1987.

Oscar Madison . . . the "slob" in the Neil Simon play/TV sitcom *The Odd Couple.*

CHAPTER SIXTEEN
How Sharing House-Power Makes Your Marriage Happier

COUPLES WHO TRY IT . . . Phone interview with Janet Hill, who also produced many of the completed questionnaires for my survey of middle-class working mothers; see author's acknowledgments.

EVERYBODY RESISTS CHANGE . . . **Psychologists have long known and long explained** . . . Examples in psychological literature are manifold. One such example is *Getting Through to People,* by Dr. Jesse Nirenberg, op. cit.

MARRIAGE PIZAZZ . . . **A Washington couple reports** . . . *50/50 Parenting: Sharing Family Rewards and Responsibilities,* by Gayle Kimball, Ph.D. (Lexington MA: Lexington Books, D. C. Heath and Company, 1988), p. 15.

The formal family research confirms . . . Men's Changing Roles in the Family, edited by Lewis & Sussman, chapter by Lamb, Pleck, and Levine, op. cit., chapter eleven, p. 70.

Arlie Hochschild . . . The Second Shift, op. cit., chapter two.

modifications in attitude and behavior may be necessary . . . Dr. Lucia A. Gilbert, op. cit., chapter fourteen, pp. 91–93.

don't need a 50-50 division of home labor to feel much better . . . "Husbands' and Wives' Satisfaction with the Division of Labor," Mary Holland Benin and Joan Agostinelli, op. cit., chapter fourteen.

Your Disappearing Battlegrounds . . . No fights among the experts on this subject . . . There are scores of marital battleground surveys. Two huge ones reaffirming money and home chores as the primary problems include: A March 1985 Ladies' Home Journal survey with 74,000 responses which reports, "The subject couples argue about most is money. For women in their twenties and thirties the second most quarrelsome topic is household chores, while for women in their forties, it's the kids, who are most often teenagers."

An article in Reader's Digest, May 1990, "How to Stop Fighting About Money," by Marie Hodge and Jeff Blyskal, which says that in "a survey of 86,000 people, 37 percent of the respondents said that money was the No. 1 problem in their marriage." It also references "another study of 131 couples . . . at the University of Denver Center for Marital and Family Studies found that money caused the most fights."

Booth, Johnson, Wite, and Edwards study quoted in "Husbands' and Wives' Satisfaction with the Division of Labor," op. cit., chapter fourteen.

Two geographers who received $122,000 . . . Dr. Susan Hanson, professor at the Graduate School of Geography in Worcester MA, together with Dr. Geraldine Pratt, a geographer who teaches at the University of British Columbia in Vancouver, have received $90,000 from the National Science Foundation and $32,000 from the National Geographic Society for their three-year study, "Geographic Perspectives on the Occupational Segregation of Women." The first phase of their research was published in the spring of 1988 and reported the work patterns cited in this chapter.

YOUR HAPPY NEW DAILY OPPORTUNITIES . . . "Life beyond middle management: No time for fun, career women complain," by Darrell Sifford, Knight-Ridder News Service 5/3/90.

"Joint leisure patterns . . ." "Leisure-Activity Patterns and Marital Satisfaction: A Further Test," by Thomas B. Holman and Mary Jacquart. Journal of Marriage and the Family, February 1988.

Working Mother magazine survey . . . "Sex & the Working Mother," May 1990.

"The more time together in activities such as eating, playing, and conversing" . . . Paul William Kingston and Steven Nock reporting in *American Sociological Review* Vol. 52, pp. 391–400.

"Shared financial control, shared family values, and shared leisure activities were associated" . . . This information is from a University of Michigan News and Information Services release, 5/1/90, reporting on U of M sociology Professor Martin K. Whyte's recent book, *Dating, Mating and Marriage*.

Yet psychologists say the family meal feeds your family's souls as well as bodies . . . "Are Square Meals Headed for Extinction?" by Betsy Morris. *The Wall Street Journal*, 3/15/88.

Two nationwide employment time-use surveys . . . These surveys were conducted independently by Gallup Organization and Priority Management. Dan Stamp is the president and chairman of Priority Management, which is headquartered in Dallas. The Gallup Organization, Inc., poll was conducted for "Accountants on Call," Park 80 West Plaza Two, Saddle Brook NJ; the results were reported by them in a press release of 8/1/90 titled "Brace Yourself, Men . . . Women Work Harder Than You," subtitled "National Survey of American Workers Finds That Women Are Significantly More Productive on the Job."

Other Ways Sharing Makes Him a Happier Man . . . **freed to indulge the interpersonal warmth** . . . **that fits rather than fights nature** . . . Reported in many psychological research reports. Some examples are found in *Passages* by Gail Sheehy.

Also, *Authors of Their Own Lives: Intellectual Autobiographies by Twenty American Sociologists*, edited by Bennett M. Berger (University of California Press, 1990). In chapter by Alice S. Rossi, p. 320, "Consistent with the Eichorn findings on middle age . . . men become more nurturing and older women become more assertive . . ."

food shopping . . . **as a means of gratifying men's primitive** . . . **food hunting** . . . Professor Peter Stein of William Paterson College in New Jersey and Herb Goldberg, an L.A.–based psychologist quoted in *American Demographics*, May 1990. "More achievement-oriented," says Seymour Lieberman, whose research company recently surveyed male food shoppers; *The Wall Street Journal*, 12/5/85, reporting a study sponsored by Campbell Soup and *People* magazine.

"calm, efficient, competent" . . . "Debunking Myths of the Male Shopper," by Marian Burros, *The New York Times*, 4/22/87, reporting on the situation in general and drawing these adjectives from the same Lieberman study cited above.

men who did housework . . . **"far healthier . . ."** Reported in the fall of 1989 by John Gottman, Ph.D., at the annual meeting of the American Association of Marriage and Family Therapy.

So What Does the Evidence Add Up To? . . . "Having, and Sharing, It All,"
New York Times, editorial, 11/17/87.

CHAPTER SEVENTEEN
Why Your Children Will Love Mother More

Headlines such as "Moms' jobs said to hurt kids" . . . "Special from the Seattle
Times," 5/2/90; "Distance Makes the Heart . . ." The New York Times,
11/7/91.

The research makes it clear the vast majority of working wives have not
separated themselves from . . . There is a mountain of evidence. One example is from Journal of Marriage and the Family, May 1987: "Socialization
into Parenthood: A Longitudinal Study of the Development of Self-
evaluations," by Reilly, Entwisle, and Doering: ". . . Women with husbands more involved in child care viewed themselves less favorably than
did women whose husbands were less involved . . . it appears that the
husband's involvement might be perceived by the women to reflect a de-
ficiency or shortfall in her own parenting."

Men more involved in child care under circumstantial duress (not the conviction
that it was a two-paycheck equity) "may increase their involvement with
their children at the expense of harmonious marital relations." From "Pro-
cesses Underlying Father Involvement in Dual-Earner and Single-Earner
Families," by Ann C. Crouter and Maureen Perry-Jenkins. Developmental
Psychology, 1987, Volume 23, No. 3, pp. 431–440. The authors at the
very beginning of their Conclusions call attention to a major "caveat,"
namely that their study is based on a small sample of blue-collar families
in the early years of child rearing. The relation between marital problems
and father involvement in childcare, they say, "may emerge only for rather
traditional couples like the ones in our study: men and women whose dual-
earner life style is a contemporary reality, but whose values, hopes, and
expectations for married life lag behind."

That is precisely the point that I am making. As long as both she and he
continue to see childcare as "women's work," pressuring or coaxing him
into doing more makes her feel she's failed in her role as a mother and
makes him angry that he has a "failed wife" and that by default he is now
being compelled to do her work.

To solve it the woman must allow herself to recognize and move him to see
that when they both work, childcare is no longer women's work; it's family
work. When you build on the summary words of the Crouter, Perry-Jenkins
study, which says their couples are living the dual-earner contemporary life
style but their "values, hopes and expectations for married life lag behind,"

you can see the need for both you and your spouse to adjust your own ideas to see that childcare is now family work, not woman's work. With Shared parenting where both of you then understand that childcare as family work is fair, you bring those lagging values, hopes, and expectations into alignment with reality. You then make it possible for him to do child care with high self-esteem and for her to accept it with high self-esteem.

Another study by Pruett, reported in *The Record*, 6/2/87, reminds us, "Despite the rhetoric of the women's movement, almost all the mothers in Pruett's study have major problems in letting go of the nurturing domain. It meant leaving a psychologically safe territory."

"When My Husband Became Mr. Mom," op. cit. "Relinquishing the housekeeping and cooking to Bill was easy; putting him in charge of our daughters was a lot harder."

"The Baby Bomb: Research reveals the astonishingly stressful social and emotional consequences of parenthood" by Carin Rubenstein, *The New York Times* Sunday "Good Health Magazine," 10/8/89. Large letter headline: "Some Women Want Their Husbands to Be More Involved, But Have Trouble Relinquishing Control of the Baby."

you may be among the majority of parents (54%) . . . This statistic and all others in that paragraph were drawn from a Gallup survey reported in *The Wall Street Journal*, 10/2/90.

satisfaction with the marriage typically takes a serious drop . . . "The Baby Bomb" op. cit. They report that "two major research projects" from California and Pennsylvania "have documented in greater depth than ever before *the astonishingly stressful social and emotional consequences of parenthood* [emphasis added]. For about half the couples marital satisfaction declined after the birth of a first child. . . . Husband and wife tend to take on traditional gender-specific roles—even if both spouses work outside the home. . . . Many husbands and wives express less affection for each other—they seldom kiss and hug or give each other compliments. Some couples become ambivalent about their marriage, doubting their feelings for each other and even questioning whether they should have married in the first place. Wives generally become dissatisfied with the marriage first, usually about six months after the baby's birth, but the husbands become equally unhappy after 18 months."

But How Competent Is He? . . . There are nearly twice as many fathers raising children alone . . . U.S. Census Bureau reports 1.2 million single parent fathers in the U.S. in late 1980s compared to just over 690,000 in 1980 and about 393,000 in 1973.

"Can a Man Raise a Child All by Himself?" by Paul Levine. *Parade*, 4/1/90: "There also is a new willingness among men to attempt the responsibilities—and rewards—of being a full-time parent, partly the result of a social climate that makes it easier for men to accept in themselves the ability to care and be sensitive." This new male comfort with their innate ability and with the emotional demands of childcare also operates among married fathers and make it that much easier for the working wife to talk up and work through with him to pleasant Shared parenting.

men have sued, won, and forced airports . . . "Pampers in the Men's Room," *Fortune,* December 1989.

American Fatherhood, "The Official Newsletter of F.A.I.R., The National Father's Organization." Their goals of increased participation in the raising of their children are self-announced and are vigorously lobbied for with front-page stories such as that in their April 1989 edition, "Children Suffer When Deprived of Fathers."

Researchers who probe father-child . . . There are multiple examples of male competence: for instance, in the book *The Daddy Track and the Single Father,* by Geoffrey L. Greif (Lexington Books, D. C. Health and Company, Lexington MA, 1990).

Also "Fathering," by Glenn Collins, *The New York Times,* 6/17/79. "Researchers from a number of disciplines using ingenious new methods now suggest that . . . there are few significant differences in the way children attach to fathers and to mothers, that fathers can be as protective, giving . . . etc." Also Dr. James Herzog, M.D., quoted in article above.

Not surprisingly . . . your encouragement and belief that he can succeed . . . "The Real 'Mr. Moms,' " *Newsweek,* 3/31/86. "Experts think one reason fathers may not spend more time with their children is that they often feel insecure about their ability to manage the routine tasks of child care."

Furthermore, sociologists/psychologists report people learn their roles from outside sources: as "Playing," by Charles D. Schewe and Anne L. Balazs, in *American Demographics,* April 1990, put it, "Roles are learned: people watch those around them to find out how to behave. Roles portrayed in movies, on television, and in commercials show people what is acceptable behavior." The flood of fathering TV sitcoms of the last few years featuring men as very involved fathers reflects the fact that Americans now seek and are comfortable in that family arrangement. The TV shows themselves support, reinforce, and spread the idea that active fathering is socially right for men. "The Family Man" is a roundup discussion of this topic by the Knight-Ridder Service's Ron Miller, 1/26/90.

Martin Gold, professor . . . *University of Michigan News and Information Services* release, 7/11/88, headed "Contrary to popular belief, most teen-agers get along well with their parents; those who don't are likely to have poor peer relationships," from Martin Gold, professor of psychology and research scientist at the University of Michigan's Research Center for Group Dynamics. "If there is no close relationship with a parent, the teen-ager may never learn how to have close relationships with others."

when men willingly do their portion of child care, you reduce the risk of divorce . . . S. Philip Morgan, in his data published August 1988 by the University of Pennsylvania.

A survey of 600 couples found . . . A national telephone survey conducted by sociologists Catherine E. Ross and John Mirowsky of the University of Illinois, reported in *Psychology Today,* April 1989.

Children who have two involved parents . . . *50/50 Parenting,* op. cit.

<small>CHAPTER NINETEEN</small>
Hiring Help When You Can't Afford It, They Won't Do a Good Job, & There's No Help Available in Your Area

After surveying 291 working parents in 30 states . . . Dr. Gayle Kimball, *50/50 Parenting* (op. cit.), found, "However, 80 percent of the dual-career couples I surveyed do not hire household help. For some people, having a nonfamily member do housework violates their sense of what it is to be a good spouse."

The pressure is off her to resort so heavily to costly convenience dinners . . . See facts/statistics quoted for chapter six in the Jensenns' section.

They hand over their paycheck and go right on asking permission . . . : My survey; also "It's 'his' money or 'our' paycheck" United Press International story by Jeanne Lesem appeared undated.

When a wife does retain some or all of her income . . . I asked readers in my survey:

"Do you use the money you earn to:

a) combine it with my husband's and it's mutual money to pay family bills;

b) keep it all for myself for things I need and maybe extras I want to buy for the family and for my private savings;

c) put about _____ ¼ · ½, how much? of my paycheck into family bills and keep rest for myself;

d) divide it just the way my husband divides his income between himself & family and that way is: _____

_____

e) other arrangement? (please describe other arrangement you have) _____

_____ "

The vast majority, 46 of the 62, chose "a." But among the others it's often clear that the result is the same as "a" but under another name.

That is, women who chose "d" usually explained both she and he were using their money for family bills and needs. But she had one account and he another. The result, though, was that her money was going for the family. Among the women who checked "b" and "c" it was not always clear where the money was really going. Two of nine "b" choices indicated they "kept it all for myself" in order to use for things like "family food shopping." And another "b" who was also theoretically keeping it for herself indicated that she used it "to pay the children's tuition."

Again, their money was going to support the family but under another name. Among the tiny group of four women who chose "c," two indicated they put three-quarters of their money into family bills; one one-half; one one-quarter. Another woman checked both "a" and "b" with no explanation. Since they are contradictory, I didn't know how to classify hers and didn't count it. Two other women didn't check anything and so also could not be counted in this portion of the survey.

One-third of Americans now say they *always* feel rushed . . . "Time Squeeze," by John P. Robinson. *American Demographics*, February 1990. Mr. Robinson is a professor of sociology at the University of Maryland, College Park, and director of the Americans' Use of Time Project. In this project, a nationally representative sample, more than 5,000 Americans in 1985, kept a one-day diary of all their activities.

***Business Week* did a cover picture story . . .** 4/27/87.

Elsewhere there are reports . . . They abound in local and national magazines and newspapers. Some examples: "The Boom in Personal Services," by Mary Rowland, *Working Woman*, November 1988; "Errand-runners will handle just about any chore," by Elizabeth Llorente, *The Record*, 1/21/90; "The New Kind of House Call," *The Sunday New York Times*, 2/19/89.

BACKGROUNDER:
How Media, Business, Government, Society Generate Working Wife Guilt & Prevent You from Solving Your Overload

***Journal of Social Psychology* . . .** Marvin E. Shaw and Stephen T. Margulis, "The Power of the Printed Word: Its Effect on the Judgement of the Quality of Research," 1974, Vol. 94.

More on the power of the printed word . . . *Personnel Journal*, February 1984, on how to put your ideas across at a business meeting: "In selecting data to support your proposal, *remember the power of the printed word* [Emphasis added]. Allen Funt of 'Candid Camera' related the episode in which he and his staff essentially closed the state of Vermont simply by placing a highway sign at the state line—'VERMONT IS CLOSED.' Due to the power of the printed word, motorists would read the sign, turn their cars around, and drive off to New Hampshire."

Al Neuharth, that shrewd student of human psychology . . . in his *USA Today* column, "Plain Talk," 9/14/90.

The Feminine Mystique . . . Betty Friedan (New York: W. W. Norton & Co., 1963).

appeared in a 1990s *Fortune* . . . "How Dual-Income Couples Cope," by Julie Connelly; the article says, "Men are confused about their roles in two-career marriages. Intellectually they accept their wives as breadwinners, but emotionally they wonder if Dad didn't have an easier time."

So total is the slant when dealing with working wives . . . **sadly it has even influenced women's best champions, their own women's magazines** . . . Some examples from the many available include: *Savvy Woman,* "Checkmate" by Ellie McGrath. "I'm a Good Mother, But a Lousy Wife," by Pamela Redmond Satran, in the "Guilt Department" of *Working Mother,* February 1990. The magazine's only comment on her guilt feelings is to reinforce them in an author's note that reads in its entirety, "Pamela Redmond Satran is a writer whose husband loves her anyway."

Another article is "I'm a Lousy Housekeeper—So Sue Me," by Linda Essig. In the "Guilt Department," *Working Mother,* October 1987. Again the magazine's only comment on her guilt feelings is to second and reinforce her guilt feelings in an author's note that reads in its entirety, "Linda Essig, a freelance writer, lives contentedly amidst clutter and cobwebs in Spring Valley, Minnesota."

"Working Mothers Share Their Shortcuts," by Brie Quinby, in *Woman's Day,* 7/7/87, assumes the truth of Rule #3, that she is responsible for home and children and offers new/better ways for her to do it all, thus reconfirming her sense of Non-Entitlement for others' efforts. Often this type of article offers some journalistic balancing asides about getting him to "help" more; but the thrust is pure Rule #3. (This is the commonest type of women's magazine treatment of the problem.)

"My Husband Resents My Job," by Janice LaRouche, *Family Circle,* 2/23/88. Though the title announces the familiar "HER career is a problem to HIM" focus, Ms. LaRouche's text is far better than most in trying to dispel her sense of guilt but apparently dares not go anywhere near far enough.

Because I've worked so long for women's magazines, I have great respect for what they've been able to accomplish for women. I believe the magazines are doing the best they can to achieve equality for women and serve their readers. But I think the general overall larger media focus is so powerfully in favor of the three one-paycheck rules for two-paycheck wives that women's magazines don't recognize how these invisible pressures are operating and are able to move away only marginally.

in a news release of a nationwide business group . . . Runzheimer International, Rochester, Wisconsin, a very respected and dependable organization that tracks business costs in "Daycare Costs Impose Additional Burden on Working Families," 10/15/90. I did not mention this organization by name in the text because this is merely an example of a widespread, nearly universal business mindset and it's not fair to pillory one company in the text. Even major women's research groups such as CATALYST adopt the same "childcare is HER responsibility" outlook. Their December 1989 *Perspective* newsletter's main headline is: *Corporate Responses to the Needs of Working Mothers.* And the *Perspective* text deals with HER need for childcare.

Or Knight-Ridder News Service 9/1/89 in a typical business story on "AT&T rethinks day care" discusses it as a working *woman's* problem . . . "illustrates the growing problem many American corporations have in attracting and retaining working mothers, women they have invested a lot of time and money."

Newsweek **ran a cover story on "Mommy Wars" . . .** by Nina Darton, 6/4/90. **And then admitted several weeks later . . .** 6/20/90.

Business Week **ran a cover story on the Mommy Track . . .** by Anne Keller, 3/20/89, pp. 126–134. Letters, 4/17/89.

Time ran another typical major story in an issue devoted entirely to *Women: The Road Ahead,* in the fall of 1990. An article called "The Great Experiment," by Philip Elmer-Dewitt, asks, "Today's parents are raising children in ways that little resemble their own youth. The question that haunts them: will the kids be all right?"

Time's article then defines the problem: "As a result, no parent is immune to the uncertainty and guilt that make the child rearing dilemma the No. 1 topic of conversation among young mothers today, and of more than passing interest to fathers . . . Should a mother stay at home, providing the values, discipline and security her children need, and let her hard-earned job skills go fallow? Or should she take a chance that her kids will be O.K. and pursue a life that brings more personal satisfaction and economic advantages?"

And there *Time* lays the anxiety and guilt on only one parent, the working mother—note, not on working fathers. Fathers, according to *Time*, have only a "more than passing interest" in whether their kids will be OK. But *Time* makes it clear that fathers do not under any circumstances have to choose career or parenthood. The men, *Time* makes clear, are Entitled to both. It is only women who should choose or worry about it; because *Time*, like all the media, is still seeing life in terms of one-paycheck Rule #3: Home & children are a wife's job. This media attitude persists despite the fact that middle-class life can no longer be lived on one salary alone and she is out there doing a significant part of his traditional male job of supporting the family.

government's one-paycheck attitude to your two-paycheck life . . . The Washington, D.C.–based research group Worldwatch Institute's study, "Women, Men and the Division of Labor," spotlights this one-paycheck government attitude. A *New York Times* discussion, undated, of that report states, "Government policies designed to ease the strain between work and family responsibilities actually do the reverse and reinforce the stereotypical division of labor (women doing most home and childcare). For example, part-time work flexible hours and child-care leaves are rarely offered to men. Rather," says the report, "they are presented as women's benefits, reinforcing the idea that home and family belong to women's sphere rather than being a joint responsibility."

A woman suffered . . . "Job Bias Ban Would Put Bite into Penalties," by Cathy Trost, 11/18/90.

"Feminist Issues Tend to Turn off Some Businesses" . . . used as lead *Business Section* headline, *The Record,* Hackensack NJ, 6/16/86. *The Record* is *the* major daily newspaper in sophisticated, upscale Bergen County, one of the ten per capita richest counties in the USA; the paper also has won a Pulitzer. So its use and positioning of such a topic carries weight and can be seen as an example of many such media treatments in influential media forums.

Survey Questionnaires
. . . .

In order not to impose on our busy working wife participants and use too much of their time, I divided the questionnaire in half, Section A-B, Section C-D. Each woman received one of the sections distributed at random. Together—A-B and C-D—provided us with important detailed information about working wives' struggle with Overload. Other facts about the survey, including sample validity, can be found in the Author's Acknowledgments.

Section A-B

Anonymous Survey for Employed Wives & Mothers

Please take this survey only if you are currently married and also have a paid job outside your home.
1) What jobs at home would you be so happy about if you did *not* have to do them? If they just somehow got taken care of.

2) What parts of the day are the hardest for you?
   What makes them the hardest?

   Why don't you make the changes that would make it easier for you?

Studies show that many working wives hesitate to pressure their husbands to do more around the house or in taking care of the children. Why do you think the women hesitate to act?

_____

_____

_____

Surveys also show that working wives and working mothers often feel guilty if their husbands do end up doing much housework or childcare. Why do you think the women feel that way?

Are there certain kinds of responsibilities with your home or children that YOU feel guilty about if your husband ends up having to do them instead of you? Yes? No?

If yes, why do you feel that way?

What kinds of jobs specifically make you feel guilty if he does them?

_____

Also lots of women say they really can't let their husbands do much at home or with the children because it turns out to be more trouble than it's worth.

Why do you think they feel it's more trouble than it's worth?

_____

_____

_____

How do you think that common husband-problem could be cured?

_____

_____

_____

_____

Do you think your husband realizes that you're really doing part of his "man's" job of supporting the family?   Yes _____ No _____

If he realized it, wouldn't he see that it is fair to do part of your "woman's" job of looking after home and children?   Yes _____ No _____

If "No," why do you think he would think it's fair for you to help support the family, and also have to do all the oldfashioned "woman's" job too?

_____

_____

_____

Circle All Answers That Apply to You & Your Family

Do you use the money you earn to:

a) combine it with my husband's and it's mutual money to pay family bills;
b) keep it all for myself for things I need and maybe extras I want to buy for the family and for my private savings;
c) put about _____ ¼, ½, how much? of my paycheck into family bills and keep rest for myself.
d) divide it just the way my husband divides his income between himself & family and that way is: _____
_____
e) other arrangement? (please describe other arrangement you have _____

_____

Circle or Fill In Answers
Your age: 20–25; 25–30; 31–35; 35–40; 41–50; 51–60; 61–70; older
Husband's age: 20–25; 25–30; 31–35; 35–40; 41–50; 51–60; 61–70; older
Married: How long _____; previous marriages? #   ; how long _____
How many children do you have living with you _____ ; Their ages are

_____

How many other children do you have that you and your husband support?

_____

ages? _____

I work full-time (35 hours or more weekly); part-time, approximately _____ hours weekly.

Education: Circle the one that describes your *last* school experience: some high school; high school diploma; some college; college degree; grad. coll. degree.

Husband's Education: Circle one that describes his *last* school experience: some high school; high school diploma; some college; college degree; grad. college degree.

Total Annual Family Income
less than $25,000; $25,000–$35,000; $35,000–$45,000; $45,000–$60,000; $60,000–$80,000; $80,000–$100,000; over $100,000.

Thank you very much.
Your answers will help other women.

Section C-D

Anonymous Survey for Employed Wives & Mothers

Please take this survey only if you are currently married and also have a paid job outside your home.

CIRCLE ALL! *(as many as you want)* ANSWERS THAT MATCH YOUR FEELINGS

1) *Because I work, I can't possibly keep our home as nice as people used to keep their homes. So when people come in and see the mess,*

a) I'm really embarrassed.
b) I feel they probably think I'm a slob.
c) I feel they probably think I'm not a good wife & mother.
d) I don't really care.
e) I think they understand that nowadays working wives just don't have time and energy to keep their homes perfectly—and also take care of the children and their paying job too.
f) I feel it's a reflection on both me and my husband because, after all, it's his home too and nothing is stopping him from doing more to keep the place looking nice.
g) I feel it's a reflection on both me and my husband because, after all, we're both bringing in money to support our family and we both should be responsible for our home and children.
h) I don't feel it's a reflection on him; it's just a reflection on me as a wife and mother.

2) CIRCLE either AGREE or DISAGREE
Trying to get a husband to change and take more responsibility for housework

and children doesn't usually work. Maybe they do you a favor once in a while but they don't really take over the responsibility.   AGREE   DISAGREE

Men are set in their ways and you can't really change them about things like housework and childcare.   AGREE   DISAGREE

Comment? _____

_____

It's really not even worth putting effort into trying to get a husband to do more around your home or in caring for the children.   AGREE   DISAGREE

You might as well be satisfied with whatever little he does. AGREE DISAGREE

Comment? _____

3) When I do try to get my husband to do more in our home or with the children, I usually say something like (write down exactly the words you usually use):

_____

_____

_____

_____

(Use additional paper if you need more space.)

He usually reacts by (saying & doing what????) _____

_____

_____

(Really describe the scene. Use additional paper if you need more space.)

One time I had a really good breakthrough where he really did change in one good way. This is what happened:

_____

_____

_____

_____

_____

(Use additional paper if you need more space.)

As far as I can figure out, the reason he did change that time was _____

_____

_____

Did you ever try the same words and actions to get him to make other good changes? Yes _____ No _____

Did it work? Yes _____ No _____

If it didn't work, why do you think it failed? _____

_____

If you've never tried to use that method to change him again, why haven't you tried it? _____

_____

CIRCLE ALL ANSWERS THAT APPLY TO YOU & YOUR FAMILY

Do you use the money you earn to:

a) combine it with my husband's and it's mutual money to pay family bills;

b) keep it all for myself for things I need and maybe extras I want to buy for the family and for my private savings;

c) put about _____ ¼, ½, how much? of your paycheck into family bills and keep rest for myself.

d) divide it just the way my husband divides his income between himself & family and that way is: _____

_____

e) other arrangement? (please describe other arrangement you have) _____

_____

CIRCLE OR FILL IN ANSWERS:
Your Age: 20–30; 31–40; 41–50; 51–60; 61–70; older
Husband's age: 20–25; 25–30; 31–35; 35–40; 41–50; 51–60; 61–70; older
Married: How long _____ ; previous marriages? #   ; how long _____
How many children do you have living with you _____ ; Their ages are __
I work fulltime (35 hours or more weekly); parttime, approximately _____
hours weekly.

Education: Circle the one that describes your *last* school experience: some high
school; high school diploma; some college; college degree; grad. coll. degree.

Husband's Education: Circle one that describes his *last* school experience: some
high school; high school diploma; some college; college degree; grad. college
degree.

Total Annual Family Income
less than $25,000; $25,000–$35,000; $35,000–$45,000; $45,000–$60,000;
$60,000–$80,000; $80,000–$100,000; over $100,000.

Thank you very much.
Your answers will help other women.

Bibliography

· · · · · · · · · · · · · ·

DIALOG COMPUTER SEARCH from the Family Resources Database: coverage of psychological and sociological literature related to the field of family studies. Includes citations to journals, various media forms, books, government documents, newsletters, instructional materials, directories.

Subject coverage includes: trends and changes in marriage and the family; family relationships and dynamics; families with special problems; family education and counseling; mate selection; marriage and divorce; minority groups; psychology and sociology.

Alberti, Robert E. and Michael L. Emmons, *Your Perfect Right* (San Luis Obispo, CA: Impact Publishers, 1990).

Applegath, John, *Working Free* (New York: AMACOM, American Management Association, 1982).

Baritz, Loren, *The Good Life* (New York: Harper & Row, Publishers, 1982).

Benderly, Beryl Lieff, *The Myth of Two Minds* (Garden City, NY: Doubleday & Company, 1987).

Bennett, Robert F. with Kurt Hanks and Gerreld L. Pulsipher, *Gaining Control* (New York: Pocket Books, 1987).

Berglas, Dr. Steven, *The Success Syndrome* (New York & London: Plenum Publishing Corporation, 1986).

Bergmann, Barbara R., *The Economic Emergence of Women* (New York: Basic Books, Inc., 1986).

Berk, Sarah Fenstermaker, *The Gender Factor* (New York & London: Plenum Publishing Corporation, 1985).

Bird, Caroline, *The Two-Paycheck Marriage* (New York: Pocket Books, 1979).

Brennan, John, *The Conscious Communicator* (Reading, MA: Addison-Wesley Publishers Company, 1974).

Briggs, Dorothy Corkille, *Your Child's Self-Esteem* (New York: Dolphin Books, 1970).

Bronstein, Phyllis and Carolyn Pape Cowen, eds., *Fatherhood Today* (New York: John Wiley & Sons, 1988).

Bryson, Jeff B. and Rebecca Bryson, *Dual-Career Couples* (New York: Human Sciences Press, 1978).

Campbell, Bebe Moore, *Successful Women, Angry Men* (New York: Random House, 1986).

Cancian, Francesca M., *Love in America* (Cambridge, UK: Cambridge University Press, 1987).

Cappo, Joe, *Future Scope* (Chicago: Longman Financial Services Publishing, 1990).

Cardozo, Arlene, *Sequencing* (New York: Atheneum, 1986).

Cowen, Connell O'Brien and Melvyn Kinder, *Smart Women—Foolish Choices* (New York: Signet, New American Library, 1986).

Crosby, Faye J., *Juggling* (New York: The Free Press, 1991).

———, ed. *Spouse, Parent, Worker* (New Haven: Yale University Press, 1987).

Curtis, Jean, *Working Mothers* (Garden City, NY: Doubleday & Company, Inc., 1976).

Dicanio, Margaret, *The Encyclopedia of Marriage, Divorce and the Family* (New York: Facts On File, 1989).

Dowling, Collette, *Perfect Women* (New York: Pocket Books, 1988).

Ehrenreich, Barbara and Deirdre English, *For Her Own Good* (New York: Anchor Press/Doubleday, 1978).

Ehrensaft, Diane, *Parenting Together* (New York: The Free Press, 1987).

Faludi, Susan, *Backlash: The Undeclared War Against American Women* (New York: Crown Publishing Co., 1991).

Friedan, Betty, *The Feminine Mystique* (New York: W. W. Norton & Company, Inc., 1963).

———, *The Second Stage* (New York: Summit Books, 1981).

Gerson, Kathleen, *Hard Choices* (Berkeley, CA: University of California Press, 1985).

Gerstel, Naomi and Harriet Engel Gross, eds., *Families and Work* (Philadelphia: Temple University Press, 1987).

Gilbert, Lucia Albino, et al. *Men in Dual-Career Families* (Hillsdale, NJ: Lawrence Erlbaum Associates, 1985).

———, *Sharing It All* (New York: Plenum Publishing Corporation, 1988).

Gilligan, Carol, *In a Different Voice* (Cambridge, MA: Harvard University Press, 1982).

Gref, Geoffrey L., *The Daddy Track and the Single Father* (Lexington, MA: Lexington Books [division of D. C. Heath and Company], 1990).

Helmstetter, Shad, *The Self-Talk Solution* (New York: Pocket Books, 1987).

Henley, Nancy M., *Body Politics* (Englewood Cliffs, NJ: Prentice-Hall, Inc., 1977).

Hertz, Rosanna, *More Equal Than Others* (Berkeley, CA: University of California Press, 1986).

Hes, Beth B. and Marvin B. Sussman, *Women and the Family* (New York: The Haworth Press, Inc., 1984).

Hochschild, Arlie with Anne Machung, *The Second Shift: Working Parents and the Revolution at Home* (New York: Viking Press, 1989).

Holmstrom, Lynda Lytle, *The Two-Career Family* (Cambridge, MA: Schenkman Publishing Company, 1973).

Kimball, Gayle, *50/50 Parenting* (Lexington: Lexington Books, 1988).

Levine, James A., *Who Will Raise the Children* (Philadelphia: J. B. Lippincott Company, 1976).

Lew, Irvina Siegel, *You Can't Do It All* (New York: Atheneum, 1986).

Lewis, Robert A. and Marvin B. Sussman, eds., *Men's Changing Roles in the Family* (New York: The Haworth Press, Inc., 1986).

Magid, Renee Y. with Nancy E. Fleming, *When Mothers and Fathers Work* (New York: AMACOM, The American Management Association, 1987).

Maglin, Nan Bauer and Nancy Schneiderwind, *Women and Stepfamilies* (Philadelphia: Temple University Press, 1989).

Martorano, Dr. Joseph T. and Dr. John P. Kildahl, *Beyond Negative Thinking* (Insight Books [division of Plenum Publishing Corporation], 1989).

Menninger, Joan and Eleanor Dugan, *Make Your Mind Work for You* (New York: Pocket Books, 1988).

Miles, Rosalind, *The Women's History of the World* (New York: Harper & Row, Publishers, Inc., 1989).

Napier, Augustus Y., *The Fragile Bond* (New York: Harper & Row, Publishers, Inc., 1988).

Nierenberg, Gerard I. and Henry H. Calero, *How to Read a Person Like a Book* (New York: Cornerstone Library, 1971).

Nierenberg, Gerard I., *The Art of Negotiating* (New York: Cornerstone Library, 1968).

Nirenberg, Jesse S., *Getting Through to People* (Englewood Cliffs, NJ: Prentice-Hall, Inc., 1963).

Osborn, Carol, *Enough Is Enough* (New York: G. P. Putnam's Sons, 1986).

Palmer, Phyllis, *Domesticity and Dirt* (Philadelphia: Temple University Press, 1989).

Rothman, Sheila M., *Woman's Proper Place* (New York: Basic Books, Inc., 1978).

Sargent, Alice G., *The Androgynous Manager* (New York: AMACOM, The American Management Association, 1981).

Schenkel, Susan, *Giving Away Success* (New York: McGraw-Hill Book Company, 1984).

Shaevitz, Dr. Morton H., *Sexual Static* (Boston: Little, Brown and Company, 1987).

Shaevitz, Marjorie Hansen, *The Superwoman Syndrome* (New York: Warner Books, Inc., 1984).

Sheehy, Gail, *Passages* (New York: E. P. Dutton & Co., Inc., 1974).

Shorter, Edward, *The Making of the Modern Family* (New York: Basic Books, Inc., 1975).

Skelsey, Alice, *The Working Mother's Guide to Her Home, Her Family and Herself* (New York: Random House, Inc., 1970).

Sutherland, Daniel, *The Expansion of Everyday Life 1860–1876* (New York: Harper & Row, Publishers, 1989).

Tannen, Deborah, *That's Not What I Meant* (New York: William Morrow and Company, Inc., 1986).

———, *You Just Don't Understand* (New York: William Morrow and Company, Inc., 1990).

Tavris, Carol, ed., *Every Woman's Emotional Well-Being* (Garden City, NY: Doubleday & Company, Inc., 1986).

Trachtenberg, Peter, *The Casanova Complex* (New York: Pocket Books, 1989).

Viscott, David, *I Love You, Let's Work It Out* (New York: Pocket Books, 1987).

Weinstein, Grace W., *Men, Women & Money* (New York: New American Library, 1986).